The Social Status of the Professional Musician from the Middle Ages to the 19th Century

FRONTISPIECE. Musician with portative organ. From "Biblia Veteris Testamenti," 14th-century miniature. (Metropolitiana, Zagreb) (See p. 13.)

The Social Status of the Professional Musician from the Middle Ages to the 19th Century

WALTER SALMEN
General Editor

Annotated and Translated from the German by
Herbert Kaufman and Barbara Reisner

SOCIOLOGY OF MUSIC NO. 1

PENDRAGON PRESS *New York*

Other titles in the Sociology of Music *Series:*

Music and Society: A guide to the Sociology of Music
Revised Edition in English by Ivo Supičíc

The present American Edition is an expanded version
of the original German version which appeared as *Der
Sozialstatus des Berufmusikers vom 17, bis 19, Jahrhundert* Kassel, 1971.

Library of Congress Cataloging in Publication Data
Main entry under title:

The social status of the professional musician from
    the Middle Ages to the 19th Century.

    Translation of: Der Sozialstatus des Berufsmusikers
vom 17. bis 19. Jahrhundert.
    Includes bibliographical references.
    Contents: The social status of the musician in the
Middle Ages / Walter Salmen -- On the social status
of the town musician / Heinrich W. Schwab -- On the
social status of the organist in Lutheran Germany from
the 16th through the 19th century / Arnfried Edler --
[etc.]
    1. Music and Society. I. Salmen, Walter, 1926-
II. Kaufman, Herbert. III. Reisner, Barbara.
IV. Title.
ML3795.S6713 1983   780'.07   82-11262
ISBN 0-918728-16-9

Contents

CONTENTS

List of Illustrations

LIST OF ILLUSTRATIONS

LIST OF ILLUSTRATIONS

Preface

This publication presents the findings of a group of specialists of the *Gesellschaft für Musikforschung.*

During the Society's Seventh International Congress in 1958 in Cologne, West Germany, a working group discussed socio-historical problems, particularly conditions of the musician in medieval society. The stimulating debate, in which experts from seven nations took part, concluded with the wish that this discourse on the social determination of music and musicians, under various conditions, past and present, might be continued, deepened, and expanded. In view of the fact that a number of special studies had in the meantime appeared in print, such an opportunity was offered at the annual meeting of the *Gesellschaft für Musikforschung,* in Coburg in 1965. It became increasingly evident that the young discipline of the Sociology of Music required the encouragement of the parent organization, in order that this special field, the concern of only a few specialists, might exert a more telling influence on musicology as a whole.

Currently, research that directs its attention primarily to the sociological aspects of music falls into two categories: either we find a collection of random facts about music and music-making, which does little towards furthering our understanding without the requisite theoretical illumination, or, on the other hand, we may read speculative outlines that are usually lacking in the necessary supporting facts. As yet, there has been neither a definitive synthesis of the empirical research which organizes data of the past and present, nor a theoretical formulation aimed at an understanding of these given facts.

This collection of monographs has a primarily socio-historical orientation. It strives to contribute towards assimilation through the transmission of new facts as well as through the codification of previously published data. (cf. *Bausteine zu einer Musiksoziologie,* Hans Engel). The intention is to make the use of established sociological concepts such as "stratification," "integration," "evolution," and "group interests" more universally accepted than before in support of theoretical formulations.

These essays, contributed by German scholars of varied backgrounds and written from the perspective of diverse locales, deal with different aspects of a single sociologic theme: the social status of the professional musician and composer. Not examined are musical masterpieces as aesthetic objects in their relationship to society.[1] Also, no consideration is given to questions of audience reception to the music. Only that aspect of the relationship of musicians to society is taken into consideration which might throw light upon how the creators and transmitters of tonal art were respected, tolerated, advanced, or impeded by their society. Several contributors chose topics which have not received even preliminary attention until now. Little was known, for example, of the various types of service and the differences in hiring standards for musicians in the society of the 17th and 18th century aristocracy and middle class. To what extent these collected essays will require further amplification, even with respect to these special topics, can be ascertained by the mere enumeration of catch-words such as "virtuoso," "dancing-master," "piano teacher," or "organist," concepts which could not be dealt with within the present volume's space limitations.

Each of the essays, presented in roughly chronological order,

---

[1] As, for example, Klaus Stahmer has attempted to do in his dissertation: *Musikalische Formung in soziologischem Bezug. Dargestellt an der instrumentalen Kammermusik von Johannes Brahms* (Phil. Diss. Kiel 1968). See also the GfMf Congress Report, Kassel 1962, p. 3 ff.

represents a painstaking effort in collecting socio-historical data. They do not have an apologetic orientation towards the "giants" of music history, but rather, are concerned with making the nameless mass more accessible. In this way general conditions can be ascertained. The attempt is made, within the framework of social history, which is the basis for sociological theorizing, to set boundaries within which one can conduct meaningful research with the aid of perspective. This approach makes it necessary to consult salary rosters, police regulations, subscription lists, registers and decrees of royal courts, as well as pictures, literary documents and records. In so far as it is still possible today, one hopes thereby to achieve an integrated view of the musician and his relationship to his colleagues and contemporaries. Biographically oriented music histories have not been consulted, for they are not particularly revealing in view of the stated sociological aims. The concern here is to obtain reliable insights into the means of existence, the working conditions, and the influence of musicians, in a society which seemed then, as it still seems today, prepared to accept them either as idols or as undeserving fools.

Walter Salmen

CHAPTER ONE

The Social Status
of the Musician
in the Middle Ages

·

WALTER SALMEN

More than all other arts, music has for centuries been expected to possess a dignity which borders on the absolute. Philosophers, past and present, have attempted to ascribe music to a world removed from all tangible things, a sphere of self-sufficient abstract expression. Yet in doing so, they have frequently overlooked the fact that the nature of music is complex and that that part which is aesthetically experienced is only one of its aspects. For music is truly as much a social phenomenon as it is a spiritual creation, one which can promote communication of common experience. As a result, music is subject not only to influences of the analytical spirit but also to conditioning factors of the natural and social environment. The creators and transmitters of music do not usually live in isolation, or in discord with the world, but quite the opposite. They have a more or less productive relationship with the world of which they are a part.

Consequently, music can be viewed from an isolated perspective, but also as a phenomenon which is an integral part of the social structure. From the perspective of this reality, music is more than something which merely exists, something which has no relation to the external world. Music has a social function to fulfill and is dependent upon society for its social significance, its purpose and its role. It is actually in part determined by that society.

The study of this aspect certainly deserves more attention than has been devoted to it. It warrants the careful attention of all who are involved with music to any degree. There is more to be concerned with than interesting biographical details, historical facts, or the investigation of peripheral areas. Music and musicians are an integral part of so many spheres of activity that they cannot be viewed in isolation.

Music and society stand in a reciprocal relationship to one another.[1] This is the subject of the following discussion, using the period of the Middle Ages as an example.

It should be made clear that at this stage, one can only consider this a preliminary study, for the state of research in this field has not yet provided sufficient data for any sort of exhaustive analysis. Indeed, the Middle Ages is a period in which radically changing social conditions had such a profound effect upon the basic position of the musician, that the consequences are to a large extent still observable today.

Although composed written music co-existed with the tradition of oral transmission during the Medieval era, a balance between non-professional musicians whose ancestry could be traced back to earliest times and professional musicians already possessed of a degree of professional class consciousness had begun to develop.

Many important factors in the lives of musicians today can be traced back to this epoch of European culture, for example, civil servant status for singers and instrumentalists, some specific kinds of middle-class prejudices against professional musicians, the organization of guild-like groups, unions, etc. These socio-historic and socially noteworthy conditions, which to date have been only sporadically researched, and whose effects are felt down to present times, should be carefully studied for, as the Dutch sociologist P. Bouman has said, "Sociological understanding is impossible without historical insight."[2]

In this review, external influences cannot be set forth in great detail; on the other hand, they must be at least considered with respect to their significance in the lives of musicians and in music. In order to form a well-rounded picture of the times, the socio-

---

[1] Some of the more recent literature in this area includes, among others: H. Engel, *Musik und Gesellschaft*, Berlin 1960; A. Silbermann, *Wovon lebt die Musik, Die Prinzipien der Musiksoziologie*, Regensburg 1957; Th. W. Adorno, *Einleitung in die Musiksoziologie*, Frankfurt 1962; W. Wiora, "Komponist und Mitwelt," in *Festgabe f. H. Mersmann*, Kassel 1957, p. 171 ff.; "Musiker," *MGG*, Vol. 9, Sp. 1,085 as well as the Report of the Berlin Congress, Köln 1958, p. 354 ff.
[2] P. Bouman, *Einführung in die Soziologie*, Stuttgart 1955, p. 14.

historical point of view is particularly important as a prerequisite for establishing an understanding of the sociology of musicians. This is particularly true since the arts were less autonomous then than they are today. Consequently, something like "anti-establishment music" was simply not possible. Music was integrated into the sphere of reality and was much less removed from the fabric of that reality.

When one objectively considers the totality of music and music-making, the forms based upon oral transmission—that is, those resulting from an immediate, specific situation—would seem to have been dominant. The distance between the musician and his listener was usually small.[3] There was everyday contact between them and good communication as far as melody and harmony were concerned. This daily multi-level contact with the real world can be fathomed only to the extent that one is familiar with those who assigned the musician his task and those who made up the audiences. In addition, we must determine who these musicians were and what assignments they had to carry out.

The social position of the medieval musician should also be ascertained since it had an effect upon the music itself. This social position must be understood in order to gain an insight into the tradition of oral or written transmission of vocal and instrumental music. The varying degrees of social integration shed light upon the music, just as the music gives us a clearer picture of the society.

The social structure of the Middle Ages was a composite of different groups, social classes, organizations and communities into which the musician was integrated and accepted to varying degrees. In the late Middle Ages, status according to profession replaced status according to birth. There was a social hierarchy in which the levels were differentiated by specific economic and political rights, as well as by an exclusivity of group attitudes. While such differences emphasized division between social levels, positions were not at all rigidly fixed. With the exception of a relatively small group at the very top of this pyramid, there was constant movement up and down within it.

The number of noble families at the very top was indeed small. In 13th-century Germany, there were probably no more than 150 such

---

3 *Cf.* Wiora, *Komponist und Mitwelt*, p. 177 ff.

5

families. This exclusive group also included the 43 episcopal sees. The resultant aristocracy was guaranteed a leisure existence through certain public functions relegated to it, not the least of which was control of the land. With the exception of the art of warfare, all forms of manual activity were looked upon with scorn. The leisure, material riches and education enjoyed by the small, privileged group made them suitable patrons for the more skillful and polished musicians. The "milte," the "largesse" of these secular and spiritual rulers provided the total (albeit insecure) material basis for this professional fraternity.

It was incumbent upon them to devote themselves exclusively to satisfying the artistic and social demands of their listeners. The sphere of the medieval musician's activity encompassed a wide range. In addition to the court of the high nobility with its many visitors and the episcopal see, there was also the densely populated town with its wealthy patricians, trade fairs and festivals, as well as the numerous cloistered orders, and other less lucrative opportunities to play for common folk at inns and taverns along travel routes, as well as for the heterogeneous class mixture of the many groups of pilgrims.

Close contact with the rulers of state, church and municipality was a necessity for the musician's existence. The musicians who made their living by "courting" the nobility, could expect to receive their compensation in the form of an honorarium, a fee, a fixed salary, a gratuity, or alms. What was actually given him is most enlightening for understanding the status of the giver as well as the social position of the recipient; alms were given to a blind beggar-singer, while an honorarium gift in the form of a fief (feudal tenure) or a gold friendship ring was given to a highly esteemed *juglar de gesta.*

Such significant relationships and differentiations have thus far not been subjected to detailed examination. The musical performer could expect a homogeneous audience in the refectory of a distinguished monastery, but would be greeted by a motley crowd in the town marketplace. The material which he presented as well as the manner of performance was likewise varied.

One must keep in mind that there existed no significant organized public interested in the arts, as for example a musical society, a concert series or concert halls solely for the performance of music. Also lacking was the second tier of official functionaries for music, such as the managers and state music inspectors of ancient China or Egypt.[4]

Audiences for musical performances ranged from individuals (e.g., a music-loving noble lady in her private chambers) to residential and family groups (for example, in a secluded castle), to professional groups, such as guilds, unions and fraternities or the general public which might be assembled in a church, town hall, dance hall, or on a battlefield. The musician had to satisfy many social groups with his artistic ability and, according to his individual capacities, perform a ceremonial, entertaining, or instructional function. His task was to suspend reality, to move his audience into another realm, as well as to arouse in his listeners a feeling for the sensual pleasures of this world.

The musicians' dependence upon their patrons, their employers, and the employment opportunities provided by festivals and daily life was, for a number of reasons, greater than it is today. One of these was that only musicians of clerical status could occupy an undisputed place and respected position in the social structure. At the height of the Middle Ages, musicians were in no way associated with a social class, caste or social station. They simply were a professional group united by the loosest professional bonds. Only in the case of a few musicians, who from the end of the 13th century joined together into corporations, can one even begin to speak of any sort of organization. Thus, the practicing musician did not enjoy the same prestige as was accorded to "musica," one of the "septem artes liberales," in the educational structure of the times.

Even distinctly creative personalities, such as the South German court singer Michael Beheim (1416-1474), were simply engaged as "servants." The musician, no matter what his station, was required to satisfy general social needs in a more or less subservient role. This included the need for emotional relaxation, social dancing, rousing communal feeling in war, elevating spirits during banquets and feasts, or heightening religious fervor in the ecclesiastical sphere.

The conditions under which he had to carry out such assignments varied greatly throughout medieval Europe. The musician, often homeless, was exposed, unprotected against the elements. In addition, the social profile also showed considerable variations, so

---

[4] Compare H. Hickmann, "Le métier de musicien au temps des Pharaons," in *Cahiers d' histoire egyptienne*, Cairo 1952 and 1954.

that material means for the support of the musician were not available in sufficient quantities from all populations. Further, there were some districts in which polyphonic or monodic compositions flourished, while in others, a multi-voiced motet or a ballade was never to be heard.

Yet performance was also facilitated by the fact that the musician's nationality or religious belief played only a minor role—for at the Spanish courts Christians performed alongside Mohammedans and Jews, and English, German, Italian and Flemish musicians worked together harmoniously in large ensembles.

The majority of medieval musicians were forced to live outside the social class system and only in the course of the late Middle Ages were able to achieve a partial integration, by means of a complex process. There was, nevertheless, an internal hierarchy reflected in what were considered subordinate, as well as superior positions. Even among those musicians who had no legal rights or privileges, there had always been a fairly rigid stratification, partly determined and respected by the society which they served. Various factors were operative in this stratification: among others, whether the musician was an itinerant or had a permanent residence, his ancestry, his level of education, his material possessions, his talent and capacity, the status of his employer, his primary performance locale, his repertoire, and not least, his particular performance instrument.

In addition to these secular social classifications, there existed a clerical categorization based upon moral-theological concepts, mainly to be found in many sermons and prayers for the examination of conscience. Such classifications have only very limited application today, since democratic or socialistic-oriented societies have eliminated many of these privileges and restrictions to which the musician of the Middle Ages was bound his entire life.

We will examine only one such factor here, that of the performance instrument. A hierarchy existed among the instruments, and this is primarily reflected in the differentiation between "hauts et bas instruments" frequently found in the sources. It was more than a simple division between loud and soft instruments. The contrast, framed by theologians as the imagined difference between the music of the angels and the music of the devil, was considered fundamental. Trumpets and trumpeters, for example, were accorded privileges everywhere, even outside of Europe. In addition, the trumpet was the special acoustical hallmark of the ruling class. A

PLATE 1. Musicians at the royal table, 1430–40. Colored drawing for Conrad von Würburg's *Argonaut Campaign and Trojan War*. (Germanisches Nationalmuseum, Nürnberg, HS 998, fol. 155V)

PLATE 2. Lute player greeting a group of guests at table. Frontispiece of a tenor song book of a French chansonnier, 16th century. (Bibliothèque Nationale, Paris, Rés. 255)

PLATE 3. Court musicians play at court dance, 1548; the round clasps on their cloaks show the coat of arms of the Hohenzollern dynasty. Rochlitzer tapestry, destroyed during World War II. (Staatliche Museen Zu Berlin, Inv. 19, 42)

hurdy-gurdy was the instrument of a lower caste musician, on the other hand.[5]

Such differentiations were important and existed well into the 17th century, for as late as the Baroque period, there were frequent disputes, particularly in middle-class settings, as to whether wind or string instruments (at considerably different rates of pay) should play at weddings and other festivities.

There were also noticeable gradations ranging from religious services and playing at the courts of nobles and rulers, to the entertainment of the middle class and the performance in the village under the linden tree. The *trobador* did not wish to be placed on the same level as the *segrel* or the *joglar*, while *menestrels* avoided identification with the less respected *jongleurs*. In Malines, in the 15th century for example, the local *biscops piper* ("Bishop's Piper"), or *stadts pijpers* ("the Town Pipers") were not the equals of the *heeren pipen* ("lord's pipers").

Whoever was capable of rendering a noble interpretation of the old heroic sagas looked with disdain upon the dance piper, while the *Minnesänger* who created verse and melody mocked the musician who accompanied him. A *musicus* was not the same as *cantor* or *artifex* or *instrumentista*.[6]* In the Middle Ages, as in antiquity and modern times, the outstanding virtuoso, master of his craft, exuded great self-assurance. By contrast, the so-called *gehrende-diet*, the itinerant beggar-musician, defenseless against arbitrary treatment, dressed in rags, and was often more mistreated by the aristocracy than the domestic animals. The classifications which have come

---

[5] An example of this hierarchy is found in a court account book in the British Library, London Arundel MSS 97, in which the "Trumpeters" are listed at the top, followed by "luter," "Rebek" and "harper," "viall" and "sagbut," as well as the lowest level of non-associated "minstrels." Also see W. Salmen, "Zur sozialen Schichtung des Berufsmusikertums in mittelalterlichen Eurasien und in Afrika," in: *Les Colloques de Wégimont 3* (1956), p. 23 ff.; E. A. Bowles, "La hiérarchie des instruments de musique dans l'Europe féodale," in *Revue de Musicologie* XLII (1958), p. 155 ff.; W. Salmen, *Der fahrende Musiker im europäischen Mittelalter*, Kassel 1960; W. Salmen, "Strukturen im Musikleben des 16. Jahrhunderts. Zur Soziologie der Musik, der Instrumente und des Tanzes," in: *Neue Zürcher Zeitung*, October 7, 1973, No. 464, p. 51 ff.

[6] This concept of division into three groups is found in writings of Johannes de Grocheo and Adam von Fulda.

*"Artifex"—worker, artisan, that is, here used in the sense of instrumentalist. *Tr. note.*

down to us from antiquity, are evident in the differentiation still made today between the *Musiker* or *Tonkünstler** (the latter a term coined by J. W. Hässler, meaning in this case an artist) and the *Musikant* (i.e. dance musician).

The 18th century contributed a further division into *Fachmusiker* (professional musicians), *Künstler* (artists), and *Liebhaber* (music lovers or connoisseurs).

The complexity of classification, despite the clear distinctions scholars have attempted to make, can be seen from a detailed examination of the relative social positions among medieval organists. Organ and portative organ were generally counted among the *altos instrumentos.* They were variously used in the Middle Ages as dance instruments during social music making, in devotional services, and as representational attributes of famous musicians (such as King David or Dufay), in portraits of St. Cecilia, or in allegories.[7]

This frequently-used instrument did not belong to a specific social level or a particular milieu with the same exclusivity as the trumpet. Indeed, the portative organ, especially, was particularly versatile and could serve for all sorts of music performances. Conversely, it was played by lay and clergy, in or outside the church.

Sources around 1400 reveal that the *orgeler* was found among the lowly itinerant players, who (as it was written in 1405 at Strasbourg) were not considered worthy of support, as well as among the more highly regarded musicians, not classified as common *ministrers.*

As befitted his particular ability and reputation, an organist (*orgelspeler*) could be found in either the upper or lower ranks of servants at a court.[8] In Aragon, as well as other places, the particularly gifted were called *magister in organis* and were accorded status separate from the "ministers."

In the cities, merchants and patricians served as organists along

---

7 See examples in H. Hickmann, *Das Portativ,* Kassel 1936.

8 See *Anuario Musical* 11 (1956), p. 38.

*This is really a German translation of Latin *ars musica* and was used from the beginning of the 18th century instead of "Singekunst," the art of singing. It took on special significance in the 19th century, differentiating between music which demanded greater artistic ability and that which was utilitarian music for entertainment. *Tr. note.*

with clerics and even ennobled artists such as Paul Hofhaimer, a highly paid servant in the imperial household, was knighted and permitted to use the title *Monachae Organistarum.* Hofhaimer was accepted as an equal among the learned humanists of his time.[9]

Since the equating of *pfeiffer und organisten* (for example, in the municipal accounts of the city of Nördlingen, 1472, Folio 33) was as customary as the previously discussed inequality between the organist and other instrumentalists, one must always be aware of local traditions and criteria.

With the exception of a few creative individuals such as Hildegard von Bingen, women in the Middle Ages were primarily instrumentalists of lowly position. Since women were also generally excluded from guild occupations, particularly in central Europe,[10] they frequently appeared as *menestrelle, chanteresse,* or dancers with itinerant groups, in spite of the strong opposition of the church. From the phrase *concubinen ofte spilfrowen* ("concubines frequently female musicians") (Münster Chron. 2.84) one can infer that many a female musician left the groups of lowly itinerant players and *moult noblement vestue* ("very finely dressed"), was able to penetrate the circle of ruling nobles. Their dancing, singing, and lute playing were frequently only a means towards gaining more intimate relationships.

The fact that in 1229 Christian women musicians were members of Friedrich II's crusade to Palestine, or that Bishop Woltger of Passau gave such women gifts in Italy in 1204, is proof of how little unanimity there was in medieval society with respect to attitudes towards women as musicians. Women shared the economic uncertainties of the profession with their male colleagues, yet were usually paid less and treated with more disdain. Only very few were able to attain any kind of respectable position through their music, as for example, *Isabel, ministrera de la senyora reyna,* who in 1384 was employed in Aragon.[11]

These few isolated exceptions might be the antecedents of the 17th-century prima donnas who attained wealth and fame in noble circles. But the gulf between the female beggar-street-singers and the bejewelled opera soprano also became wider.

---

[9] H. J. Moser, *Paul Hofhaimer,* Stuttgart 1929, p. 10 ff. and p. 90 ff.

[10] Compare K. Bücher, *Die Frauenfrage im Mittelalter,* Tübingen 1910, p. 13.

[11] *Anuario Musical* 11 (1956), p. 44.

Between the connoisseur and the professional musician, wholly dependent on playing for his living, there were several intermediate categories in the Middle Ages. Singing or playing an instrument was, after all, a pastime for all social groups and in some cases even a second occupation. In certain areas of Europe, as for example in Estonia, musicians never developed beyond this intermediate stage of the semi-professional classification.

One might cite a few examples of this from the lower social classes. There is an entry dated 1442 in the Registry of the Deceased in St. Lambrecht, Austria, which indicates that a shoemaker by the name of Cunrad was the *cantor rusticorum*, that is, a leader of the choir, an honorary post which has maintained itself in out of the way areas up to the 20th century. It undoubtedly brought Cunrad nothing in addition to the honor.[12] In Ireland in olden times, professional dirge-singers participated in funerals, as they also did in Karelia and elsewhere.[13] From England we learn about "Sunday-pipers".[14]

Examples of bourgeois avocational music-making are very numerous. For example, the Florentine wood-engraver, Baccio Cellini, was engaged as a *piffero della signoria.*[15] In 1430 an announcement in Strassburg stated: "da sind ettliche in unser statt huselich und hebelich gesessen, die antwerck könnent und tribent, und die sich dar zu pfiffer werck annement..."[16]* A tailor in Frankfurt in 1499 was also known as a *trometer* (trumpeter).[17] This class of amateur musicians is to this day still actively performing on weekends in small taverns and inns and at country festivities.

---

12 H. Federhofer, "Musikleben in der Steiermark," in: *Die Steiermark*, Graz 1956, p. 226.

13 *MGG* VI, Sp. 1406.

14 W. L. Woddfill, *Musicians in English Society from Elizabeth to Charles I*, Princeton 1953, p. 125 and p. 131.

15 M. Wackernagel, *Der Lebensraum des Künstlers in der Florentinischen Renaissance*, Leipzig 1938, p. 313.

16 M. Vogeleis, *Quellen und Bausteine zu einer Geschichte der Musik und des Theaters im Elsass 500-1800*, Strassburg 1911, p. 99.

17 K. Bücher, *Bevölkerung von Frankfurt a. M. im XIV. und XV. Jahrhundert*, I, Tübingen 1886, p. 420.

*"There are numerous [citizens] in our town, permanently settled and paying taxes here, who accept work as pipers [musicians]." *Tr. Note.*

The musical performances of the Tyrolean knight, Oswald von Wolkenstein (?-1445) exemplify this same avocational musicianship within the ranks of the nobility, as do the works of the Benedictine monk, Hermann (or Johannes?) von Salzburg, who composed songs for the prince's *Freudensaal* (the entertainment hall) in Salzburg and possibly performed there himself.[18]

At this stage it is impossible to define precisely what was professional or avocational, amateur or recreational, especially if one also takes musicians in holy orders into account. Clerical musicians are found in the most diverse positions and places as cantors, organists, composers, conductors, university teachers, itinerants, or even Minnesingers, (such as the Canon of Zofingen, Hesso von Rinach).[19] It is therefore not possible to make a clear-cut division, for frequently there were also *clerici, qui histriones faciunt in publicis spectaculis per instrumenta musicalia* ("clerics who performed at public spectacles on musical instruments").[20] Thus, a valid distinction cannot be drawn between realms of music only for clerical or lay musicians. There was an overlapping of the secular and sacred sphere: clerics wrote profane songs, while secular itinerants sang the legends of saints.

The few musically knowledgeable people were most often found among the educated clergy; yet they could not be considered professional musicians since the daily liturgical and non-liturgical song was part of a monk's way of life. This is equally true for much of the musical activity of the cantor and the choir master.

Yet the Cantor was, as *laudator Dei* (e.g., Amalarius von Metz) professionally trained and sometimes even possessed outstanding solo capabilities. But he fulfilled only one very specialized function, that role which was assigned him by the division of labor in the monastery.

The situation for the *cantores palatii* ("palace singers"), who were, as *capellani* ("members of the chapel"), part of the retinue of kings and emperors, was quite different. They performed at cathedrals and collegiate churches. In most instances they were the conductors and trainers of the medieval sacred choruses, except on those

---

[18] See *MGG* VI, p. 223 ff. as well as W. Salmen, "Werdegang und Lebensfülle des Oswald von Wolkenstein," in: *Musica Disciplina* 7 (1953), p. 147 ff.

[19] C. Brunner, *Das alte Zofingen und sein Chorherrenstift*, Aarau 1877, p. 41; MGG VI, Sp. 223 ff.

[20] J. Gmelch, *Die Musikgeschichte Eichstätts*, Eichstätt 1914, p. 19.

occasions where such duties were delegated to the *succentores* ("choral vicars") and *magistri puerorum* ("masters of the choristers"), and they themselves assumed an administrative and supervisory role over the organization and execution of the church service. They received an income from canonical sources. They wore a distinctive cantor cap as well as the *baculus* ("staff"), for their *officium* had become very rigidly defined through regulation and custom, and was already at the time of the Carolingians a very respected one.

The church also set up educational prerequisites which led to distinctions between *cantores per artem* and *cantores per usum. Cantores* can be traced from the 8th century on in the Carolingian court chapel. During the course of the entire medieval period, esteemed cantors repeatedly rose to high positions, even becoming bishops. In the year 806, for example, the *cantor palatii* Johannes became bishop of Cambrai, while in the year 1505, Philipp von Rosenberg (?-1513) was elevated to bishop and cantor of the cathedral of Speyer.[21]

As *vassi,* that is, servants to the king in the imperial palace, the cantors were counted among the most esteemed chaplains of high rank. Music-loving rulers such as Otto the Great sought to obtain chaplains who were also creative musicians for their retinue. In some churches the post of the cantor carried with it the status of a dignitary. In the school regulations of the late Middle Ages, the cantor's post was ranked just under the rector's and later just under the assistant rector. He had the active assistance of the *succentor* ("choral vicar") or *maître de chant.*[22]

The spreading secularization from the time of the Reformation on forced clerics out of such activities, by and large. In the schools, secular *magistri* ("schoolmasters") replaced the cantors, and in the churches, *musica figuralis* ("contrapuntal music") was more and more relegated to the *maestri di cappella,* who were not ordained priests. In the monasteries, however, the *cantor* continued to be chosen from among the ranks of the monks, and for the cantor whose interest was primarily oriented towards *musica practica,* art was the preeminent mediator between God and man.

It is to be questioned to what extent the encyclopedic music

---

[21] For further sources see, for example, W. Salmen, *Musikgeschichte Schleswig-Holsteins von der Frühzeit bis zur Reformation,* Neumünster 1972, p. 25 ff.

[22] Compare *MGG* I, Sp. 669 as well as H. Federhofer, "Der Musikerstand in Österreich von ca. 1200 bis 1520," in: *Dt.Jb.d. Musikwiss. für 1958,* p. 92 f.

scholar of the Middle Ages should be subsumed under the professional musicians, since the designation *musicus* was one the latter sought to reserve to themselves, the implication being that they were the sole interpreters of the muses. The social position of the *musicus* was the honorable one of an academic scholar and thinker, who was motivated idealistically by an inner vocation. His primary occupation was not music-making, but rather to discover the mathematical laws which governed the properties of *musica* as an intellectual discipline. From this point of view, music was both a matter of metaphysics and sensory perception.

The scholar-musician thus represented, as the *musicus theoricus*, the field known as *scientia musicae* which occupied, along with the doctrine of salvation, an exalted position.[23]

Music as a matter of culture and learning had as little to do with performance as the contrast between the terms *ars* and *usus*. The *musicus theoricus*, as the only scholar-musician who was also learned in the laws of mathematics and logic, thus held a very respected special position. It could happen, for instance, that the great academic professor of music, Johannes de Muris, was placed as a musician "not among the professionally trained *cantores*" but among the amateurs.[24]

Not until the late Middle Ages do the *sacerdotes* ("priests") appear as performers. One example, Conrad von Zabern, taught as a travelling scholar at several universities while active at several monasteries and convents as a reformer of choral practices.[25]

The absolute precedence accorded the theoretical speculations of the scholar-ecclesiastic *musicus* over any practical performing ability did much to lower the status of the executant musician. Only relatively few church composers were an exception to this rule, and among them one could cite the *canonicus* John Dunstable, the bishop Philippe de Vitry, the *chaplain* Antoine Busnois and the *capelláan y cantor* Juan de Anchieta.[26]

---

[23] Also see W. Gurlitt, "Zur Bedeutungsgeschichte von musicus und cantor bei Isidor von Sevilla," in: *Abh. d. Geist. u. Sozialwiss. Kl. d. Akad. d. Wiss. u.d. Lit. in Mainz* Jg. 1950, No. 7.

[24] *MGG* VII, p. 1, and 112.

[25] K. W. Gümpel, *Die Musiktraktate Conrads von Zabern*, Mainz 1956, p. 150 ff.

[26] *MGG* I, Sp. 454.; E. Timm (Trier University) compiled a list of composers of the 14th and early 15th centuries in 1973. Of the 134 names at least 69 could be verified as men of the church.

The composer of the Middle Ages was either a *dyner* ("servant") of the church or of a noble court; "he always had a trade, a post."[27] He had to curry favor with the powerful of the moment since there was no such thing as independent existence for an artist. Art and artist had not yet attained that degree of autonomy, common today, which permits "l'art pour l'art" (art for art's sake). The artist was not permitted to lead a self-centered existence, finding fulfillment only in the creative drive arising from inner necessity.

As a consequence, music was rarely used to satisfy aesthetic needs alone. It was performed most often for a specific function, either in church, banquet hall, or out of doors. The social purpose and specific implications for limited concrete occasions had a marked effect on creative activity.

Rarely was there a concern for the common man, and much was reserved for the ears of the knowledgeable and initiated in exclusive circles. In addition, the composer's individuality was naturally quite often concealed behind the anonymity of a school or the typical qualities of the style of a social class. The *facere* of compositions was determined by the commission and the employer, such as the chapter and the order of service with the congregation in the background. No composer could ignore factors such as the acoustical properties of a given church, the emphasis on the personal importance of the particular patron, the heightening of reality into the spiritual, or the gregarious working together of the *valentes cantores* ("hearty singers"). These are concepts of art with which composers today are much less concerned.

The medieval composer addressed himself to a relatively small circle who were educated to respond with a receptive ear to the sophistication and cryptic details of highly developed forms. There were few cities, monasteries, and estates where the highly developed art of Notre Dame or the Italian Trecento could find suitable audiences. At that time, when there was no printed music and little monetary gain could be expected from the composition of music, the goal of reaching a broad public could not exist.

---

[27] H. Engel, *Musik u. Gesellschaft*, 1960, p. 110. John Dunstable, for example, was in service of Count John Bedford as *canonicus* and *musicus*, while G. Binchois served as *kaplan* in the Burgundian Court. José Anchorena, known as a composer of Masses, was *maestro de infantes* in Pamplona. A. Brumel was active as *heurier matinier* in Chartres, and the composer of ballades and virelais, Jacomi, even served as menestrel at the court of Aragon.

Not until the 15th century did the role and position of the *compositor* (Johannes von Affligem), whom Tinctoris defined as *alicujus novi cantus editor* (i.e., anyone who issues a new piece of music) undergo a change. One of the first important *cantores* who can be said to have been conscious of his individual role as a great musician was Johannes Ciconia, who grew up during the Renaissance (?-1411). An indication of his growing class consciousness is demonstrated in his motet commissioned by the city of Venice, *Venecie mundi splendor*,[28] which culminates with the composer's name prominently mentioned in the work (measure 85 ff.). Thus this cleric, a native of Liège and a traveler to Italy, steps out from behind the anonymity of a servile fulfiller of commissions, makes himself known audibly, and proclaims with proud self-confidence his right to be known as the composer of the work. This is in contrast to the then-prevalent depreciation of the creative *musicus practicus*.

This new development is carried on by Oswald von Wolkenstein who, in a manuscript containing an index of his collected works, even includes a portrait of himself.[29] From then, through the period of the ennobled Conrad Paumann, Arnold Schlick, Paul Hofhaimer, Ludwig Senfl, and into the early 16th century, the word composer had become more frequently used, denoting an honorable profession.[30]

Also of importance is the socio-legal position of secular musicians, among whom the Minnesinger was preeminent. Here one must distinguish between the professional singer and the creatively talented amateur. The latter was a member of the upper nobility (perhaps a knight), while the professional singer generally came from among the ranks of the landless *Ministerialen* class (i.e., precursors of today's civil servants).

Singers from the upper nobility such as Bertran de Born and those from the lower echelons or ministerial class, such as Peire Vidal or Marcabru, contribute to the distinguished profile this branch of the

---

[28] S. Clerc, *Johannes Ciconia*, Tome II, Bruxelles 1960, p. 183 ff.

[29] H. Moser and U. Müller, *Oswald von Wolkenstein, Abbildung zur Überlieferung 1: Die Innsbrucker Wolkenstein-Handschrift B*, Göppingen 1972.

[30] In the "Bürgerbuch" of Salzburg in 1528 there is an entry "Hans Clarwegg of Nördlingen, Composer."

art boasts. Itinerant singers, such as Walter von der Vogelweide, performed for a salary, lodging, and food, as did all itinerants. They were differentiated by the social classes they served and classified as *cantores* if they served the upper class exclusively and as *joculatores* if they also served the lower classes.

The lord of the manor thought of his own poetry and composing as a perfectly suitable activity, whereas he left painting or building to his artisans.

A great deal of training and discipline was required, particularly for the itinerant, in order to hold his art of the *Minnesang* separate and above the ordinary love songs of lower-class musicians. Both groups lived in constant competition for the favors of the ruling class. Yet the lines of distinction were fluctuating ones and many a *jongleur* learned the art of the *trobar*, (the baker's son, Bernard de Ventadour, to mention but one) and made a name for himself as a troubadour. In turn, nobly born troubadours such as Arnaut Daniel often had to eke out a living as itinerant musicians. Only a few, such as Ulrich von Lichtenstein or Hugo von Montfort, possessed inherited properties. The ownership of a horse or the proud rejection of used clothing as compensation often made a clearer distinction between the *Spielmann* and the *Minnesänger* than the actual quality and art of their performance.

The German *Minnesingers* are, from a sociological-historical point of view, predominantly the *dienstmannen* ("the servants") of the upper classes.[31]

It is most difficult to describe the other secular musicians who are generally classified en masse as *Spielleute*. In this instance, such an oversimplification is less than justified, for the relationship of this diverse group towards medieval society was a most complex one. The total population could be counted as their audience, for they were a part of festivals as well as the daily routines from birth to death. Among the *joculatores* were those schooled in theology, men of noble birth, artisans' sons, as well as runaway scholars, blind beggars, and gypsy musicians.

Permission to perform at a court or in the village dance hall was not based upon social origin, but solely upon the nature of the musical offering and the manner of its performance. Consequently, in the 15th century, gypsies played at the Hungarian court while

---

[31] Kluckhohn, *Ministerialität und Ritterdichtung*, in ZfdA 52 (1910), p. 147.

clerics occasionally played for peasants at dances. The itinerant musician had no firm engagement anywhere, but in a real sense was, as it fittingly says in the song, "aller werlt ein gast," (a guest everywhere).[32]

This mobility increased the musicians' sphere of influence, something the performer with a fixed position did not enjoy. Thus the itinerant musician was the journalist of his day, the international transmitter of styles, melodies, standards, and values. These landless itinerants fell roughly into three groups: those who were homeless only for a period of time, those who since birth had never had a permanent home, and those who through epidemics, wars, or other catastrophes were forced to take up the life of a wanderer. In addition, one must distinguish between those musicians who were on the road out of free choice and those who were sent away or perhaps recruited by another nobleman or court.

The nobles often treated the musician the way one would a song bird, which might be traded from court to court, from one district to another, according to some whim. Some traveled as individuals, while others were part of a retinue of *Minnesänger,* amateur musicians, legations, or travel groups. Among them one might find a *stolczer spilman* ("proud harper") and others, who took on the title of *magister* or *mester.* An unusual stage name was already a common occurrence in the Middle Ages.

Despite the disdain heaped upon the musician who found himself outside of all medieval class designations, he was nevertheless an indispensable part of the way of life. Weddings, for example, were not legally recognized without his participation, and many a social custom was unthinkable without him. For the nobility, the visual and aural show on festive occasions, banquets, and tournaments was indispensable.[33]

The *Spielmann's* work was completely bound to daily life and its demands. He had to be able to improvise at a moment's notice, to have a rich imagination, an inventive mind. Yet for him, there was only the real world, a direct relationship with his listeners. His contact with his audience took place at dinner, at a theatrical

---

[32] For more details on this see W. Salmen, *Der fahrende Musiker im europäischen Mittelalter,* Kassel 1960.

[33] *Anuario Musical* II (1956), p. 38.

performance or in church, and consequently, under highly differing conditions.

The musician who was himself part of a group dance while performing was certainly more intimately related to his audience than, for example, the musician at the Byzantine court who performed separated by a curtain from his noble audience. This was the custom in other places as well.

The compensation which a musician could expect differed considerably since his work could not be evaluated as an artisan craft. As a result, compensation was completely dependent upon the whim of the public or the employer. For those who appeared, as in the case of the *Heldensänger* ("bard"), as part of a social custom at court, there was no salary but rather compensation in the form of gifts which frequently had a greater qualitative than tangible value. This differentiation between qualitative and quantitative compensation is important because it was a major point of distinction between the more noble *cantores* and the beggar musician who was first and foremost concerned with the amount of his compensation. For others, a gift of friendship, such as a ring, was more significant than a sack of coins. In the one case, the musician was considered the recipient of condescending compensation; in the other, he was thought of as an honored guest to whom one gave a token of one's appreciation. This singing and playing for a salary was a sore point with all itinerants in the Middle Ages, for the proverbial phrase *Gut für Ehre nehmen* ("take goods above honor") was always used to denounce musicians whenever anyone wanted to bring out something reprehensible about their profession.

Goods consisted of clothing, horses, gold, room and board, or even the investiture with real property, depending upon an individual's rank and reputation. In the case of compensation with money, one can, from a socio-historical point of view, make the most accurate and informative comparisons. The following typical figures are of interest in this respect: In Nijmegen in 1427, the *trumpener, Meister Peter,* received twice the salary of the pipers.[34] This ratio also existed at that time at the court in Salzburg.[35] In St.

---

[34] H. van Schevichaven and J. Kleijntjens, *Rekeningen der Stad Mijmegen 1382-1543,* Nijmegen 1910, p. 394.

[35] H. Spies, "Beiträge zur Musikgeschichte Salzburgs im Spätmittelalter und zu Anfang der Renaissancezeit," in: *Mittl. d.Ges. f. Salzburger Landeskunde* 81 (1941), p. 44.

Gallen, in 1490, a trumpeter received 18 Gulden per annum, while the two *Amtsbürgermeister* ("mayors") each received only 10 Gulden.[36] In England, a royal minstrel received approximately the same pay as lower officials.[37] The compensation for musicians who took part in military campaigns was often greater than that of the mercenary soldier.[38] A marriage regulation in Frankfurt set the fee for musicians as follows: 2 Gulden for trumpeters, 1 Gulden for the lute player and 1/2 Gulden for fiddlers and bag-pipers.[39] That some singers rode on horseback, dressed in costly furs, and maintained a retinue of servants or even slaves, is just parenthetically indicated here.

The majority of itinerant musicians had goods which were easily transported and expendable. Yet there were a considerable number who had a house and land, acquired through purchase or as a gift from the nobility. In 13th-century Hungary, for example, the *joculatores regis*, part of the royal court, were landowners.[40] Irish harpers were citizens who owned property and were obligated to pay taxes.[41] Pipers, fiddlers, and trumpeters were homeowners and taxpayers who proliferated in great numbers in German cities from the late 13th century on. The frequently-read comment that the medieval musician was penniless simply cannot be justified.

One way, often a prerequisite, for a musician to ascend the social ladder was to become involved in activities which lay outside his specialty. The citizen who considered work valuable and meaningful if it had a concrete purpose and produced something tangible often made use of the otherwise disdained musician. Records reveal that musicians were often used as messengers and even as spies during wars. In tight situations, musicians were often successful mediators between warring parties. In epics one frequently finds

---

[36] K. Nef, "Die Stadtpfeiferei in St. Gallen," in: *Schweiz. Musikzeitung u. Sängerblatt* 39 (1899), p. 322.

[37] Th. Wright, *A history of domestic manners and sentiments in England during the middle ages,* London 1862, p. 182.

[38] F. Ernst, "Die Spielleute im Dienste der Stadt Basel im ausgehenden Mittelalter" (bis 1550), in: *Basler Zs.f. Gesch. u. Altertumskunde* 44 (1945), p. 192.

[39] C. Valentin, *Geschichte der Musik in Frankfurt am Main,* Frankfurt 1906, p. 40.

[40] B. Szabolcsi, "Die ungarischen Spielleute des Mittelalters," in: H. Abert-Fs., Halle 1928, p. 157 as well as Z. Falvy, "Spielleute im mittelalterlichen Ungarn," in: *Studia Musicologica* I (1961), p. 29 ff.

[41] *MGG* VI, Sp. 1409.

that musicians' clothes were used as a disguise by people in flight. In addition, musicians were often active as house servants (for example, at the court of Navarre),[42] chamber servants,[43] scribes,[44] language teachers, or even as "quack" doctors.

The medieval itinerant musician was not eligible for military service. Travelling musicians, without legal rights and considered dishonorable, were treated as murderers, highway robbers and other antisocial types. Legally, their disenfranchised status of being considered honorless (*ehrlos*) meant a loss of creditability and did not permit them to take an oath.[45] Consequently, itinerant musicians could not be witnesses and were excluded from the *Landfrieden*, the public peace proclaimed by the emperor in medieval times, as for example in Bavaria after 1244.[46] They were denied both legal rights and compensation. Some cities (Regensburg around 1350) prohibited them from carrying knives, swords or from wearing armor,[47] while others forbade their entering through the town gates (Montpellier in 1321). And, according to the statutes of Siena, a person who violently attacked a *Spielmann* would not be punished.[48]

The children of musicians were excluded from laws of inheritance (Goslar in 1219). Trade guilds required a so-called proof of lineage in which one had to prove non-descent from a musician.[49] As late as 1540, even the resident piper of Nördlingen wore the colors of the bailiff as an identifying stigma. It was thus necessary to have the personal protection of a powerful patron if one wished to survive as a musician in the Middle Ages.

Musicians were not only outside the legal system but also excepted from the moral and custom codes. In this respect the

---

[42] *MGG* I, Sp. 1377.

[43] K. Wiemann, *Die Ministerialität im späteren Mittelalter*, Leipzig, 1924, p. 78.

[44] *MGG* II, Sp. 230.

[45] See R. His, *Geschichte des deutschen Strafrechts bis zur Karolina*, München 1928, p. 93.

[46] W. Schnelbögel, *Die innere Entwicklung der bayerischen Landfrieden des 13. Jahrhunderts*, Heidelberg 1932, p. 304 ff.; M. Gondolatsch, "Die ältesten urkundlichen Nachrichten über das musikalische Leben in Görlitz, 1375-1450," in: Zs. f. Musikwiss. 2 (1920), p. 450.

[47] *Monumenta Boica* 53 (1912), 724.

[48] G. Bonifacio, *Giullari e Uomini di Corte nel 200*, Napoli 1907, p. 20.

[49] For examples see J. Hennings, *Musikgeschichte Lübecks*, I, Kassel 1951, p. 12.

church was their sharpest adversary, both in the east and in the west. The *Spielmann* was thought of as a devil's minister, thus unworthy of heaven. To many churchmen he was a bearer of heathen traditions and attitudes. According to Thomas of Cabham and later writers, only those who at court celebrated the *gesta principum et vitae sanctorum* ("the Deeds of the princes and the lives of the saints") might, under certain circumstances, be tolerated by the church. When Tinctoris wrote *musica est ars divina* ("music is a divine art"), he was nevertheless a musician oriented towards earthly things and presumably captured his listeners with the temptations and unrestricted joys of this world. Thus he was considered to have misused the divine art most crudely. As a willing assistant of the devil on earth, he only led men astray. Yet despite such condemnations, there were few bishops and abbots who did not maintain their personal musicians and few processions, pilgrimages, or festive religious services that did without the services of participating musicians.[50]

Properly understood, this social and moral rejection of the profane musician is closely connected with Th. W. Adorno's concept of Mimetic Taboo (which has been traced back to Antiquity), because the so-called *Spielmann* removes himself, as a homeless and independent individual, as far as possible from social pressure.

Although the musician is economically dependent on the ruling society, he is nevertheless not completely subservient; he often comments upon society or abandons it according to his whim. To be a *Spielmann* meant to lead a restless existence. Such a natural, uncontrollable "Mimesis" was felt to represent an offensive relapse into a disorderly, heathen-like existence. The *Spielmann* was thus a nuisance, a sinister figure, constantly attempting to remove himself from the power of the collective society, from established norms. Yet this was also a direct consequence of the treatment accorded him, for as the weaker one, he had to surrender himself to fate without being able to plan his life rationally. He had to forego a striving for a solid existence.

---

[50] Further evidence in W. Salmen, *Geschichte der Musik in Westfalen bis 1800,* Kassel 1964 and W. Salmen, "Zur Geschichte der Ministriles im Dienste geistlicher Herren des Mittelalters," in: *Miscelánea en homenaje a Mons,* H. Anglés, Vol II, Barcelona 1961, p. 811 ff.

Such a relationship between citizen and itinerant musician was particularly observable in the late Middle Ages when the vagrant existence was especially objectionable to a growing middle-class morality based upon specific virtues. Pay without useful labor, an existence without walls or power, but with independence and freedom to travel aroused such resentment that in many places musicians were denied a decent burial or the last rites. This irrational and unreasonable nuisance of a musician, whom the power structure opposed, was nevertheless a constant magnet to which one was emotionally drawn.

In the late Middle Ages there was an attempt to do away with this paradoxical problem by incorporating the cause into controllable institutions with fixed regulations. This bringing of the itinerant as well as the resident musicians into the fold occurred in a number of ways, e.g., court ensembles, bands, Town Piper organizations, and *Spielmann* fraternities.

Within the court organizations there developed a working relationship of toleration between the sacred and secular musicians. Trumpeters who had for centuries been in the service of the courts as individuals were, along with entertainers and singers, gradually absorbed into the existing ensembles and henceforth known as *ménestrels*. They were now, like the other artisans, workers, and artists, working for the court, strictly bound to specific assignments, traditions, and to the whims of the master.

Some were also composers while others were strictly performers. Dressed in the liveries of their masters, the average court musicians belonged to the class known as *povres officiers*. As late as 1585, the court organist and the court trumpeter at Oldenburg sat at the "third table."[51] In comparison to the place of honor given the *Skomorochen*** at the court in Kiev in the late Middle Ages, this was indeed a modest position.

As the founding of court music ensembles enabled the musician to aspire to some degree of social advancement, the organization of the Town Piper somewhat appeased the middle classes and made the musician's life more bearable too. The resident musician

---

[51] G. Linnemann, *Musikgeschichte der Stadt Oldenburg,* Oldenburg 1956, p. 110.

*Skomorochen, possibly related to Molière's *Scaramouche* and its Italian antecedents, may be understood here as a collective term for court musician or jester. *Tr. Note.*

advanced to the status of civil servant and received those rights and obligations. The Town Pipers were representative of an independent municipal government, particularly if the members also included trumpeters. Parallel to the craft guilds, these musicians formed an interdependent hierarchy of apprentices, journeymen, and masters, while also attempting to monopolize performance rights. In this way they sought to keep out foreign competitors, as well as those who were not members of the guild. Attempts to establish exclusive residential areas, known as *Pfeifer- und Trompetergassen*, aimed in this direction.

The Town Piper was a servant of a political community. His compensation was in the form of money or goods. In Basel, in 1410, the *Ratspfeifer* ("municipal piper") received a weekly salary of 16 Groschen, a relatively large sum, for a non-skilled servant received 10, while a watchman received only 4.[52] The Town Piper assumed a rank somewhere between a guild worker and those who were non-affiliated.

Thus, from the 13th century on, even the musician's desire to lead a free, mobile existence could not withstand the pressure towards organization and the guild structure. With the growing awareness of common professional interests, strengthened by the stubborn opposition from the other side, the prospect of improved living conditions was too powerful to resist.

Fraternities organized over larger geographical areas were united for the pursuit of a number of goals. They attempted, through association with the church, to raise the moral reputation of their members. In other cases, they sought protection of a temporal lord against legal encroachments. Internally, there was the attempt to sort out the incompetents, as well as those who, through their poor performance capability or objectionable life-styles, brought the organization into disrepute. In addition, profit motives, the securing of external group prestige, development of the competitive spirit, and the organized supervision of the education of future members were all aspects of the growth of *confréries* ("fraternities").

These musicians who had always moved about, free and independent, now assumed responsibilities within their organizations, leadership roles which even had titles such as *Spielgrafen* or

---

[52] Ernst, *Spielleute im Dienste der Stadt Basel*, p. 93.

Spielmannskönig—Count of Musicians, King of Musicians. These "kings" formed a professional ruling class, borrowing their titles from the worldly powers. It is characteristic of the then-prevalent attitudes that the real kings and counts raised no objection to such designations; indeed, as the ruling powers they strongly supported the fraternities.

This brief survey of the social status of the medieval musician must be viewed as a preliminary study in view of the present state of research. Only with an increased body of data can one hope to achieve a more complete picture.

CHAPTER TWO

The Social Status of the
Town Musician

·

HEINRICH W. SCHWAB

From the Flensburg municipal court records of 1685, we learn of a misdemeanor whose genesis is similar to the one which provoked the famous women's quarrel in the *Nibelungenlied*.* The wife of a local businessman lodged a complaint against the town musician's wife, claiming that she had not respected her right to precede her into church, and had "laid claim to superior status." The testimony given in court reveals details which are quite significant with respect to the social position and standing of the town musician. The musician, Lorentz Schwensen, in defending his wife, stated that the complainant had "in public spoken disparagingly about them, saying: 'Who do this *Spielman's* wife and her husband consider themselves to be?', not to mention her other insinuations." He further claimed that "having been classified by the Council, in view of his upright calling, not as a *Spielman* but as a Town Musician, he had consequently been accepted as a Master, dedicated to the liberal arts.[1]

---

[1] Flensburg, Stadarchiv, document 35/8, p. 513 ff. 2. Mai 1685; c.f. H.P. Detlefsen, *Musikgeschichte der Stadt Flensburg*, Kassel 1961, p. 16 n. 2.

*Heroic epic of about 1200, written by an anonymous poet for performance at an Austrian court. The reference here is to a quarrel between the two queens, Kriemhild and Brunhild, about the merit and valor of their respective husbands, Siegfried and Gunther. The feud is based upon Brunhild's false assumption that Siegfried is the vassal of her husband, Gunther. Matters come to a head when the two queens approach the church one day at the same time. "The two processions met before the minster [church] and the lady of the land, prompted by great malice, harshly ordered Kriemhild to halt. 'A liegewoman may not enter before a Queen!' " (prose translation by A. T. Hatto). *Tr. Note.*

This deposition illuminates not only the difference perceived as important by the *Spielman* and by the Town Musician, but it also emphasizes the recurring middle-class prejudice against the musician's profession in general. To the itinerant "histrio"* is attributed the actual ancestry of the guild; consequently, the entire group is relegated to the lowest social and artistic level.

If one speaks of an improvement in the general position of the town musician at a later time as compared with medieval *Spielleute*, it must be kept in mind that derogatory prejudices have survived into the twentieth century, albeit below the surface, and could reappear at a moment's notice, something due to that same stimuli which evoked similar responses in the past. In the novel *Musicus curiosus* of 1691, even the modest prosperity of the town piper "was envied by those citizens, who do not like to see a musician flourish and enjoy good fortune."[2]

The Flensburg court record cited above also shows that musicians' titles represented a primary means of achieving sought-after social status; Town Musician was only one of many names for the musician who was a municipal employee. The striving for higher social status, as well as the growing social recognition of the instrumental musician from the late Middle Ages on, can in part be deduced from the changes in such professional designations that have been documented by Arno Werner.[3] Among the oldest designations are those relating to the concept of *Spielmann* or minstrel, as in 1335 in

---

[2] Mimnermo [W. C. Printz], *Musicus curiosus, oder Battalus, der vorwitzige Musicant,* Freiberg 1691, p. 157.

[3] A. Werner, *Vier Jahrhunderte im Dienste der Kirchenmusik. Geschichte des Amtes und Standes der evangelischen Kantoren, Organisten und Stadtpfeifer seit der Reformation,* Leipzig (1933), p. 266: "Minstrel, Performer, Town Piper, Organist, Cantor, Court Musician, Concert Master, Conductor, Director of Music**—this was, in the eyes of the public, the ascending evaluation of those who had cultivated music from the Middle Ages to the beginning of the nineteenth century." Compare also: H. J. Daebeler, *Musik und Musikpflege in Rostock von der Stadtgründung bis 1700,* unpublished Diss. Rostock 1966, p. 15 f. [**The term *Director of Music,* here translated literally from *Musikdirektor,* should not be confused with *Kapellmeister.* The *Musikdirektor* (as for example Telemann, in Hamburg) had the overall administrative responsibility for the music life in a given locale. This might or might not include the job of *Kapellmeister* or conductor. *Tr. Note.*]

*The word "histrio" is a rather ambivalent term roughly equivalent to the word minstrel. *Tr. Note.*

Lüneburg: *figellatori consulum* ("council pipers");[4] in the municipal archives of Basel in 1375: *fistulatoribus nostris* ("our pipers");[5] in Wismar in 1490: *des rades spelman*;[6] or as late as 1578 in Paderborn: *stadt spielmann*.[7] That one had begun to differentiate among *Speilleute* both socially and artistically is shown by the annotation in the *Sachsenspiegel* of 1563.[8] From the late sixteenth century on the official designation *Spielmann* fell more and more into disuse in favor of more objective titles such as *Zinkenist, Pfeyfer, Musicus, Musicant,* or *Instrumentist, Stadtpfeifer,* and *Stadtmusikus,* as well as *Kunstpfeifer,* or *Kunstgeiger,* through which a specific skill, as well as the obligation towards the "artes liberales," were emphasized.[9] In Rostock the titles for musicians in the service of the municipal senate changed from a uniform *fistulator** (1348/49 until 1363/64), *piper* or *basuner* (1421-1469, authenticated until 1530) to *de heren spellude* (1478), *stadt spellude* (1541/42), *Stadtspielmann* and *Herr Spilmahn* (1577), *Kunstpfeiffer* (1578), *Stadtpfeiffer* (1584), *Instrumentist* (1596-1662), and from 1638,

---

[4] W. Reinecke, Alte Kämmereirechnungen, in: *Lüneberger Museumsblätter* III (1928), p. 324.

[5] K. Nef, Die Stadtpfeiferei** und die Instrumentalmusiker in Basel (1385-1814), in *SIMG* X (1908/09), p. 395. [**The word *Stadtpfeiferei* refers to the organizational structure of the Town (Municipal) Pipers. It is not synonymous with the term "guild," for it did not have the same functions. *Tr. Note.*]

[6] E. Praetorius, "Mitteilungen aus norddeutschen Archiven über Kantoren, Organisten, Orgelbauer und Stadtmusikanten älterer Zeit bis ungefähr 1800," in: *SIMG* VII (1905—06), p. 211: Blomekenblaw. In Lübeck one finds "for the first time the concept, Councilor's Musician" in the document for the watchman, Hans Kyle, in the expression "des rades spelluden." (J. Hennings, *Musikgeschichte Lübecks,* Vol. I, Kassel 1951, p. 74).

[7] W. Salmen, *Geschichte der Musik in Westfalen,* Kassel 1963, Vol. I, p. 86.

[8] F. Vogt, *Leben und Dichten der deutschen Spielleute im Mittelalter,* Halle 1876, p. 32: "But understand by the word *Spielmann* lute and fiddle players—yes, know that the jugglers and magicians are also known as *Spielleut,* ut infr. art. 51 in glossa. Do not apply it however, to those who play stringed and other instruments from the music...." Compare also: *Sachsenspiegel auffs newe ubersehen... Durch den Hochgelarten Herrn Christoff Zobel,* Leipzig 1582, fol. CXXII. I am indebted to Dr. A. Buschmann, Kiel, for this reference.

[9] H. P. Detlefsen, *Flensburg,* p. 30; A. Schering, "Die Leipziger Ratsmusik von 1650 bis 1775," in: *AfMw* III (1921), p. 17 f. In Lübeck, the town musicians were known as *Ratsinstrumentisten* ("the council's instrumentalists") "officially from the year 1610." (J. Hennings, *Lübeck, p. 75).

*The word *fistulator* is used here to mean a flutist who performed on a variety of flutes, including what is today referred to as a recorder. *Tr. Note.*

also *Musicant.*[10] The leader of a municipal ensemble, the principal musician of a town, might also have the special designation *Director der Instrumentalen Music* or *Stadtmusikdirektor.*[11] The career of a musician employed by a municipality culminated in the post and title of *Stadtmusikdirektor.* His function was that of composer, practicing instrumentalist or conductor, and teacher of music.

From the eighteenth century until the abolition of the post of town musician in the nineteenth century, the established professional designations remained basically unchanged, even though the rise of the virtuoso and developments in musical composition had created a new situation. The growth of the instrumental virtuoso, judged by his peers to be of greater skill, brought with it new professional designations[12] which only rarely embraced the catego-

---

[10] H. J. Daebeler, *Rostock*, p. 13,17,48,148 and 233.

[11] K. Koppmann, "Die Rostocker Stadtmusikanten," in: *Beiträge zur Geschichte der Stadt Rostock* II (1897/98), p. 87: "An essential change took place in 1623 through the hiring of a Music Director when, on the 29th of September, the council appointed one Balthasar Kirchhof 'musician and instrumentalist, as fourth master and Director of Music' for our community."—H. Biehle, *Musikgeschichte von Bautzen bis zum Anfang des 19. Jhs.*, Leipzig 1924, p. 33, 116; E. Praetorius, *Mitteilungen*, p. 252: Zuber (Wismar 1692/93 "Director Von der Instrumental-Music"); K. Nef, *Stadtpfeiferei*, p. 398; K. W. Niemöller, *Kirchenmusik und reichsstädtische Musikpflege im Köln des 18. Jhs., Beiträge zur Rheinischen Musikgeschichte* vol. 39, Köln 1960, p. 238 f.: Michaels Frantzen als "Directeur de Musique," 1801; H. Kätzel, *Musikpflege und Musikerziehung im Reformationsjahrhundert dargestellt am Beispiel der Stadt Hof*, Göttingen 1957, p. 72: 1871 Carl Gottlob Scharschmidt "Städtischer Musikdirektor." The fact that the title of "Director of Music" did not enjoy protection can be read from a Prussian court proceeding dealing with the use of the title, "Director of Music," stating, "We indicated some time ago (see p. 16) that the bearing of the title 'Director of Music' was not illegal. Only is this the case with the unlawful use of the title 'Royal Director of Music' as was previously stated by the highest judicial authority, The Supreme Tribunal of Berlin" (*NZFM* 57, 1862, II, p. 200); compare here also D. Krickeberg, *Das protestantische Kantorat im 17. Jh.*, Berlin 1965, p. 104 ff.

[12] J. H. Zedler, *Grosses vollständiges Universal-Lexicon aller Wissenschaften und Künste*, Leipzig and Halle 1739, vol. 22, col. 1386 f.: "Musicanten are those, according to an old and genuine definition, who play a composed piece of music from the notes. In view of this description, one would not be doing an injustice if one were to designate even the foremost virtuosi and music-connoisseurs *Musicanten.* But because contemporary usage associates this term only with those musicians who play at weddings or who serve in country taverns and pubs as fiddlers and pipers, those who are in the service of royal or princely courts are displeased to be considered in this category and would much rather be designated as music-Experts, musici or virtuosi. So one is prone to permit them these designations as a means of differentiation, even though they be in part borrowed from other languages, for it is their due as citizens."

ry of the town musician.[13] The artistic stagnation of the town musician is historically verifiable and is reflected in the external aspects of professional designations.

Integration and evolution are the processes which determine the social status of the town musician. The historical stages indicate the direction of this evolution. The town musician's artistic stagnation, beginning in the early eighteenth century, was not the only reason for the limits placed on his social evolution. In his relationship to professional instrumental competitors, the town musician took up a typical and, to him, satisfactory position in the midst of the organists, choir masters, court musicians, oboists, dancing masters, student players, and amateurs. He was subservient to the church musician[14] as long as sacred music had priority over secular instrumental music in the eyes of the town councils. At the same time, he persecuted the unlicensed performers of music as far as the law courts, regardless of whether their music was better or poorer than his. In view of their guild-like privileges, the town musicians generally avoided musical rivalry that offered a challenge and spurred one on to greater accomplishments. Unlike the medieval *Spielmann*, the town musicians had recourse to legal complaint. The more gifted among them, and those who were also interested in a broader musical repertoire, often became part-time or permanent servants in aristocratic households. This rise to being a court musician could involve some social risk in comparison with municipal employment, for service at a court was considered most insecure. "For there are numerous courts which, at the least sign of stress, will lay off or reduce their staff to such an extent that the entire court must dissolve as a result. Consequently, there are many court musicians who long to be town musicians if the compensations were as great. For what is more splendid than stability?"[15]

---

[13] G. Linnemann, *Celler Musikgeschichte bis zum Beginn des 19 Jhs.*, 1935 p. 91.

[14] Compare A. Werner, *Vier Jahrhunderte*, p. 219.

[15] J. Beer, *Musikalische Discurse durch die Principia der Philosophie deducirt*, Nürnberg 1719, p. 17f.; Compare also G. Ph. Telemann in his autobiography in Mattheson's *Grundlage einer Ehren-Pforte*, Hamburg 1740, ed. by M. Schneider, Berlin 1910, p. 363: "I don't know what moved me to leave such a select court as the one in Eisenach, but I remember hearing at that time, 'Whoever might want a life-time position should settle down in a republic.' Thus I went to Frankfurt am Main in 1712 as conductor at the Baarfüsser Church and accepted the post . . . and the loss of fine

From a socio-historical point of view, a more important problem for the town musician was that of integration into middle-class society. Since he was not considered an original member of the urban community and had to prove repeatedly and well into the nineteenth century how essential and useful he and his function were, it is understandable that establishing himself and achieving social recognition in the eyes of the town clerics, officials, and businessmen was of great concern to him.[16] The numerous records and accounts which have come down to us only rarely concern themselves with artistic matters. As a rule, they deal with trials about privileges and defamation, or with administrative and salary questions. They report on matters of discipline such as disputes with apprentices, or the precise determination of day-to-day and special duties. They depict the musician as an artisan and citizen. The town musician wanted to be recognized as a citizen with equal rights, and not be counted as an outsider. He sought middle-class status to the extent that he desired his activities to be considered as "honest" craft and set himself, understandably, apart from the non-middle-class, free-lance, unreliable, non-guild member, such as the roving fiddler who played in beer and dance halls.

In promoting his own reputation and sharing middle-class prejudices, the town musician did much to keep the discriminatory attitude towards the medieval *histrio* alive. The trait with which the town musician emphasized his superiority over the itinerant players was the one cited above by the Flensburg town musician Schwensen: "his upright calling." This calling implied a relationship entered into by town musician and municipal council that is comparable to the "guild roster," the judicial foundation of which guaranteed the municipality dependable service and promised economic security to the musician.[17] In Oldenburg in 1610, a town musician who had customarily sealed his obligation "with a handshake" requested, on

---

virtuosi which I suffered ... was replaced by a pleasant sense of a free life." [No attempt has been made to reconcile contradictory views of the various authors of these essays. In quoting from Telemann's autobiography, Schwab attempts to establish that greater musical demands were made of the court orchestral musician. In a similar manner Mahling attempts to show the opposite (p. 253 fn. 117), that "In the court orchestras ... a musician was hardly ever dismissed because of poor performance, but rather because of improper behavior." *Tr. Note.*]

16 A. Werner, *Vier Jahrhunderte*, p. 238.

17 Compare with article "Zunftwesen" in: *MGG* XIV, 1968, col. 1441 ff.

being victimized by unfair competition, "the elimination of such abuses by written agreement, whereby he, like all others, would be genuinely obligated."[18]

An evaluation of the artistic recognition and social position of the town musician suggests a comparison taking into consideration his relationship to professional colleagues and fellow citizens. One difficulty with this method becomes apparent when, as is frequently the case, one is confronted with contradictory documentation. Conditions in German regions varied considerably from city to neighboring city within any given time period, so that a uniform picture is difficult to establish.[19] Furthermore, natural differences in ancestry, education, talent, and character from one town musician to the next could in some instances do away with prevailing class or social barriers. Nevertheless, it is possible to sketch a very general professional profile of the typical town musician. Toward this end, our investigation concentrates on relevant historical sources—for example, documents pertaining to appointments, professional organizations, privileges, or forms of service—whose social content might be revealed through prognosticative or retrospective interpretation. Such an attempt is undertaken here with respect to Appointment, focusing primarily on North and Central German sources.

I • PRECONDITIONS FOR APPOINTMENT

The dual signature of an "Appointment-Document" was not the first stage of employment. In order to be accepted as a town musician, certain prevailing character standards and moral obligations had to be fulfilled. Of primary importance in this respect was proof of "honest" and "legitimate" birth.[20] According to article 11 of the

---

[18] G. Linnemann, *Musikgeschichte der Stadt Oldenburg,* Oldenburg (Oldb.) 1956, p. 146.

[19] Compare to the conditions generally outlined here a strikingly different situation in the city of Oldenburg, G. Linnemann, *Oldenburg* p. 143 ff.

[20] Flensburg, Stadtarchiv, document 34/19, p. 74, 13. March 1688: H. V. Schutt requests a testimony of birth for his stepson "Johann Mathies Musicantengesell" because he (J. Mathies) "desires to settle in Elbingen, Prussia." The Regulations for the Order of Cornetto Players of 1721 in Württemburg contained as their first point: "Whosoever wishes to pursue a profession of music from here on, and be accepted as

Statutes (ratified in 1653) of the Saxon "Kunstpfeifer," even apprentices should "not only be of legitimate birth, but (should) also not of their own accord have committed any act which could be considered against the law."[21] As late as 1803 a Catholic, Johann Christoph Demuth, had to "obtain the required dispensation because of his birth place and his religion."[22] The first condition pertained because he was not a "native son," having come from Silesia. At the same time, this former music director of the Schleswig Court Chapel Orchestra was also informed that his wife would have to give up her position at the theater.[23]

A Jew in the position of town musician has not, up to now, been recorded. It is likely that this, like other municipal posts, was forbidden to him. On the other hand, a foreigner, the Frenchman Roger Morell, could hold the position of town musician in Wismar in 1694, though he had to admit in his candidature "that his knowledge of music, in the French manner, was quite different from the German music here."[24]

The technical prerequisites included completion of a prescribed apprenticeship as well as the passing of an "audition," usually in public. For the latter, the examiners were generally the local choir directors and organists,[25] and in the duchy of Gotha during the eighteenth century, also the Director of the Court Orchestra; "rarely did the Pastor or Councilmen concern themselves with the

------

a boy into apprenticeship, must be able to show proof of legitimate birth, which the Master will retain until completion of the apprenticeship period, to return it with the indentures." (J. Sittard, *Hochfurstlich-Württembergische neue Zinckenisten-Ordnung von 1721 sowie einige Urkunden bezüglich der Anstellung der alten Instrumentalisten in Stuttgart*, in *MfM* XVIII (1886), p. 27.)

21 R. Wustmann, "Sächsische Musikantenartikel" (1653), in: *Neues Archiv für Sächs. Geschichte u. Altertumskunde* XXIX (1908), p. 111.

22 Flensburg, Stadtarchiv, document 34/52, p. 311, 22 Nov. 1803; compare the same demand by C. Hanke, 1782 (H. P. Detlefsen, *Flensburg*, p. 68).

23 Flensburg, Stadtarchiv, document 34/52, p. 319 ff., 29 Nov. 1803.

24 E. Praetorius, *Mitteilungen*, p. 241.

25 G. Linnemann, *Celle*, p. 94; W. Prillwitz, "Ratzeburger Stadtmusikanten," in: *Lauenburgische Heimat N.F.* XX (1958), p. 15; A. Werner, *Vier Jahrhunderte*, p. 213; H. Techritz, *Sächsische Stadtpfeifer. Zur Geschichte des Stadtmusikantenwesens im ehemaligen Königreich Sachsen*. Diss. Dresden 1932, p. 9; E. Pomsel, "Die alten Kieler Stadtmusikanten," in: *Mitteilungen der Gesellschaft für Kieler Stadtgeschichte* No. 48 (1956), p. 129.

accomplishments" of the applicants.[26] In Greifswald in 1777, the examination committee consisted of "Professor Rehfeld and his two brothers, Professor Weigel, Councilman von Platen, School Director Piper, Choir Director Filenius, Secretary Dittmar, the Merchant Brünstein, and others."[27] The composition of this group can be explained, above all, by the special interest in new concert formats which the high-minded middle class wanted for its city at that time.

Upon notification[28] of a vacancy for a town musician, the interested candidate could write his own letter of application[29] or present himself as a candidate with the help of a recommendation of third parties.[30] In Celle in 1691, eight musicians applied for a vacant position. Among the letters of recommendation there are documents written by choir masters, established town musicians, and a doctor of medicine. They testify to accomplishments on a number of instruments (violin, viola d'amore, viola da gamba, harp, oboe, flute, cornetto, tympani, and trumpet); they speak of experience "at the opera" or testify to a "changeover to a quiet, virtuous life-style." The one calls himself a "native son," the other, an experienced traveler, having served "fourteen years abroad as a journeyman."[31] Because of the publication of compositions in the area of Leipzig, the already well-known violinist ("Kunstgeiger") Johann Pezel was appointed as principal musician in Bautzen in 1680 without having to play an audition,[32] whereas his two applications for the post of town

[26] A. Werner, *Vier Jahrhunderte*, p. 213 f.

[27] H. Engel, *Musik und Musikleben in Greifswalds Vergangenheit*, Greifswald 1929, p. 17.

[28] G. Linnemann, *Celle*, p. 77; H. Techritz, *Sächsische Stadtpfeifer*, p. 9.

[29] C. Stiehl, *Gesuch des Peter Grecke um Verleihung einer Rathmusikantenstelle*, in: *MfM* XX (1888), p. 111 f.; H. Bienle, *Bautzen*, p. 43; Tangermünde, Stadtarchiv, document III, 41: Bewerbung des Musicus G.Ph. Rost, 1749; Flensburg, Stadtarchiv, Stadtmusikanten A290: Bewerbung des Trompeters J. F. Winckler, 23 Juni 1831; G. Linnemann, *Celle*, p. 87; H. Engel, *Greifswald*, p. 12; H. Techritz, *Sächsische Stadtpfeifer*, p. 20.

[30] E. Praetorius, *Mitteilungen*, p. 211: Bertram; G. Linnemann, *Celle*, p. 85, 87; compare also O. Richter, "Dresdner Stadtmusikanten-Bestallung 1652," in: *Dresdner Geschichtsblätter* XIV (1905), p. 23: "Accordingly, in view of the fact that the honorable and artistic Johann Leutering . . . has made application for the available position and we (Mayor and City Councilman) found him, upon audition . . . and other experts' recommendation to be capable . . ."

[31] G. Linemann, *Celle*, p. 81 f.

[32] H. Biehle, *Bautzen*, p. 35.

musician in Dresden in the years 1675 and 1679 had been turned down.[33]

This independent application for a city music post is radically different from earlier hiring practices in towns. In Freiburg im Uechtland in 1453, Konrad Ritter was given sixty shillings for his trip to the principality of Strassburg "for the purpose of hiring the two new musicians."[34] In the same manner, in 1464 in Hamburg the municipal pastry chef received as a recruiting fee the sum of 10 ₰/ "upon the acceptance of the new musician into the town service."[35] In this case the agent was given an honorarium, but not as an expert in music. Even the candidates who failed in their efforts were subsequently compensated with an allowance to cover "travel expenses" incurred in coming to the auditions.[36]

"Because a number of applicants have applied for the position as town musician here," the City Council in Kiel in 1738 established a procedure whereby there "first be a public audition and that consequently the person with the best ability be appointed by means of a regular voting procedure."[37] The voting took place after the reading of letters of recommendation,[38] "subject to a plurality"[39] "in the Town Council."[40] Only then were the appointment papers signed, again unless it was necessary first to negotiate about specific clauses.

---

33 K. Kreiser, *Allerlei aus der Geschichte der Dresdner Stadtmusici*, in: *Dresdner Geschichtsblätter* XXXVII (1918), p. 18.

34 K. G. Fellerer, *Mittelalterliches Musikleben der Stadt Freiburg im Uechtland*, Regensburg 1935, p. 82.

35 K. Koppmann, *Kämmereirechnungen der Stadt Hamburg von 1350-1562*, Hamburg 1869 ff., vol. II, p. 228.

36 W. Lidke, *Das Musikleben in Weimar 1683-1735*, Weimar (1954), p. 24; H. Biehle, *Bautzen*, p. 35; K. G. Fellerer, *Freiburg*, p. 78.

37 Kiel, Stadtarchiv, Ratsprotokoll I/3, S. 978, 13 April 1738; compare E. Pomsel, *Kieler Stadtmusikanten*, p. 129. With respect to audition music, see A. Schering, *J. S. Bach und das Musikleben Leipzigs im 18 Jh.*, Leipzig 1941, p. 151.

38 A. Werner, *Vier Jahrhunderte*, p. 214. H. Engel, *Greifswald*, supplies very detailed information on auditions, p. 16 ff.; compare also H. Techritz, *Sächsische Stadtpfeifer*, p. 23 f.; W. Braun, "Musikgeschichte der Stadt Freyburg (Unstrut)" in: *Wiss. Zs. der Martin-Luther-Universität Halle-Wittemberg* IX, 4 (1960), p. 491.

39 G. Linnemann, *Celle*, p. 88.

40 A. Werner, *Vier Jahrhunderte*, p. 214.

*It cannot be clearly established that this symbol for currency had a single meaning. At times it means, for example, Florin, Gulden or Taler. *Tr. Note.*

II • THE "APPOINTMENT-DOCUMENT"

At the beginning of the 16th century there was an increase in the number of municipal contracts made with musicians. Here were itemized not only the traditional duties and obligations, but also such items as the obligation to carry identification at all times.[40a] Formally, these Appointment-Documents were drawn up according to a model that remained unchanged into the 19th century. Particularly noticeable are later corrections and emendations to the basic document made for the purpose of adaptation to new conditions, in part negotiated by the town musician himself, though the basic format remained intact.[41]

In the first instance, "mayor and city council" acknowledged that the named party had been "accepted and appointed" by them as town musician.[42] Then followed a listing of individually numbered "Conditions." In the first part, the various duties are itemized ("Firstly, he is required to . . ."), while the second part contains the obligations of the town towards the musician and his rights resulting therefrom ("In return we have promised and added . . ."). A central point is financial compensation, generally stipulated in such a manner that the musician is guaranteed, in addition to variable sources of income such as weddings, a fixed sum, paid quarterly, semi-annually, or annually. In the event that music-making might have to be "terminated" or forbidden because of war or national

---

[40a] Compare here also records from Regensburg, 1409 (R. W. Sterl, *Musiker und Musikpflege in Regensburg bis um 1600*, Regensburg [self-published] 1971, p. 107).

[41] Itzehoe, Stadtarchiv, Abt. 97, No. 12, Anstellungsdekret 1751 (1789); Dresden, Stadtarchiv, Sig. CXXIV 214a, p. 34a-37a, *Der Stadtpfeiffer zu Dresden Ordenung* (1606); O. Spreckelsen, *Die Stader Ratsmusikanten*, Stade 1924, p. 13; H. P. Detlefsen, *Flensburg*, p. 18 f.

[42] Compare here, and for what follows, the Appointment-Documents from *Halle*, 1513 (W. Sérauky, *Halle*, I, p. 156 f.)—*Zwickau*, 1569 (A. Werner, *Vier Jahrhunderte*, p. 275 ff.)—*Flensburg*, 1609 (H. P. Detlefsen, *Flensburg*, p. 18 f.)—*Rostock*, 1623 (H. J. Daebeler, *Rostock*, p. 212 ff.)—*Soest*, 1627 (W. Müller, *Geschichtliche Entwicklung der Musikpflege in Soest*, Emsdetten 1938, p. 149)—*Riga*, 1648 (C. J. Perl, "Drei Musiker des 17. Jhs. in Riga," in: *ZfMw* I (1918/19), p. 710 f.)—*Dresden*, 1652 (O. Richter, *Stadtmusikanten—Bestallung*, p. 23)—*Eisenach*, 1671 (F. Rollberg, Joh. Ambr. Bach. Stadtpfeiferei zu Eisenach von 1671-1695, in: *Bach-Jahrbuch* 24 [1927], p. 135 f.)—*Stade*, 1673 (O. Spreckelsen, *Stader Ratsmusikanten*, p. 13 ff.)—*Celle*, 1726 (G. Linnemann, *Celle*, p. 88). The following quotations refer to the Flensburg Appointment-Document.

mourning, the town musician could expect financial "satisfaction" upon the submission of a "supplication."[43] With a corroborating phrase ("This is to be faithfully complied with"), the date, seal of the city, and signatures of the authorized town official and the musician, the document comes to a close.

In the form presented, the "appointment" is a legal public contract between the city as employer and the town musician as employee. The taking of an "oath" is no longer mandatory, and sources indicate that the taking of an oath appears to have been primarily used, or considered necessary, in connection with the older *Town Pipers Orders*[44] which were still drafted in the form of a council decree. The swearing-in of the look-out or watchman appears to have persisted the longest.[45]

As to content and form, the Appointment-Document represents a significant step forward over the older *Ordnung der Spelelude*—the Rules for Musicians, as they are transmitted to us from Wismar,[46] for example. This document, dated February 1, 1343, is a resolution of the town council, not even addressed to the players, but speaking rather to the citizens of the town. The players are here merely objects in a fixed relationship of citizens and senate. In two places there is mention of "joculatores...qui hic in Ciuitate iacere solent," meaning players who happened to reside within the city limits, but were not accepted into service by the town council itself. With respect to compensation for musical performances, the council prescribed to the citizens (not to the players) what the musicians

---

43 Kiel, Stadtarchiv, Prot. publ. I, 1, p. 175, 25 Mai 1685: "Upon the pressing appeal of the musicians, the Council... has agreed, in view of the current year of mourning, to appropriate the sum of ... 12."—H. Biehle, *Bautzen*, p. 111 f.

44 Compare here, W. Serauky, *Musikgeschichte der Stadt Halle*, vol. I, Halle 1935, p. 54: Der 'pfifer eyth' (1461) and p. 281 f.: 'Eydt der Stadt Pfeiffer oder Hausleuten uffm Thorme.'

45 Compare also K. Nef, *Stadtpfeiferei*, p. 396: 1545; E. Praetorious, *Mitteilungen*, p. 251: Chr. Westphall, 1586; *Das Kieler Denkelbok*, edited by F. Gundlach, Kiel 1908, p. 150, No. 178 "Thormans eydt" (until about 1570); W. Salmen, *Westfalen*, vol. I, p. 91 f.: Brilon 1595.

46 O. Kade, "Ordnung der Spelelude [Joculatorem] in Wismar vom Jahre, 343," in: *MfM* XIV (1882), p. 111 ff.; B. Busse, "Eine Ordnung für Spielleute aus dem Jahre 1343 in Wismar," in: *Beiträge zur Musikwissenschaft* III (1961), p. 67 ff. The quotations are taken from the later edition. Compare the corresponding regulations in an order in Bremen from 1303 (A. Arnheim "Aus dem Bremer Musikleben im 17. Jh.," in: *SIMG* XII (1910/11), p. 377).

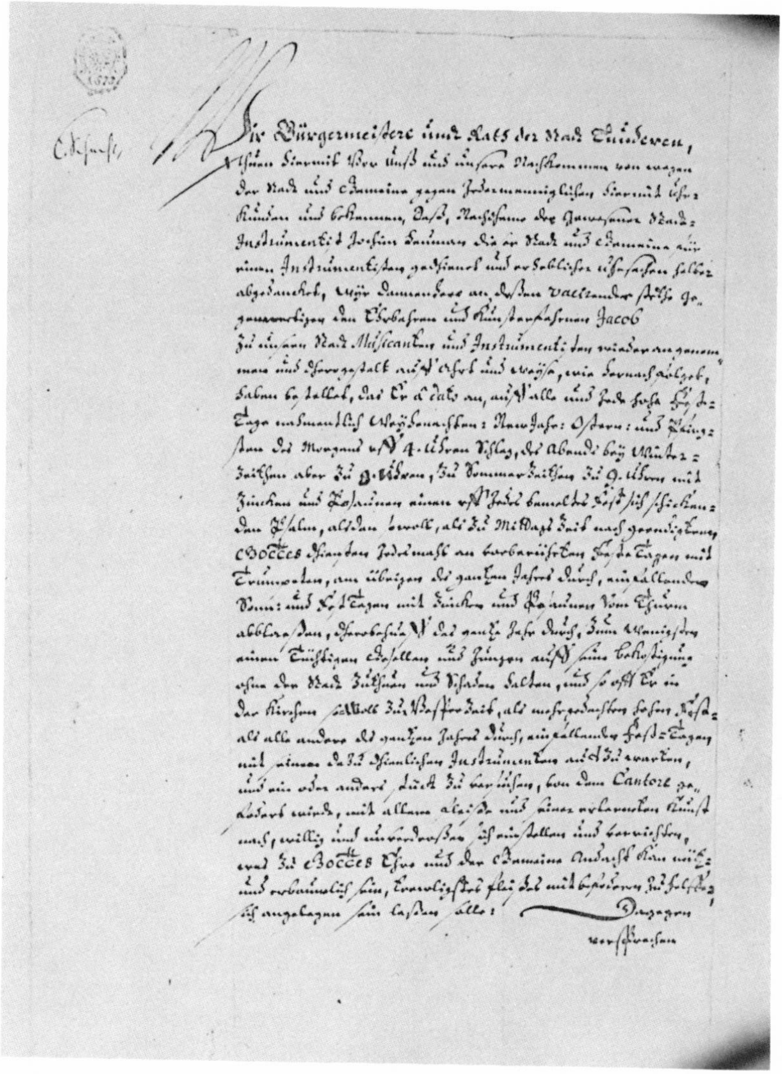

PLATE 4. Facsimile of the Appointment-Document of the town musician Jacob of Tondern, from the year 1670. (Abenra, Landsarkivet)

PLATE 5. Wedding procession in Bremen, with four municipal musicians, 1618. (Bremen, Staats- und Universitatsbibliothek)

PLATE 6. Four municipal pipers of Nürnberg in official uniform, ca. 1600, (Nürnberg, Stadtbibliothek)

PLATE 7. Four municipal pipers of Nürnberg with a procession of city merchants, early 18th century. (Nürnberg, Germanisches Nationalmuseum)

PLATE 8. New Year's serenade by Nürnberg pipers and drummers, 19th century. (Nürnberg, Stadtbibliothek)

PLATE 9. Municipal trumpeters from Amersfoort—a folkloristic tradition revived as a tourist attraction in 1963. (Amersfoort, Fremdenverkehrsverein V.V.V.)

PLATE 10. Detail from a canvas by Anthonis Sallaert, early 17th century. (Museés Royaux des Beaux-Arts, Brussels, Inv. 409)

PLATE 11. Military and (town) municipal musicians in a procession in Brussels. Canvas, 1615. (Museés Royaux des Beaux-Arts, Brussels, cat. 408, Inv. 172)

might be paid as maximum (*non magis quam*, i.e.). While on the basis of the Appointment-Documents one can speak of *municipal musician*, the *Spielmann* or minstrel must still be classified as a "day-laborer." As the itinerant musician, he is compensated merely for a specific performance,[47] without even being able to count on a minimum fixed sum. He can make no demands. If he is not willing to play for the money offered, he can leave town ("Si vero aliquis illorum pro tanto Ciuibus nostris seruire nollet, ille suam mansionem hic diucius habere non deberet."). Indeed, the minstrel was permitted to reside within a town only as long as he was prepared to remain in attendance to the citizens' wishes. The minstrels of Wismar had "no rights," as indicated by Otto Beneke, Josef Klapper and Walter Salmen.[48]

In order to hold excessive exploitation somewhat in check, the Wismar councilmen made one concession to guarantee some measure of security for the musicians ("Ut autem ipsi cum dicto precio eo melius se possint sustenare" [In order that they might better be able to support themselves on the compensation which was established]). They freed the musicians, who had resided in the town for some time, from having to fight the additional competition of newly arrived players, by establishing that "Ciues nostri nullos alios joculatores ad suas nupcias conducere debent preter illos qui hic in Ciuitate iacere solent [Our citizens are obliged to hire no other players for their marriage ceremonies except those who normally reside here in the city]." Even though an exception to this resolution was made when a citizen might wish to hire players of instruments not available locally, or when the desired musicians were occupied elsewhere, this phraseology, guaranteeing a closed shop for musicians, is important as a model for later Appointment-Documents.

Prior to the time when such preference over outside competition became an established part of the contracts,[48a] protectionist clauses

---

[47] Compare W. Salmen, *Der fahrende Musiker im europäischen Mittelalter*, Kassel 1960, p. 140 ff.: Compensation of Itinerants.

[48] C. Beneke, *Von unehrlichen Leuten*, Berlin 1889, p. 24 ff.; J. Klapper, "Die soziale Stellung des Spielmanns im 13. und 14. Jh.," in *Zeitschrift für Volkskunde* XL (1930), p. 115 ff.; W. Salmen, *Der fahrende Musiker*, p. 86 ff.

[48a] An early bit of evidence comes from Chemnitz (W. Rau, "Geschichte der Chemnitzer Stadtpfeifer," in: *Mitteilungen des Vereins für Chemnitzer Geschichte* XXVIII [1931/32], p. 36).

were secured separately. Around 1430, the Council of Lüneberg proclaimed in favor of their own town musicians: "Todem ersten sso enscall neyn spelman pipen este trumpen to Hochttyden edder kumpanien bynen luneborgh ane des Rades Spellude edder he endede dat mit eren willen . . ."[48b] ("Local town musicians shall have priority over outsiders at weddings and parties and all such outsiders must receive the permission of the town musician, in any case.")

III • RIGHTS, PRIVILEGES, AND STATUS SYMBOLS OF TOWN MUSICIANS

The social position of town musicians can be ascertained in one sense by the catalog of duties with which they were charged, a roster which could extend to moral responsibility and liability for the journeymen and apprentices they accepted.[49] Duty in the tower (*Turmdienst*) was considered particularly degrading when it was not performed by a watchman (*Türmer*). When the council at Delitzsch in 1658 wanted to assign additional duty as caretaker in the tower to an applicant for a town musician's post, the applicant declined the post.[50] Also treated with disdain were the duties which brought the town musician into contact with the executioner. Before the town musicians in Kiel would "beat their drums" for the erection of a new gallows in 1726, they had their superiors give them a warranty to assure them that this was, "in fact, honorable work and that no one, now or later, could make reproach."[51]

If it becomes clear to what depths the town musician had to stoop professionally, on occasion, so on the contrary, the rights confirmed to him in writing reflect the social advancement possible. The

---

[48b] H. Walter, *Musikgeschichte der Stadt Lüneburg*, Tutzing 1967, p. 20.

[49] H. P. Detlefsen, *Flensburg*, p. 94: The town musician Timmermann in 1756 was fined 45 ℔ for a violation because his apprentice, Ernst Wichmann, had caused the pregnancy of a maid in his house; compare also p. 38 Alexander Schmidt.

[50] A. Werner, *Vier Jahrhunderte*, p. 215. In a document from Oldenburg (1669) (Oldb.) there is a reminder of the duties of former "town watchmen and musicmen, as they have been known from times past," admonishing them to tower duty: "And this be a verifiable fact, which none among the musicians can deny." (G. Linnemann, *Oldenburg*, p. 158).

[51] Kiel, Stadtarchiv, Copialbuch 5256, p. 311.

privilege to perform is the first and oldest professional right given to the town musician. The guarantee, "Item dor ober, so sol keinen frembden pfeiffern und Spielleuten hinder yne und on yre bewust, inn der stadt zu pfeiffer oder zu spielen verstatet werden" [that no outside pipers or players shall be permitted to play in the town instead of local players or without their knowledge],[52] placed the town musician on the same level as, for example, the carpenters who, as members of a guild, were the only ones permitted to do all available carpentry. Economic existence was based upon this privilege, since it created work. The magistrate supported such a guarantee whenever it was at all possible. As late as 1833, the administrative authority of Flensburg, at the request of a town musician, Heinrich Rudolph Julius Demuth, resolved to place "a notice of public warning in the weekly newspaper against all infringements on the exclusive rights of the town musicians for supplying music at local weddings and dances."[53] The gradual undermining of this privilege from the early sixteenth century on by "beer-fiddlers," students, military musicians, instrument makers, traveling virtuosi, and dancing masters, and its extinction in the wake of the French Revolution, together with the gradual introduction of complete freedom to exercise a trade, led ultimately to the elimination of town musicians. After the privilege had remained for a time a right on the part of the employed town musicians to license others to perform, it was finally abolished as such and transferred completely to the city administration.

The financial compensation, when compared to that of other municipal employees, or to the general buying power of money, is an especially opportune indicator from which social position can be ascertained.[54] Equally significant, however, are the additional earnings, *Accidentien*, i.e., cash income derived from such items as

---

[52] Employment or Appointment-Document of the Town Pipers in Halle of Nov. 8, 1513, in: W. Serauky, *Halle*, vol. I, p. 156 f.

[53] Flensburg, Stadtarchiv, Ratsprotokol 34/56[b1], Nov. 18, 1833. The warning appeared in the *Flensburger Wochenblatt* of Nov. 23, 1833.

[54] R. Petzold, "Zur sozialen Stellung des Musikers im 17. Jh.," in: *Bericht uber den 7. Internationalen Musikwissenschaftlichen Kongress Köln 1958*, Kassel 1959, p. 210 ff. Yet one cannot use the fixed salary as the sole measure for comparison. This is shown by examination of the income record maintained by a Schleswig-Holstein town musician over a period of twenty years. (cf. H. W. Schwab, *Das Einnahmebuch des Schleswiger Stadtmusikanten F. A. Berwald*, Kassel 1972).

funds for music and clothing, *Noten-und Kleidergeld,*[55] money for bathing, *Badegelt,*[56] the sanctioned processions at Martinmas and Christmas,[57] or the income derived from participation in church services and performances at court concerts and the theater.[58] In Swiss Fribourg in 1451 the Council undertook the payment of 60 s. for treatment of an ailing town musician.[59] What the Saxon-Thuringian town musicians might expect to receive in additional allowances was itemized by Arno Werner:[60] free lodging, use of a garden plot, allocations of wood and grain, and exemption from watch duty and special taxes. The musicians of Emden received sheep regularly every year.[61] To its first "Director of Instrumental Music" the Council of Rostock resolved in the year 1623 to award

> as an annual payment, the sum of eighty gulden from the public funds upon the signing of the customary receipts. Further, to supply for the period he be in service, free quarters, to be administered through St. Mary's Church, and that he be further relieved of the obligation to pay tax, and of tours of duty digging,* tower watch and

---

[55] A. Werner, *Vier Jahrhunderte,* p. 233 f.; H. Techritz, *Sächsische Stadtpfeifer,* p. 5. Compare for *Kleidergeld* also A. Kappelhoff, "Der Emder Organist und Stadtspielmann Cornelius Conrady und seine Vorgänger," in: *Jahrbuch der Ges. f. bildende Kunst u. vaterländischer Altertümer zu Emden* XL (1960), p. 47 ff., 72.

[56] W. Serauky, *Halle,* vol. I, p. 156: Urkunde vom Jahre 1513.

[57] H. P. Detlefsen, *Flensburg,* p. 64: In 1785, the magistrate determined that the "collection and processions of local musicians, customary up until now at Martinmas and Christmas be completely stopped"—instead they would receive a fixed sum of 100 Rthl. from the city.—H. Techritz, *Sächsische Stadtpfeifer,* p. 7; E. Pomsel, *Kieler Stadtmusikanten,* p. 136.

[58] Compare here especially A. Werner, *Vier Jahrhunderte,* p. 234 ff.: G. Linnemann, *Celle,* p. 90.

[59] K. G. Fellerer, *Freiburg,* p. 82.

[60] A. Werner, *Vier Jahrhunderte,* p. 233 f.; H. Techritz, *Sächsische Stadtpfeifer,* p. 5; Compare here also the complaint of the Danziger town musicians. "There are none in this city, famed far and wide, so poorly paid as we. In the first place, we have no free lodging, no wood, clothes, grain for bread, as is customary in other cities. Those [musicians] in Torn receive 5 floren per week in addition to free lodging, grain for bread and as much wood as they need. Item . . . also 6 suits of clothing . . ." (H. Rausching, *Geschichte der Musik und Musikpflege in Danzig,* Danzig 1931, p. 88).

[61] A. Kappelhoff, *Der Emder Organist und Stadtspielmann,* p. 47 ff.

Grabengehen was an annual collective obligation for all citizens to help clean the municipal sewage canals. *Tr. Note.*

sentry service at the town walls. That he further receive six yards of cloth as his colleagues also receive, and that he may bake cake [at the municipal ovens] when the turn comes to him."[62]

It was also quite customary that additional special gifts or new instruments, to be bought by the town, were items added to the list.[63] The instrumentalists of Stettin were quite upset when, in 1720, they had to come up with *Nahrungsgelder*—money for sustenance—and called attention to their centuries-old *Freiheit in der Accise*[64] (tax-exempt status). For a time, the musicians of Flensburg were exempt from the payment of burial fees (*klockengelt, Fanengelt*), from the quartering of soldiers, and the assumption of burdensome civic duties such as that of church juryman.[65] "During the current heavy billeting" in the year 1700, however, use was also made of the town musician's house.[66]

One social security arrangement was the granting of what was called a "widow year" or "year of grace." Upon the death of a town musician, the widow continued to receive his income for a specified time. In Emden, Danzig and Flensburg, the "widow year" was specified as twelve months;[67] in the cities of Bremen, Wismar, Leipzig, Eisenach and Greiz, as six,[68] and in Celle as three.[69] During this period of time, the widow had the responsibility of seeing to the

---

[62] H. D. Daebeler, *Rostock*, p. 213.

[63] H. Rausching, *Danzig*, p. 88.

[64] W. Freytag, *Musikgeschichte der Stadt Stettin im 18 Jh.*, Greifswald 1936, p. 94.

[65] H. P. Detlefsen, *Flensburg*, p. 32, 29 f.; compare also O. Spreckelsen, *Stader Ratsmusikanten*, p. 16; E. Pomsel, *Kieler Stadtmusikanten*, p. 136. According to the contract of May 30, 1695, the town musician of Rendsburg was "relieved of all payment of all taxes and donations" (K. Friedrichs, "Von den ehrenfesten und kunsterfahrenen Stadtmusikanten," in: *Die Heimat* LXV [1958], p. 286). Compare also W. Müller, *Soest*, p. 149: "M. Herman Creutzkampf [1627]. . . is to be relieved of the burdensome duty of providing billeting, as well as watchman's duty."

[66] H. P. Detlefsen, *Flensburg*, p. 44.

[67] A. Kappelhoff, *Der Emder Organist und Stadtspielmann*, p. 48 f.; H. Rauschning, *Danzig*, p. 91; H. P. Detlefsen, *Flensburg*, p. 32.

[68] A. Arnheim, "Aus dem Bremer Musikleben im 17. Jh.," in: *SIMG* XII (1910/11), p. 377; E. Praetorius, *Mitteilungen*, p. 209: Joh. Armentrick; A. Werner, *Vier Jahrhunderte*, p. 240.

[69] G. Linnemann, *Celle*, p. 88, 90.

administration and maintenance of the service. The wife of the deceased town musician Hussfeldt in Güstrow in 1767, preferred to "maintain the local musical post" herself, giving up the *douceur* ("settlement") offered by the successor.[70] In order to be relieved of the responsibility for supporting the wife and minor children, cities were happy to relax the strict conditions for employment of a new candidate, if he was prepared to marry the widow or a surviving daughter.[71]

As a rule, municipal employment was of a permanent nature and provided security if the musicians did not violate any of the stipulations of the employment contract, or do anything contrary to the strictly enforced middle-class code of ethics. The town musician Pezel dismissed an apprentice in 1682 summarily "because he had not attended" him properly.[72] Since he had "violated the sixth commandment," the piper Christoph Pahrmann was dismissed in 1637 in Güstrow by the town—and for the same transgression the musician Peter Boye[73] in Wismar in 1659. The employment contracts, on the other hand, also made provision for the musician's giving notice. It was frequently called into use when a musician foresaw a possibility of better employment. Heinrich Pape made it known to the Council in Flensburg in 1667, that he "was able to obtain another position in Husum, and that [he] would like to give notice a half year early."[74] A six month period of notice was

---

70 E. Praetorius, *Mitteilungen*, p. 247: H. Ch. Stolberg.

71 A. Werner, *Vier Jahrhunderte*, p. 213. To what peculiarities this custom could lead is reported by E. Pomsel from Kiel; the wife of the deceased town musician (1688) Böhrens had become the spouse of a successor in 1724 for the third time. At that time she was already over 50 years old, her new husband just 26. (p. 128, 144).

72 H. Biehle, *Bautzen*, p. 32. Article 15 of the "Order of Cornetists" stated that "a master was not permitted to dismiss his apprentice arbitrarily; however, if there be significant causes, it be in the power of the master to summarily dismiss the apprentice." (J. Sittard, *Zinckenisten-Ordnung*, p. 29).

73 E. Praetorius, *Mitteilungen*, p. 233, 212; compare here also p. 225: A. Kirchhoff, *Rostock*.—The town piper of Eilenburg was dismissed in 1624 "because on the occasion of the Elector's journey through the town, he had not sounded [a fanfare] and that further he had insulted the Council." (quoted from A. Werner, *Vier Jahrhunderte*, p. 216).

74 H. P. Detlefsen, *Flensburg*, p. 37.

considered the norm.[75] The Appointment-Document of the first music director in Rostock in 1623 states: "And we have mutually reserved the right to give six months' notice of termination and so state expressly herewith." This was a marked improvement over the earlier quarterly notice clauses, reserved for the employer only, as was stated in the contract of musicians Frey, Amsel and Grunewald in Rostock in the year 1579.[76]

Not expressly stated in the employment contracts, but suggested by them later, are certain external indicators which testify to a heightened social prestige of the town musician. While the itinerant players were forbidden to carry weapons, and a trumpeter in Basel in 1397 was punished because he had "carried a sword on his person,"[77] the town musicians could enjoy this right—an indicator of the free man with the right to bear arms. In the case of the Saxon Town Pipers, the emancipation was proclaimed through a ceremony in which "the apprentice was given a box on the ear, to symbolize granting him his freedom, and then the new Town Piper was decked out with a dagger."[78] In Hannover, Lüneberg, and Celle as well, the journeymen could carry weapons. When in Celle, in 1731, a government decree sought to do away with this prerogative, the music-journeyman Friedrich Brendel was able to secure, with the support of the council, permission "to continue carrying his dagger and was also excused from the payment of the imposed fine."[79]

In their external appearance, town musicians substituted carrying weapons for the older mark of musicians, the wearing of coats of

---

[75] E. Praetorius, *Mitteilungen*, p. 252: Ch. F. Zietzmann, 1773.—The town pipers in Basel in 1547 were, "in the event th y did not remain in service, to give a quarter year's notice and, lacking special permission of the council, not to be relieved of their duties prior to this time." (K. Nef. *Stadtpfeiferei*, p. 396). In Soest in 1627, the period of giving notice was set at one year. (W. Müller, *Soest*, p. 149).

[76] H. J. Daebeler, *Rostock*, p. 214 and 211: "We have reserved the right, in the event that we no longer require your services or the stipulations of the contract have not been properly complied with, to give notice of a quarter year. You, however, are to be considered unquestionably guilty for leaving the post [prior to the expiration of the contract].

[77] F. Ernst, *Die Spielleute im Dienste der Stadt Basel im ausgehenden Mittelalter*, Basel 1945, p. 120; compare here also W. Salmen, *Der fahrende Musiker*, p. 87.

[78] A. Werner, *Vier Jahrhunderte*, p. 210.

[79] G. Linnemann, *Celle*, p. 90.

arms and shields.[80] Whether the latter was from the beginning recognized everywhere as identification remains to be substantiated. It is known that a town musician in Rostock "did not hold to the wearing of a coat of arms, and that he was ashamed of it."[81] The law historian Karl Gustav Homeyer has pointed to the ancient German custom "that the humble status of a person was recognizable by a given, particular emblem."[82] Rarer and rarer from the late 16th century on is the stipulation that a town musician must be supplied with cloth and material.[83]

Also with respect to the dress of town musicians, there was a movement away from the uniform to the simple clothes of the citizen. For the town musician, it must have seemed an obstacle to his sought-after integration into middle-class society, to be identified with the conspicuous multi-colored plaid service uniform[84] of earlier times. And it must have seemed outright discrimination if the clothing were anything like that of the town pipers of Nördlingen, who in 1540 had to wear the colors of the bailiff.[85] The half distinctive and half ordinary "Mi-parti" dress of the earlier *Spielmann* is no longer found among town musicians. However, an additional external status symbol can be identified in the individual,

---

[80] M. Geisberg, "Das alte Ratssilber," in: *Quellen und Forschungen zur Geschichte der Stadt Münster i. W.*, vol. III (1927), p. 323 ff.: "IX. Die Spielmanns-Wappen" (with two illustr.); W. Salmen, *Westfalen*, vol. I, p. 88 f.; K. Fellerer, *Freiburg*, p. 71; H. Rauschning, *Danzig*, p. 20; R. Nissen, "Silberne Boten- und Spielmannsabzeichen und ihre Träger, in: *Westfalen* XXXVI (1958), p. 167 ff., also same reference XLVII (1969), p. 1 ff.

[81] H. J. Daebeler, *Rostock*, p. 50 f., p. 207: around 1562.

[82] G. Homeyer, *Die Extravaganten des Sachsenspiegels*, Berlin 1961, p. 247.

[83] In Braunschweig in 1500, three town musicians received 1 m, 10s for the purchase of "ten yards of red and green cloth" (H. Schröder, *Verzeichnis der Sammlung alter Musikinstrumente im Städtischen Museum Braunschweig*, Braunschweig 1928, p. 53). In Basel in 1547, the town pipers were, "at the taking up of their duties, granted five yards of cloth for the purpose of making a suit of clothes." (K. Nef, *Stadtpfeiferei*, p. 396); compare also Salmen, *Westfalen*, vol. I, p. 86; W. Serauky, *Halle*, vol. I, p. 53: In accordance with the charter of 1461, the pipers received "two types of clothing, to each person ten yards of cloth, to serve for dress for a period of seven years."

[84] W. Salmen, *Der fahrende Musiker*, p. 55 f.: Spielmannskleidung.

[85] W. Salmen, "Die soziale Geltung des Musikers in der mittelalterlichen Gesellschaft," in: *Studium Generale* XIX (1966), p. 101.

presumably unique seal that the town musicians of Bremen displayed.[86]

The town pipers of Dresden were engaged in 1572, "for the sake of music and as a credit to the town at large."[87] For the towns, musicians were prized as acoustical and visual symbols, particularly when dressed in the town colors or displaying the town coat of arms on their dress or instruments.[88] The desire of a given town to exhibit itself ostentatiously was no small factor in promoting the higher social status of its musicians. Significantly, the *Hamburg-Chronicle* of Kunrat von Hövelen speaks of "the Council's and City's most elegant musicians" being "particularly well regarded, and like other places, Hamburg has musical artists for its pleasure and esteem."[89]

Everywhere there were the well-wishers and the jealous, fellow citizens who were proud of the town musicians and others who felt ashamed of them. The Council of Nordhausen enviously found fault with a town musician, Ernst, in 1712: "When he bought his house, the windows of the 'Nordhäuser' type were not good enough for him; he had stately windows built for himself, and on the exterior, an ornamental fence. Then a garden had to be purchased, in which he could promenade with his sweetheart."[90] Social levels within the municipal middle-class society can be measured by "police ordinances" issued for a town, permitting some citizens to wear a velvet band prohibited to others from a lower class. In Flensburg in 1646, the wife of the town musician Heinsen was denounced because she had "draped her bed with taffeta curtains, which were above her station."[91] In particular, the minutely detailed mourning, lodging,

---

[86] W. C. Müller, "Versuch einer Geschichte der musikalischen Kultur in Bremen," in: J. Smidt, *Hanseatisches Magazin*, vol. III, Bremen 1800, p. 152; O. Spreckelsen, *Stader Ratsmusikanten*, p. 18.

[87] H. Techritz, *Sächsische Stadtpfeifer*, p. 3. A similar remark is to be found in the records of Soest, to the effect that a town musician has been appointed "for the honor of this city" (W. Müller, *Soest*, p. 149).

[88] Compare the pictorial sources of town musicians of Nürnberg in: H. Zirnbauer, *Musik in der alten Reichsstadt Nürnberg*, Nürnberg 1966, p. 24 and 41. The musicians of Emden wore the town colors of yellow, red and blue (A. Kappelhoff, *Der Emder Organist und Stadtspielmann*, p. 44).

[89] K. V. Hövelen, *Der Uhr-alten Deutschen Grossen und des H. Röm. Reichs-Freien An-See und Halndel-Stadt Hamburg...*, Lübeck 1668, p. 77 ibidem p. 78 states: "Having such beautiful music is no small sign of nobility."

[90] A. Werner, *Vier Jahrhunderte*, p. 239.

[91] H. P. Detlefsen, *Flensburg*, p. 33.

dress, and luxury codes were closely tied to or actually determined by ordered middle-class social stations, and defined petty social distinctions. The hierarchy to be observed often stands in marked contrast to what is transmitted to us in the payroll records. For example, in the financial accounts of Ratzeburg, the town musician holds second rank after the municipal secretary; however, with respect to salary, he stands below the court clerk, the clock setter, the policeman, the cowherd, and the swineherd.[92]

There exists for the city of Flensburg a "ranking order for citizens and inhabitants . . . and their wives"[93] confirmed by King Friedrich IV in 1718, which recalls the wives' dispute cited earlier. The publication of this decree appeared to be necessary because, "among the citizens and inhabitants of our city of Flensburg, and in particular among their wives, rank-precedence quarrels have led to unnecessary, extensive and costly litigation." Therefore a "ranking" was determined and fixed "by which the entire citizenry of whatever profession, trade or calling, together with their wives, have to abide." The town musician is now taken into the "first rank of citizens" which is also the one designated for "writing and mathematics instructors at German schools," the "merchants who have some 9,000 ℳ in assets," and the "building and bridge inspectors." Above them, in a special class, there are "royal servants, doctors, court and county lawyers, provosts, priests, school principals, mayors, council associates, bailiffs, hospital administrators . . . municipal secretaries and lecturers in the Latin schools." Beneath them, there is the "other class . . . merchants with less than 9,000 ℳ in assets, craftsmen who are members of a guild or holding a post licensed by us, and also seamen, goldsmiths, painters, woodcarvers and other artists who gain their livelihood with such professions." In a third class of citizens are ". . . workers who have no post and are not guild members, day-laborers, working people, bumboat peddlers and the like."

As is shown by this order, the quarrel over rank among the Flensburger wives was no isolated incident on the occasion of a

---

92 W. Prillwitz, *Ratzeburger Stadtmusikanten*, p. 15.

93 *Corpus Statutorum Slesvicensium oder: Sammlung der in dem Herzogthum Schleswig geltenden Land- und Stadt-Rechte, nebst den für diese Gegenden erlassenen neueren Verfügungen, Zweyter Band* (2nd vol.) 1795, p. 324 ff., Nr. 15—compare here also the ranking orders which agree with the above in the essentials for Hadersleben (1719) and also Apenrade (1733); in same ref. see p. 532 ff. and p. 438 ff.

Sunday church attendance. Precedence at table at court had its parallel in the seating order at church. While it was generally accepted that the wives of men of the second and third rank had to arrange themselves "according to the rank precedence of their husbands," the order also determined that for wives of husbands of the first rank, their order in seating would be set "according to the seniority of their marriage." Thereby the attempt was made to equalize carefully the social differences between the higher ranks. Nevertheless, the trial between the well-to-do merchant's wife and the town musician's wife ever living in financial straits, expanded into a battle for social prestige: an apparently eternal struggle between the claims of position and wealth.

CHAPTER THREE

The Social Status of
Organists
in Lutheran Germany
from the 16th
through the 19th Century

.

ARNFRIED EDLER

I • THE ROLE OF THE ORGANIST

The organ played an important role in Christian worship from the earliest times. Nevertheless, the function of the organ and its evaluation by the Christian church underwent numerous changes, and consequently, the status of the organist was also strongly affected by changing attitudes in the social climate.

Until the 17th and, to some extent, the beginning of the 18th centuries, the role of the organ in the church was fundamentally different from the one assigned to it today: harmonic support and direction of congregational singing. This function was actually the product of a long process of musical re-thinking, historically identified with the concept of the figured bass. The beginning of this development coincides fairly closely with the much-cited "style change" around 1600,[1] and it was not completed in some regions until the end of the 18th century, e.g., in Schleswig-Holstein and Mecklenburg.[2]

---

[1] Georg Rietschel, *Die Aufgabe der Orgel im Gottesdienste bis in das 18. Jahrhundert,* Leipzig 1893, p. 47 ff. — Martin Blindow, *Die Choralbegleitung des 18. Jahrhunderts in der evangelischen Kirche Deutschlands,* Regensburg 1957, p. 1 ff.

[2] In Kiel, for example, it was not decided until March 24, 1800, that organists were required to perform at all services and to lead the congregation in song. Congregational singing had "sunk so low . . . that it is unthinkable without the support of the organ; it turns into something wild, unbearable, a disrupting cacophony which destroys all reverence." Stadtarchiv Kiel, Nikolaikirche 112, Bl. 106.

Organists gradually came to take over the role of the precentor, and as the sole leaders of congregational singing were the most important, indeed, the indispensable guardians of an ecclesiastical musical inheritance. This inheritance, a shrunken liturgy in the form of congregational chorales which had been capriciously manipulated from church to church, was all that was left to the late 18th and 19th centuries.

Originally the organ was not at all associated with congregational singing in the Christian service, for the medieval church had no place for such singing in the liturgy.[3] In those few churches of the Middle Ages where there was an organ, the instrument was used for the display of formal polyphonic church music. Indeed, it was used *alternatim* and thus assumed an antiphonal relationship to the florid counterpoint and chant of the choir. As with the members of the choir, the organists, ranked as musical equals of singers, were primarily recruited from the clergy,[4] although there were numerous non-clerics among them, in church as well as court posts.[5] The organist of the Middle Ages was forced to accept the authority and control of the cantor, who organized and directed all music in the church. The cantor's control was based upon the assumption of his superior *eruditio*, both in theological matters as well as in general knowledge. This was the attitude into the 17th century and once again in the 20th century, when large churches attempted to revive sacred music.[6]

---

[3] See Bruno Stäblein, "Gemeindegesang," in *MGG*, Vol. 4, Sp. 1637 ff.

[4] Around the middle of the 15th century, the cathedral organist in Schleswig was counted among the 16 vicars; and at the beginning of the 16th century, the court organist in Gottorf held the rank of chaplain. W. Salmen, *Musikgeschichte Schleswig-Holsteins von der Frühzeit bis zur Reformation*, Neumünster 1972, p. 49. —In Lübeck too, the cathedral organists were probably vicars, or at least men with formal theological education, as for example a Magister Nikolaus, mentioned in 1348; see W. Stahl, *Musikgeschichte Lübecks*, Vol. II, Kassel 1952, p. 15. As late as 1531 a first priest and prebendary (canon) in Schleswig, a certain Reinhold Westerholt, was entrusted with "service" at the organ and given additional compensation for it. (Hist. Pfarrarchiv Schleswig II, 2 b, No. 7).

[5] W. Salmen, "Musiker," in *MGG*, Vol. 9, Sp. 1087. Even in larger churches such as the Nikolaikirche in Kiel, it was possible for non-clerics to be organists. This is confirmed in the records for the year 1458; compare U. Haensel, *Musikgeschichte Kiels im Mittelalter*, Bonn 1971, p. 31, note 87. The organ's significance in the sphere of secular music, still considerable in the Middle Ages, saw a steady decline after the Reformation.

[6] Johannes Piersig, *Beiträge zu einer Rechtssoziologie der Kirchenmusik*, Regensburg 1972, p. 46.

The Reformation did not take a uniform position with respect to the role of organ music in the church service. It considered the organ symbolic of all the musical abuses of the old church. As a result, organ playing was eliminated wherever possible. Though the organ did assert itself in many Lutheran districts, Luther's personal position towards it was considerably less enthusiastic than was his attitude towards vocal music.[7] Yet it was most likely the pedagogue in him which kept him from drawing the conclusions made by Calvin and Zwingli with respect to the organ.[8] In contrast to their radicalism, Luther overcame his aversion to the "organs and trickery" of the "clerics and monks." He was convinced of the correctness of Aristotle's teaching with respect to the existence of certain things (including organ music) which, though from the perspective of absolute truths might be of second rank, because of their capacity to attract can serve to lead towards such truths: "Thus we have organs for the sake of the young, as one gives children apples and pears."[9]

II • THE SOCIAL CLASSIFICATION OF ORGANISTS THROUGH THE REFORMATION

As a consequence of this basic decision to keep the organ, it became necessary to redefine its role in the service, as well as the social and professional status of organists. Both aspects were considered by many, though by no means all church orders. Without taking into consideration here the numerous local differences,[10] it can be said that the Reformation took over the usages of organ playing for the service with no basic changes. However, under the new concept of the function of music and the resulting needs, the role of the organ

---

[7] Oskar Söhngen, "Theologische Grundlagen der Kirchenmusik," in: *Leiturgia, Handbuch des evangelischen Gottesdienstes*, Vol. 4, Kassel 1961, p. 39.

[8] Compare: Georg Rietschel, *Die Aufgabe der Orgel im Gottesdienst bis in das 18. Jahrhundert*, Leipzig 1893, p. 18 f.

[9] Quoted after Christoph Wetzel, "Die Träger des liturgischen Amtes," in *Leiturgia*, Vol. 4, p. 303, note 240.

[10] The author is currently preparing a study for the area of Schleswig-Holstein-Lübeck-Hamburg and the Duchy of Lauenburg which attempts to establish in detail, on the basis of records available, the organists' work in a socio-historical context.

was modified and considerably expanded. This expansion was concerned primarily with transferring the antiphonal concept to the basic new element of the Lutheran service, the chorale sung in alternation with the congregation.

Usually the Lutheran organist was no longer a cleric; indeed, church regulations prescribed the hiring of men "well versed in their art and upright." This meant that musical ability and technical knowledge rather than academic or theological background were considered the essential prerequisites. It was also pointed out, however, that it was forbidden "to play worldly, disgraceful and unsuitable songs in church,"[11] a precaution which was thought particularly necessary in view of the fact that lay professional musicians were closely associated with the ranks of itinerant players. (Such traveling *Spielleute* had, from the Middle Ages, been subject to considerable social prejudice.) In Lübeck, for example, the close relationship between organists and these other instrumentalists was maintained into the 19th century. In fact, it was not until 1815 that the department of municipal music was abolished there. The majority of the organists at the Ägidienkirche, as well as many others in Lübeck, were both organists and also *Ratsmusikanten*, municipal musicians identified with all the features of the civil service. In the course of the 16th and 17th centuries, many were given the supervisory post associated with the title of *Spielgreven*.[12]

The close relationship between both musical professions became especially evident later, in the careers of members of "musical dynasties," such as the families Bruhns, Zinck, Kuntzen, Paulsen, and Kortkamp, among others, in which the children learned to master a large number of instruments. In this way one was ready for all possible musical demands, and it was consequently often a matter of chance whether one became an instrumentalist or a municipal or court organist.

---

11 "Hamburger Kirchenordnung des Superintendenten Aepinus von 1556," quoted in: Emil Sehling (ed.), *Die Evangelischen Kirchenordnungen des XVI. Jahrhunderts*, Vol. 5, Leipzig 1913, p. 547.
12 W. Stahl, *Musikgeschichte Lübecks, Vol. 2/Geistliche Musik*, Kassel and Basel 1952, p. 32, 73, 115. —J. Hennings, *Musikgeschichte Lübecks, Vol 1/Weltliche Musik*, Kassel and Basel 1951, p. 21, 76.

III • THE TRAINING OF ORGANISTS

The Age of the Reformation viewed the activity of the organist as only a part-time one. As a result, it was thought even then that the organist should augment his income from other sources, primarily in the area of music pedagogy.[13] Only in a small number of cases, however, did he teach keyboard instruments to interested dilettantes. It was not until the end of the 17th, and above all, the 18th centuries that, in many circles, it was considered essential to a proper upbringing to be able to play a keyboard instrument.[14] It was much more likely that the majority of their students were people who required a knowledge of organ playing for their training as craftsmen in organ building. The "art" of the organist at that time included and was indeed judged to a considerable degree by his technical competence as an organ builder, and this is documented by the fact that many an important organist of the 16th century is designated as a "master."[15] This recognition served to counterbalance the socially unacceptable musical element with which organists as a class were still identified. Organists such as Barthold Hering were both the builders and players of their instruments. Such ideal combinations became ever more impossible with the increasing musical specialization from the 17th century on.

Accordingly, training in the art of organ playing bore those patriarchal features which had developed in the crafts in pre-industrial times. The guild-craft approach towards the acquirement of skills is as observable among organists as it is with Town and Court Musicians. In contrast to other musicians, however, the organist was never eager to form professional associations after the

---

[13] Thus, one can read in the Hamburg church regulations of 1529: "They [the organists] can easily earn additional income, especially can they teach their art to others, since they only play on holy days, so that they have the other days free." E. Sehling, *Kirchenordnungen V*, p. 512 f.

[14] O. Kinkeldey, *Orgel und Klavier in der Musik des 16. Jahrhunderts*, Leipzig 1910, p. 82.—F.W. Riedel, *Quellenkundliche Beiträge zur Geschichte der Musik für Tasteninstrumente in der zweiten Hälfte des 17. Jahrhunderts*, Kassel and Basel 1960 (*Schriften des Landesinstituts für Musikforschung Kiel*, Vol. 10), p. 14 f.

[15] Examples are: Meister Andreas (Smedecke) at the Dom in Hamburg, Meister Peter at the Katharinenkirche in Hamburg, ca. 1500-1521, Meister Andreas (Wirck) at Hamburg's Nikolaikirche 1505-1530, and Meister Barthold (Hering) at Lübeck's Marienkirche, ca. 1515-1556.

model of the guilds.[16] The organist was just as self-reliant in the pursuit of his social and material goals as he was in playing his instrument, with the exception that, due to his additional employ- ment, he might be a member of another professional organization. This individualistic approach continued and grew in the 18th century due to the rapid disintegration of church administration, and also accelerated the decline in the social and material conditions of the organist.

IV • THE ORGANIST AND THE SCHOOL SYSTEM

In those communities where the organist was only partially burdened by his duties as organist and builder, he was often also the sexton as well as the school master. Such combinations took on many forms. In an affluent area such as the farming, region of Dithmarschen, where in the 16th century even small villages boasted numerous organs, the instruments were played by the local school master who, as the only literate person besides the pastor, also frequently was required to take care of church correspondence.[17] In cities, the school activity of the organist was most often limited to providing help to the regular teachers.[18]

In view of the many differences, it is not really possible to speak in general of an "organists' school" or "sextons' school" during the period of the Reformation.[19] Organists might well be employed in

---

[16] H.W. Schwab, "Zunftwesen," in: *Die Musik in Geschichte und Gegenwart,* ed. F. Blume, Vol. 14, Sp. 1442.

[17] So it was that the organist in the village of Busen in Dithmarschen, in the year 1582, received a fixed income of 40 Ml (Marks "lübsch"), money in the Lübeck currency, so that he could "diligently instruct the boys in school 2 hours daily, one in the morning and one in the afternoon." In addition he had to be "chapel secretary and read correspondence."—E. Rolfs, "Aus Dithmarsischen Visitationsprotokollen," in: *Schriften des Vereins für Schleswig-Holsteinische Kirchengeschichte Reihe II,* Vol. 5, p. 426.

[18] In Lauenburg in 1581 the organist was required to help in "school service." The church inspectors required of him, as of the sexton, who served in the same capacity, that they "be assigned as regular 'colleagues in the school' under the supervision of the school master."—*Landesarchiv Schleswig,* Sect. 218, No. 654 (Kirchenvisita- tionsbericht für das Fürstentum Niedersachsen 1581), p. 15.

[19] For example, P. v. Hedemann-Heespen, "Des Kirchenspiel des Kreises Westensee," in: *Heimatbuch des Kreises Rendsburg,* 1922, p. 391.

the "German Grammar School" of small and larger cities,[20] in the "Klipp" and "Winkel" schools (meaning here, in part, obscure private institutions) in the countryside, as well as in the "Latin Schools."[21] In fact, it was not considered beneath the dignity of a *Rektor* of a Latin school also to hold a post as organist, as was the case with Magister Laurentius Thomae of Apenrade (Denmark/North Schleswig-Holstein).[22]

V • ORGANISTS AS ECCLESIASTICAL ADMINISTRATORS

Particularly in small towns, organists frequently held the post of church secretary, though frequently it was a joint responsibility with the local school master. In the three main churches of Hamburg—St. Petri, St. Jakobi, St. Katharinen—this practice can be traced from the second half of the 16th century[23] through all of the 17th and part of the 18th centuries. There were only a few exceptions, notably that of Johann Adam Reinken who, as successor to his teacher Heinrich Scheidemann at the Katharinenkirche, rejected the secretarial post in 1666, stating that it was "burdensome and moreover not fitting his profession."[24] This attitude of Reinken, accepted by the society, was the result of an artistic self-confidence which went far beyond the prevalent convention for organists. It later supplied the mocking pen of Johann Mattheson with evidence for his unfounded contention concerning the false ranking of organists.

The secretarial records of organists in Hamburg, among them manuscripts of Jakob and Hieronymus Praetorius, provide valuable information with respect to liturgical repertoire at the Jakobikirche in Hamburg in the 16th century. In Lübeck, such organists' records

[20] So it was in the St. Nikolaischule in Hamburg, where the organists also served as "monitors." L. Krüger, *Die Hamburgische Musik-organisation im XVII Jahrhundert*, Leipzig-Strassburg-Zürich 1933, p. 134.
[21] In Flensburg, the organist at the Marienkirche, Frederick Lutter, is said to have taught at the Latin school until it was converted into a German school in 1566. H.P. Detlefsen, *Musikgeschichte Flensburgs*, Kassel and Basel 1961, p. 110.
[22] L. Andresen, "Des Petrus Fabricius Leben," in: *Die Heimat* Jahrgang 39 (1929), p. 268 f.
[23] Liselotte Krüger, "Johann Kortkamps Organistenchronik," in: *Zeitschrift für Hamburgische Geschichte*, No. 33, 1933, p. 194. —H. Leichsenring, *Hamburgische Kirchenmusik im Reformationszeitalter*, doct. diss., Berlin 1922, p. 68.
[24] L. Krüger, *Hamburgische Musikorganisation*, p. 163.

reflect the all-inclusive activities of the *Werkmeister,* ("general overseer"), with figures for materials purchased, as well as the financial and general administration of the church.[25]

In Kiel, the organist Jakob Kortkamp was given the responsibility for administering the church-owned brickworks, and an error in his bookkeeping, in connection with the insolvency of a debtor, brought him to financial disaster; the church held him fully responsible, holding back his full pay from 1652 until 1660, and forcing him and his family to exist on bread and water.[26] In such rural areas as Schwabstedt (near Husum in Schleswig-Holstein), the organist was used by the church administration as the "granary scribe."

VI • THE POSITION OF THE ORGANIST IN THE CHURCH HIERARCHY

To the extent that 16th-century church regulations dealt with the organist at all, they reflect a social ranking with the sexton, on the level of "lower church servants." Such rankings were determined by the pastors, church elders, and *Juraten* ("elders") of a parish. Pastors were designated as their direct superiors "to whom they owe obedience."[27] Yet this relationship appears to have been contested, and it is noteworthy that in 1529, in Bugenhagen, regulations for sextons emphasizing such obedience to pastors did not apply to the organists. In 1585, regulations of Lauenburg mention "petulant, rebellious complaining" among organists. In spite of differing regional conditions, organists rebelled against pastors, particularly with respect to the choice of music, length, and tempi, well into the 19th century.

As might be suspected, there was relatively little cause for disagreement as long as the organist was assigned a distinct and separate place in the service, removed from other musical performers. When he was employed to accompany and conduct congrega-

---

25 W. Stahl, *Dietrich Buxtehude,* Kassel and Basel 1937, p. 17.

26 E. Pomsel, "Die Organisten der Kieler Nikolaikirche von der Reformation bis zum Ausgang des 19. Jahrhunderts," in: *Mitteilungen der Gesellschaft für Kieler Stadtgeschichte,* Vol. 53, 1959, Heft 1/2, p. 50 f.

27 "Hamburger Kirchenordnung des Aepinus, 1556," in: Sehling, *Kirchenordnungen,* Vol. 5, p. 547.

tional singing, however, many opportunities for misunderstandings arose.

The appointment of an organist was generally made by the church council of elders (known as *Juraten* and *Conservatoren*), as well as the mayor or some other secular authority representative. In the case of patronage churches, the patron had the decisive voice into the 19th century. The pastor or pastors of a church had no legal role in the hiring of organists or in the determination of their duties. This was reserved for the competent prior or provost.[28]

These relationships were maintained in a relatively stable manner into the 19th century, and a dispute in 1818 between the well-known theologian Claus Harms and the organist Georg Christian Apel in Kiel was clarified by a member of the church council. It was stated that no subordinate relationship existed between "church officials" and pastor, but that the duties of the former were determined by the pastors, and that the pastors' duties and authority were limited to making certain "that the official comply with and carry out the task in accordance with church regulations."[29]

On the other hand, it was a fact that in small places where organists' duties were combined with those of the sexton, the man holding such a combined post was cast in the role of servant to the pastor.[30] Then too, in his role as school master, the sexton-organist was viewed by the Reformation as the pastor's representative, one who had under his direct supervision the task of carrying out religious instruction.

The ecclesiastical duties of a sexton seemed so degrading to the organist of Mölln, Joachim Heinrich Haacke, a man thoroughly convinced of the dignity of his musical post, that in 1697 he used a portion of his income to pay someone else to do the sexton's work. In view of the fact that the city refused to separate the two functions, the organists of Mölln continued to make this sacrifice during the 18th century in spite of increasing material hardships, in order to demonstrate that the social recognition due the organist was being

---

[28] Investiture of the organist Christian Wendeler in Hadersleben in 1653: *Hadersleben Radstue-Arkivet.* In Hamburg the collegium of church-coroner jurymen was the organists' governing authority, as is verified by investiture records.

[29] Stadtarchiv Kiel, Records of the Nikolaikirche, No. 12.

[30] It was one of the duties of organists in the small Johanniskirche on the outskirts of Flensburg to assist the pastor in dressing.

unjustly denied. One organist[31] carried matters so far that he took up a hopeless battle with the town elders, the so-called *Feuergräfen*,[32] in the year 1738. He demanded for himself the right to take his place at funeral processions directly behind the mayor and councilmen, that is, ahead of the *Feuergreven*. After a long-winded trial, which in its records reflects the whole problematic question of artistic self-confidence and social status of the 18th-century organist,[33] the government of Ratzeburg decided that the organist could not "presume to take a place between the municipal magistrate and the most aristocratic citizens of Mölln, namely the *Feuergräfen*." Since he was a servant of the church, both in his capacity as organist and sexton, it was not to be permitted that he, unlike the staff of the municipal school, follow directly after the magistrate.[34]

VII • ORGANIST AND CANTOR

The organist and cantor had separate and distinct duties, the latter being responsible for vocal music. Since the Reformation, the cantor had been assigned two basically related functions. He led the total contrapuntal and choral music of the church, and was also responsible for developing the school choirs which formed the basis for contrapuntal church singing. In other words, he also had a pedagogic function at the Latin schools. As a full-fledged colleague at such schools, he taught his discipline, music, as a science, the aspect from which it had been viewed since the Middle Ages. In

---

31 Christian Georg Müthel, father of the well-known composer and student of Bach, Johann Gottfried Müthel, was organist in Mölln after 1717 and also took on the post of Town Musician in 1735.

32 The "Feuergreven" were six respected citizens of the city; among them were frequently found mayors and councilmen, who were charged with the supervision of municipal fire protection and who, on the basis of this, possessed certain rights, received revenues, and even were empowered with punitive authority. After 1598 they had their own church seat, embossed with their coat of arms, and in the Town Hall a "Feuergrevenbuch," a book of names, was kept. E. Kemmler, *Johann Gottfried Müthel (1728-1788) und das norddeutsche Musikleben seiner Zeit*. Marburg 1970, p. 216, note 5.

33 A detailed description of the legal proceeding is given in a work currently in preparation by the author on the social history of organ music in Schleswig-Holstein, Hamburg, Lübeck and Lauenburg.

34 *Stadtarchiv Mölln II*, No. 117, letter dated, October 9, 1738.

addition, like other teachers, he taught a number of other subjects. Thus the cantor, as an elevated member of the church and school hierarchy, enjoyed numerous freedoms from the routine obligations to which the municipal and rural population were subject. As was the case with pastors, cantors did not have to earn the rights of citizenship, and they were also automatically exempt from military service as well as watch duty.[35]

In contrast to conditions in central Germany, the cantor in northern Germany during the 16th and early 17th centuries was primarily utilized as a teacher. Composition, a matter of course in central Germany, played a lesser role in the life of a cantor in the north. As a result, the organists here found it possible to demonstrate their musical superiority over the scholar-cantor. The extant collections of vocal church music of Hamburg of the 16th century are not primarily written by cantors but by members of the Praetorius Dynasty of organists.[36] Even the *Hamburger Melodeyengesangbuch* of 1604, a hymn-book of great significance in the history of Protestant congregational singing, was a joint project of four organists of Hamburg's main churches. It introduced the "Kantionalsatz," a primarily four-voiced homophonic composition, as well as the concept of organ accompaniment (*in den Gesang*

---

[35] D. Krickeberg, "Das protestantische Kantorat im 17. Jahrhundert," *Veröffentlichungen des Musikwissenschaftlichen Instituts der Freien Universität Berlin* (ed. A. Adrio) Vol. 6, Berlin 1965, p. 78.

[36] Jacobus Praetorius, who was organist and secretary of the Jacobikirche (from 1554-1586), assembled in 1554, under the title "Cantilenae sacrae," the monophonic church songs then currently in use. Included was the accompanying antiphonal organ part (Königliche Bibliothek Kopenhagen, Mskr. Thott 151 fol.). In 1566 he undertook the task of collecting the contrapuntal repertoire of the choir of the Johannisschule, a group which sang at Hamburg's main churches. This was an opus in four parts (Katalog der Ausstellung *Die Musik Hamburgs im Zeitalter Seb. Bachs*, Hamburg 1921, p. 46). The assumption based upon this, made by L. Krüger (*Hamburgische Musikorganisation*, p. 24), that Jacobus Praetorius must have been a cantor at the Johannisschule for a time before he accepted the post as organist, is unlikely, in view of the fact that this would have meant a social regression. Jacob. Praetorius' son, the famous Hieronymus Praetorius, organist at Hamburg's Jacobikirche (1582-1629), compiled a similar work of that city's "lateinischen Chorale und Kirchenmelodeyen," which was printed in 1588 by the cantor of the Johannisschule, Henricus Eler, without mentioning Praetorius' name. The work was known in Lübeck and Lüneburg as well. L. Krüger, *Musikorganisation*, p. 31 f.

[37] F. Blume, *Geschichte der Evangelischen Kirchenmusik*[2], Kassel ... 1965, p. 87. — G. Rietschel, *Die Aufgabe der Orgel im Gottesdienst*, p. 52 f.

spielen).[37] Cantors were not involved in the creation of this hymn-book. Similarly, the notorious quarrel between the organist in Danzig, Paul Siefert, and the cantor Kaspar Förster arose primarily from the fact that Siefert refused, as a composer, to assume a subservient position to the non-composer school cantor.[38]

The socio-historical significance of this case is not so much a matter of a composer-organist denying due respect to an untalented cantor, but rather that here, at a relatively early period, the art of musical composition was assigned such significance that the degree of its mastery was used as a standard to measure social status. At an earlier time composition had not previously been accorded such significance, and even Siefert was not successful in asserting his demands. Still, the tendency was clearly established that the cantor was to be an all-around teacher, and thus was established a direct competitive relationship between cantor and organist, as well as other musicians. Towards the end of the 17th and beginning of the 18th centuries this development led to the well-known problem faced by cantors, that of asserting themselves against the increasing influence of operatic music. In this connection it should be noted that two organists were intimately involved with the founding of the first municipal opera house in Germany in Hamburg in 1678: Johann Adam Reinken was an important advisor and threw his musical prestige on the side of opera against the theological opposition, while Jürgen Bronner, organist and sexton at the Holy Ghost Hospital, was active as co-entrepreneur and composer at the opera.

Organists were also a moving force in the development of public concerts, of which the most significant precursor, the *Collegium Musicum*, was first distinctly defined in North German Lutheran areas by the organist of the Jacobikirche in Hamburg, Matthias Weckmann. During the 14 years of its existence (1660-1674), this forum placed Hamburg in the position of musical leader in northern Germany for decades to come. Weckmann's activity in the *Collegium Musicum* is of socio-historical relevance insofar as one can observe here a changeover from music-making in the service of the church to public musical activity, privately sponsored.[39]

---

38 M. Seiffert, Paul Seiffert, in: *VjfMw.* VII, 1891, p. 405 f. —H. Rauschning, *Geschichte der Musik und Musikpflege in Danzig,* Danzig 1931, p. 144 f.

39 J. Habermas, *Strukturwandel der Öffentlichkeit, Untersuchungen zu einer Kategorie der bürgerlichen Gesellschaft,*[5] Neuwied 1971, p. 45, 56.

Based upon the Hamburg model, *Collegia Musica* were established in a number of places, mostly under the direction of organists or Town Musicians. Here professionals as well as amateurs were engaged in learning the newest music, gradually developing a feeling for aesthetic judgment.

The kind of comprehensive musical education which was to be received in these *Collegien* was described by J. Mattheson, using Tondern (a small town on the west coast of Schleswig-Holstein) as an example. This was the place where, as a young boy, the organist Raupach performed contemporary music "sometimes playing thorough-bass, sometimes the violin, but also singing."[40] Mattheson himself set the standard in his writings, for example, in the two editions of his *Organistenprobe* (1719, 1731), with respect to the qualifications for an organist, including the performance of church music and improvisation, but beyond that, he had to have knowledge of thorough-bass playing and be familiar with the latest concert and operatic music.

Thus, in contrast to the cantor, the 17th-century organist represented the progressive musical force within the religious sphere. This development assigned to organists a new function, and they rose from a subordinate role to one of equality with cantors. Indeed, the musical work of organists was frequently superior, both in composition and performance.

The fact that most *Kantoreien* ("school choral groups") had deteriorated greatly during the Thirty Years' War (1618-1648), and had either been eliminated or drastically reduced in size and reorganized, resulted in a situation which aided organists in setting up independent musical productions. These often brought in professional musicians, either itinerant or local singers and instrumentalists.[41] Most often performed were purely instrumental compositions or cantatas for a few voices. Prior to the establishment of opera and public concerts, organists were the sole transmitters of modern music. Thus, they took on an important function in

---

[40] J. Mattheson, *Grundlagen einer Ehrenpforte*, Hamburg 1740, Neudruck Berlin 1910, p. 283.

[41] The best known description of such "organistenmusik" in the 17th century is given by the writer Johann Rist for the town of Wedel (near Hamburg). He describes the playing of the violinist Johann Schop with Heinrich Scheidemann in Hamburg's Katharinenkirche in 1658. M. Seiffert, "Matthias Weckmann und das Collegium

preparation for what was later to become the impetus for public musical presentations. With the establishment of the opera, the organists' concerts lost this function and, sixteen years after the founding of the Hamburg opera, were abandoned as being too costly. For decades they had alternated with cantoral music. Now one had to be satisfied, once again, with "ordinary cantoral music."[42]

Yet in Lübeck, where a permanent opera theater was not established until the 19th century, the organists of the Marienkirche provided a substitute in the form of "evening musicales" whose form approached the opera and oratorio more and more during the course of the 18th century.[43]

It should not be assumed from this growing importance of organists in a few larger cities that they enjoyed a general growth of musical and social prestige. Organists could achieve a leading musical position and compete for the title of "Director of Music" in the church only in such places and under such conditions where they were able to fill a need felt by an urban population growing in self-confidence and desirous of prestige. This was the case in relatively few places, and in most smaller cities the lack of concert or operatic music was noticed infrequently or at a later time.

This is corroborated by F. Krummacher, whose research revealed that only three organists in northern Germany are represented in the area of vocal music, with a sum total of 10 works, while the bulk of vocal contrapuntal music, even in the 17th century, was composed by cantors.[44] As a rule, the cantor was the "Director" of church

---

Musicum in Hamburg," *SIMG* II, 1900/01, p. 107 f.

[42] L. Krüger, *Hamburgische Musikorganisation*, p. 127.

[43] The concept of a "public" must be used with reservation here, for the audiences of these "Abendmusiken" or evening concerts underwent numerous changes during the course of the 18th century, and their description goes beyond the scope of this study. Compare also the article by G. Karstädt, "Abendmusik," in: *MGG* I, Sp. 34. Karstädt is currently preparing a detailed study, "Die Lübecker Abendmusiken von Buxtehude bis Königslöw" for the series, *Quellen und Studien zur Musikgeschichte Schleswig-Holsteins*.

[44] The three organists are Franz Tunder, Dietrich Buxtehude (Lübeck, Marienkirche) and Matthias Weckmann (Hamburg, St. Jakobi), of whom it is known "that they had a very special need for vocal music for the *Hamburger Collegium* and the Lübecker *Abendmusiken*." F. Krummacher, "Orgel—und Vokalmusik im Oeuvre norddeutscher Organisten um Buxtehude," in: *Dansk aarbog for musikforskning 1966/67*, Kobenhavn 1968, p. 82.

music, while the organist was required either to serve as continuo player at prearranged events or to be available at all times. The arrangements varied from place to place, but he would receive a fixed fee from the cantor.[45] This does not mean, however, that the organist was generally subservient to the cantor. The cantor was able to command and direct him only with respect to execution of the thorough-bass accompaniment for contrapuntal music. In no other area did he have authority over the organ and its music.[46] This was emphasized by the organist of the Katharinenkirche in Hamburg, Johann Adam Reinken, a man who probably achieved the height of social prestige and material recognition among North German organists. Mattheson reports mockingly that he did not simply call himself an organist as others did, but rather "Organi Hamburgensis ad. D. Cathar. Directorem," and even added the word "celebratisimum."[47] Despite the arrogance which his contemporaries attributed to him because of the presumptuousness of this description, there is some justification for the "director" title, since in Hamburg, as in numerous other large cities, the Town Musicians (municipal musicians) were at the disposal not only of the cantor but of the organist as well, and evidently for his own musical performances.[48] At the same time, it can be observed that these

---

[45] Theodor Voss, "Petrus Laurentius Wockenfuss, Cantor at St. Nikolai in Kiel 1708-1721," *Mitteilungen der Gesellschaft für Kieler Stadtgeschichte*, Heft 33, Kiel 1926, p. 202.

[46] This can be verified by the numerous disputes between the two church musicians. For example, the organist Friedrich zur Linden of Husum reprimanded the cantor and his choir in 1673 and called his compositions "the work of an ass." Heinz Kölsch, "Nikolaus Bruhns," *Schriften des Landesinstituts für Musikforschung Kiel*, Vol. 8, Kassel/Basel 1958, p. 29.

[47] J. Mattheson, *Grundlagen einer Ehrenpforte*, p. 293.

[48] At the Jakobikirche in Hamburg there is verification of viol players at the organ from 1602/03 (L. Krüger, *Hamburgische Musikorganisation*, p. 122), and as early as 1563, four wind players ("Bassuner" and "Diskanter," continuo and upper voice) had been assigned to "blow with the organ." In Lübeck's Marienkirche, the viol player Simon de Tree performed with the organ in 1594. W. Stahl, *Musikgeschichte II*, p. 32. —In Flensburg the Town Musician Hein Heinsen was obligated, as part of his appointment in 1609, to "on occasion let himself be heard on the organ" in addition to his service with the cantor. H.P. Detlefsen, *Musikgeschichte Flensburgs*, p. 23. —In Husum, according to the specification of the office, the Town Musician Johann Ohrem, in 1552, was obliged to perform "in church on Sundays and holidays, or whenever required by the cantor and organist to assist with choir or organ." Joh. Lass, *Sammlung einiger Husumischer Nachrichten*, Flensburg 1750, p. 14.

municipal musicians, who were known to perform on the most diverse instruments, often as skillfully on keyboard as well as on strings and winds, more and more frequently moved into positions on a par with church musicians. For example, the cantor in Hamburg's Johanniskirche, Joachim Gerstenbüttel, supervised church music in the main churches but was not able to obtain the directorship of the Cathedral which required very specific up-to-date church music. This directorship was assigned to a Town Musician rather than the cantor.[49]

VIII • ORGANISTS AND MUSICIANS

In the first half of the 18th century the church musicians' consciousness of their superior rank with respect to other musicians was gradually undermined, and in an early capitalist society was replaced by the concept of productivity. As a consequence, Town Musicians, as municipal employees, assumed a competitive role with organists as they attempted to combine both services. In the area of instrumental instruction in particular, an increasingly important aspect, they tried to draw off pupils from church musicians.[50]

Even in the field of composition of occasional music, secular musicians demanded equality. Particularly informative is the position taken by a Town Musician in Glückstadt in 1715 against the prominent organist Rosenbusch, who had disputed his right to compose "funeral music." The Town Musician of Glückstadt claimed that "any man, be he of elevated or of modest station, is free to compose music requested of him, even though he might not be an

---

[49] L. Krüger, *Hamburgische Musikorganisation*, p. 241 ff. and especially p. 243.

[50] For example, at the beginning of the 18th century it became necessary to delineate the respective areas of competence or privilege for the organist of Neumünster and the Town Musician of Kiel. Th. Voss, *Petrus Laurentius Wockenfuss*, p. 198.—In the year 1710, a municipal decree in Flensburg assured the Town Musician equal rights with the organist and the cantor, with respect to additional income derived from playing at weddings. H.P. Detlefsen, *Musikgeschichte Flensburgs*, p. 44. In the year 1728, the council of Flensburg determined that organists and Town Musicians were "dependent on each other" in that it was "not possible for one to maintain a music program without the other." Consequently, their fees were required to be equal. Nevertheless, the Flensburg organists complained that more and more citizens turned to the Town Musician and his apprentices instead of hiring the organist at weddings. H.P. Detlefsen, loc. cit., p. 107, 120.

organist. If it should also come to me that I might earn an occasional shilling in this manner, this should also be permitted me."[51]

The degree to which 18th-century organists were at the mercy of the laws of supply and demand can be judged from the fact that, with very few exceptions, it was not thought necessary to adjust their fixed income to a rising cost of living, a practice which had been customary in earlier times. They were simply told to seek income from private "sources." As a consequence, and because of the fact that charlatans and any incompetent could give music lessons, the material condition of many organists became more and more critical. They felt it necessary to invade the domain of secular musicians in order to improve their income. From the social point of view this meant a definite loss of prestige, for now the organist performed for the citizenry for pay, that is, a salary, which automatically removed him from the upper-level social ranks to which he had belonged at the beginning of the century.[52]

IX • NON-MUSICAL ACTIVITIES

More than other musical professionals, municipal organists since the Reformation were involved in working at extra-musical activities in order to improve their income. The ample free time at their disposal made this possible, and from the time of the Reformation, such outside income was considered in calculating the organists' fixed income.

In addition to money derived from the rental of seats in the organ gallery, something which was taken for granted in both city and village churches after the 17th century, organists frequently earned considerable income from the leasing out of church lands which

---

[51] Schleswig, *Landesarchiv A III*, Abt. 11, No. 1817, 103/104.

[52] This is evident from the previously mentioned dispute between the organist Christian Caspar Müthel in Mölln and the local "Feuergreven" in 1738 ("Feuergreven's" letter, dated Oct. 9th). *Stadtarchiv Mölln II*, No. 117. By issuing certificates of apprenticeship to his students aspiring to become musicians, Müthel attempted to bestow a certain dignity upon the profession, emphasizing the "guild-like" aspect of their training and activities. Yet even this attempt, coming at a time of general decline of the whole guild system, did not have much chance of success, even though in Berlin, for example, such certificates were employed to attempt to gain higher fees (1739). See D. Sasse, "Berlin" in: *MGG* I, Sp. 1710.

went with the post. Quite often organists also served as legal advisors and notaries.[53] It should be added that the organist's prestige was enhanced by the fact that such titles most often required a completed university education, which in some cases can be verified.[54]

Such learning and the ability to master the rigid stylistic rules of the legal bureaucracy made organists ideal candidates for posts as municipal secretaries, and indeed, they even held positions as mayors.[55] Occasionally organists were also innkeepers and merchants dealing in chemicals and alcoholic beverages. In such cases, however, there was always the danger that their earnings would in fact be diminished or neutralized through the loss of certain privileges and exemptions.[56]

The school regulations of Holstein in 1747 prohibited schoolmasters (and consequently many organists) from earning

[53] The cathedral organist in Hamburg, Johann Daniel Decker, held the title "Advocate and Registered Royal Swedish Notary." His activities between 1669 and 1693 were far more dictated by juristic duties on behalf of the church than those of organist, even to the extent that on occasion he left them to "female persons," something which represented a terrible scandal for the time. L. Krüger, *Hamburgische Musikorganisation*, p. 175. A similar situation prevailed with respect to maintenance of the two posts by the cathedral organist, Ludwig Wehreisen in Lübeck. He was even given the official title of "Camerarius." Stahl, *Musikgeschichte Lübecks II*, p. 73.

[54] Such was the case with the organist Daniel Twitemeyer of Rendsburg, who had studied at the University of Helmstedt until 1581. K. Friedrichs, "D. Organisten an der Marienkirche in Rendsburg," in: *Heimatkundliches Jahrbuch des Kreises Rendsburg 1960*, p. 24.

[55] In 1585 the Rendsburger organist Thies Moller was also municipal secretary (W. Stahl, "Musikgeschichtliche Beziehungen zwischen Gottorf, Husum und Lübeck," in: *Lübeckische Blätter 82*, 1940). In Dithmarschen, organists were frequently assigned clerical duties in the church (E. Rolfs, "Aus dithmarsichen Visitationsprotokollen," in: *Schriften des Vereins für Schleswig-Holsteinische Kirchengeschichte II*, Vol. 5, p. 426). Johann Crantz, organist at the Marienkirche in Rendsburg, became mayor in 1713, after he had been a town councillor for four years. (K. Friedrichs, *Die Organisten der St. Marienkirche in Rendsburg*, p. 27). It is also possible that an organist mentioned in a church inspection document, dated 1593, a Daniel Blanckebiel of Plön, is the same person as a mayor who bore that name *(Kinder, Urkundenbuch zur Chronik der Stadt Plön 1890*, p. 148 B. Engelke, *Musik and Musiker am Gottorfer Hof I*, Breslau 1930, p. 33, note 2.).

[56] The cathedral organists of Ratzeburg had for ages sold "Rommeldeuss" (a kind of beer) as well as wine, but the abuse of this privilege led to its repeal at the beginning of the 18th century. (F. Hellwig, in: *Vaterländisches Archiv für das Herzogtum Lauenburg*, Vol. 4, Heft 1, 1893). A cathedral organist in Ratzeburg, Franz Benten the elder, who served from 1576 to 1617, was also the alchemist for the administration of

additional income from the sale of beer and spirits.[57] Nevertheless, organists repeatedly sought to engage in all sorts of commercial enterprises.[58] Some obtained lottery franchises, ran address-services,[59] or were active in the more lucrative field of painting portraits.[60]

X • THE ORGANISTS' PLACE IN MIDDLE-CLASS SOCIAL ORDER

The extent of outside spheres of activity was expanded even further. In Hamburg, for example, organists were also writers, music publishers, and opera managers. Such a broad spectrum makes it apparent that a clearly defined, consistent social status for organists was not possible. The limits of prestige went from recognition and acceptance by the highest circles and institutions of society (particularly during the 17th century in Hamburg, but also in

the ducal house of Mecklenburg (Mitteilung des Ratzeburger Domarchivars W. Prillwitz). —When the organist of Kiel's Nikolaikirche, Claus Dengel, opened a tavern in his home in 1676, he had to subsequently pay the house tax from which he had previously been exempt as a servant of the church. (E. Pomsel, *Die Organisten der Kieler Nikolaikirche,* p. 51). In Flensburg the organist of the Marienkirche, Joh. Friedrich Meister, built a house outside of the city gates where he was allowed to sell "French wine and brandy as well as foreign and other beer." It was in vain that the council complained to the king against the establishment which was, they claimed, turning into a refuge for shady elements. H.P. Detlefsen, *Musikgeschichte Flensburgs,* p. 118.

[57] F.M. Rendtorff, "Die schleswig-holsteinischen Schulordnungen vom 16. bis zum Anfang des 19. Jahrhunderts," *Schriften des Vereins für Schleswig-Holsteinische Kirchengeschichte I,* Vol. 2, Kiel 1902, p. 113.

[58] For example, with the sale of candles and twine, Ratzeburg 1750 (Stadtarchiv Ratzeburg V 33), with optical instruments, static electricity devices, Glockenspiels and barrel organs, Flensburg 1793 (Detlefsen, *Musikgeschichte Flensburgs,* p. 159), as well as in retail trade with the organists' acceptance into the shopkeepers' association of Lübeck around 1770 (Stahl, *Musikgeschichte Lübecks II,* p. 114).

[59] Kopenhagen, Riks Arkivet, *Deutsche Kanzlei, Patenten-Extrakter* 1748, No. 28.

[60] Balthasar Joachim Reimers, organist at the Marienkirche in Rendsburg, received official royal approval upon his appeal in 1748 that he be permitted to improve his material status through portrait painting, and was even allowed a substitute at the organ. K. Friedrichs, *Die Organisten an der Marienkirche in Rendsburg,* p. 28. —In connection with his application in Hadersleben, the following judgment was made of him: "He paints better than he plays the organ, and he is very old-fashioned." Hadersleben, *Radstue-Arkivet XII 3,* "Letter of the Rendsburger Rektor Wagner to the municipal secretary Neuhöffel, dated Feb. 4, 1766." Reimers was even engaged as court-miniature painter at the palace in Kiel.

smaller cities, such as Lübeck and Husum[61]) to an attitude which regarded the organist as a servant and included all the aspects of disentitlement associated with that status. In part, this can be attributed to prejudices dating back to the Middle Ages and negative attitudes towards the itinerant player which, to some extent, were based upon the lack of legal status and occasional activities bordering on the criminal by members of this class.[62]

It was decided variously, from place to place, whether an organist was to be considered a citizen, a member of the middle-class, or whether he was to be thought of as a servant of the church and—like the precentor—consequently freed of the burdens and legal obligations of the citizen (in other words, whether he was to be ranked outside or even above the middle class social order). Though organists were constantly endeavoring to obtain such recognition, it was denied them in most instances. Even those who held the most respected posts, for example, that of organist at the Marienkirche in Lübeck, had to struggle for full citizenship.[63]

---

61 In the 17th century, organists often came from the upper levels of the social structure, that is, from the church hierarchy, or they married women from such levels. As an example, Samuel Kuhlmann in Rendsburg, brother of the local provost, as well as Caspar Ferkelrath of the Marienkirche in Flensburg, both married into well-to-do merchant families.

62 Particularly among the Flensburger organists of the 17th and 18th centuries there was a tendency towards corruption, slander and quarrelsomeness. Through administrative as well as legal activity, there was the temptation to participate in irregularities, as well as to gain favor through their connection with influential families.

63 F. Blume, "Buxtehude," in: *MGG* II, Sp. 551. In 1636 the organist in Plön, Johannes Einfalt, abruptly resigned his position. The citizenry required of him that he "must return to the city everything which has been acquired improperly." The most important argument for this measure was that "the organist occupied a public office, since he received an annual salary from the town for his service in the church." *Kinder, Urkundenbuch zur Chronik der Stadt Plön*, p. 250f. On the other hand, during the occupation of Flensburg by Brandenburg troops in 1658-60, churches, schools, hospitals and alms-houses, and their employees were exempted by the Elector from quartering troops. A listing of exempted houses included, besides those of the pastor and German and Latin school masters, those of the organists and instrumentalists. *Stadtarchiv-Flensburg*, 946, 947. —In cities with strong traditions, such as Mölln, rules set forth in 1770 were observed well into the 19th century, to the effect that "The organist, as well as pastor, rector and cantor, are exempt from all contributions [taxation]." *Stadtarchiv Mölln II*, 112. Even the church regulations of the small duchy of Sonderburg-Plön in 1732 affirmed these "Freedoms and amnesties" for organists and sextons and their equalization with pastors, with respect to immunity from secular judicial jurisdiction. *Fürstliche Plönsche Kirchenordnung*, Plön 1732, p. 66 f.

This was clearly defined in the social ranking which was devised in numerous cities at the turn of the 17th and into the 18th centuries. In the Flensburg regulations of 1712-18 the organist was not listed among those considered outside the middle-class citizenry, persons such as "Royal servants, doctors, court and district advocates, priors and priests, the school rector, mayor and council staff, town magistrate, pharmacist's assistant and director of the hospital..., town clerk and faculty of the Latin school," but rather, the organist belonged to the first rank of citizens, that is, among the more prestigious merchants and the school masters at the German school.[64] Such ranking conformed to other German districts such as Braunschweig, where organists were ranked with the "most prestigious artists and artisans."[65] Among musicians, the organist was closest in rank to the Town Piper.

These official rankings must be viewed in narrow temporal and geographic limits. Krickeberg has shown that such hierarchies within a given municipality could change numerous times over the span of a century. What is more, he established that over and beyond such official scales, there were "unofficial" standards with respect to social prestige which must be taken into consideration.[66] These latter attitudes can only be indirectly reconstructed, and then only in specific instances. To a great extent they depended on the personality of the individual involved. In the country as in the towns, the social status of organists was not the same everywhere. In districts where organists also had definite administrative posts, as in various places in Dithmarschen, an agricultural area, they belonged to the group permitted to conduct church inspections. Yet this was on the basis of their administrative position, not their musical function.[67] This does testify, however, to a relatively high place in the

---

64 H.P. Detlefsen, *Musikgeschichte Flensburgs*, p. 109, 215 f. In Plön in 1703, the sexton was "awarded" the rank beneath that of the organist "because he is not only employed by the main church but is also versed in the Holy Scriptures, and beyond that, because he is soon to be appointed as a teacher in the municipal school." *Kinder, Urkundenbuch zur Chronik Plöns*, p. 364. —In contrast to these regulations, in central Germany the cantor also belonged to the citizenry ranks, and though above him, was closer in rank to the organist. D. Krickeberg, *Das protestantische Kantorat im 17. Jahrhundert*, p. 81, 97, 111.

65 D. Krickeberg, *Das protestantische Kantorat*, p. 111.

66 D. Krickeberg, loc. cit., p. 79, 81, 97, 109 ff.

67 C. Rolfs, "Aus alten dithmarschen Visitationsprotokollen," in: *Schriften des Vereins für Schleswig-Holsteinische Kirchengeschichte II*, Vol. 5, p. 244.

hierarchy and naturally, like clerics, they were exempt from taxation and civic duties. Moreover, they were not subject to secular legal jurisdiction but solely to the church authority (Consistorium and Calandt).[68]

During the second half of the 17th century, such administrative functions of organists became less common. With the coming of an epoch of rationalism and the consequent diminishing of the church officials' authority, the municipal as well as the rural population was clearly no longer prepared to entrust public administrative duties to musicians whose primary activity was far removed from such assignments.[69]

XI • MATERIAL CONDITIONS

Looking at the material condition of the organist, one can also draw only very limited conclusions with respect to his social status. On the one hand, it is most difficult to ascertain a precise total income, which often came from a variety of widely dispersed activities. On the other hand, in making comparisons of fixed salaries, it is not always clear what might have led to the situation in which a particular organist might have been paid more or less than a cantor, deacon, school master, or other comparable professional. What can be definitely determined is the following:

---

[68] A. L. J. Michelsen, *Urkundenbuch zur Geschichte des Landes Dithmarschen,* Altona 1834, p. 400.

[69] As for example in 1669, when numerous villages in the district of Rellingen (Dithmarschen) refused to permit inspection visits by pastors and organists to continue in the traditional manner. E. Frytag, "Zur Geschichte der Ausgliederung der Dörfer Heist und Glinde aus dem Kirchspiel Rellingen," in: *Schriften des Vereins für Schleswig-Holsteinische Kirchengeschichte II,* Vol 18, p. 66. In 1666, in addition to the pastor, the organist Caspar Engel also conducted hearings in witches' trials in the district of "Probstei" (vicinity of Kiel). This was subsequently forbidden him in a ruling by the law faculty of the University of Kiel. *Schleswig-Holsteinische Blätter für Polizei und Kultur,* Vol. I, 1799, p. 72 f., 76 f. In the city of Eutin, the post of town clerk was linked to that of organist until 1719. When the holder of the post, Johannes Cordesius, then committed a small irregularity by overextending his holiday, the post was immediately taken from him, and it was thereafter separate from that of organist. For the municipal organists of Eutin this meant a significant reduction of social prestige as well as material hardship. *Schleswig-Holsteinisches Landesarchiv Schleswig,* Sect. 11, Part 2, 1.

1. Income differed from place to place, even within the same area of a given city, from church to church, often to a considerable degree. In the 17th century some organists were also able to increase their salaries significantly during the period of their tenure.
2. As with pastors, deacons, cantors, and sextons, organists' incomes were earned only partly in cash. Indeed, the major portion of their subsistence was received in kind (*Naturalien*). This included grain, eggs, sausages, bread, flax, firewood (earlier, even whole trees), tracts of land, free housing, and even additional monies gathered from foundations, collections in church, as well as legacies. Though there was sometimes some additional income through *Akzidentien*, monies derived from service at official functions such as weddings, funerals, and similar occasions, it was not as important a source of income for the organist as it was for the Town Musicians.[70]

At the time of the Reformation, the fixed salaries for organists in the main churches of Hamburg and Lübeck were set at "50 Mark lübsch,"[71] with express reference to the fact that these organists had many additional sources of income at their disposal during their ample free time.[72] Included with the cash income, however, was a guarantee of free lodging. Such figures must be understood as basic contracts which were always supplemented. In the 16th century, school masters and organists in rural districts report a "basic salary" of 40 Marks per year, but to this was added income from church clerical work.[73]

---

[70] Compare, H. W. Schwab, "Das Einnahmebuch des Schleswiger Stadt-musik-anten Friedrich Adolph Berwald," in: *Kieler Schriften zur Musikwissenschaft XXI*, Kassel 1972, p. 96 ff.

[71] The currency of Lübeck was the standard exchange in districts bordering on the southern Baltic until the end of the 18th century.

[72] E. Sehling, *Die evangelischen Kirchenordnungen V*, p. 512. As a comparison: The Superintendent's assistant received the same 50 Ml (marks in the Lübeck currency) as the organist; the "cappellane" (chaplains) 100 Ml, the pastors, 200 Ml, and the Superintendent (the prior) received 300 Ml. While the regulations did not specify beyond the guarantee of free housing for sextons and organists, the pastor's residence is described in detail (it should be comfortable, with bed chambers, heat and tile stoves and windows). Also, quarterly payment was prescribed for pastors but not for sextons and organists. In effect, this meant discrimination; organists often lived in poor, temporary housing, and in hard times were not paid regularly.

[73.] E. Rolfs, *Aus dithmarsischen Visitationsprotokollen*, p. 426.

In larger cities, during the 17th century, organists' income increased, corresponding to the growth in musical and social prestige. Similarly, as the organist's importance decreased from about 1670 on, there was also a decline in income. The income of the organists at the Katharinenkirche in Hamburg reached a peak under Heinrich Scheidemann and J. A. Reinken, with continuous increases up to 1666—as high as 400 *Reichstaler,* that is, some 1200 Marks in the Lübeck currency. This represented the high point in salary for the North German-Lutheran area. Yet this too was supplemented by payment in kind, free lodging, donations, and 200 Marks for burial services.[74] Except in this extreme case, the average fixed cash income at the main churches of Hamburg and Lübeck was somewhere between 300 and 900 Marks.[75]

In the smaller churches of Lübeck, as well as in cities the size of Flensburg, Kiel, and Husum, organists' fixed incomes during the middle of the 17th century were somewhere in the neighborhood of 300 Marks, and consequently higher than those of cantors. In small towns such as Ratzeburg or Tondern, records indicate salaries between 100 and 200 Marks, and, as a rule, organists in rural areas received even less in cash, though there was obviously a heavier reliance on payment in kind for these organists, which in some instances represented almost the total income in the more remote areas.[76]

In the 18th century, increases in salary for Hamburg organists were the exception, though they were still granted in smaller churches of Lübeck and Flensburg. On the whole, however, the economic situation for the 18th-century organist deteriorated rapidly, and there is much evidence that these musicians lived under the most abject conditions.

The fact that there was less and less interest in the musical

---

[74] L. Krüger, *Hamburgische Musikorganisation,* p. 164. The data supplied by Krüger indicate that the Johannisschule cantors Seele and Bernhard scarcely received more than 500 Ml. in income. Though their supplementary pay may have been greater than that of the organists of Hamburg's Katharinenkirche, one may assume that the latter earned twice as much as the cantors. cf. L. Krüger, loc. cit. p. 40 f., 67.

[75] At the Marienkirche in Lübeck, the combined salaries of Franz Tunders and Dietrich Buxtehude as organists and construction supervisors were approximately 880 Ml. after 1646. —W. Stahl, *Dietrich Buxtehude,* Kassel, no date, p. 16 f.

[76] Additional examples will be found in the author's work previously mentioned and now in preparation.

achievements of organists was reflected economically from about 1685 on, and organists' posts in Hamburg were sold to the highest bidder. This deplorable custom, which continued until the early 19th century, led to a situation where candidates, sometimes offering grotesque sums, wound up hopelessly in debt.[77]

In smaller cities and villages, prospects were also poor. Since organists' salaries were in no way adjusted to the rapidly climbing cost of living in the 18th century, there was only the possibility of obtaining a post as school master and other sidelines to assure the family's livelihood.

XII • COURT ORGANISTS

As a group, court organists played a considerably less significant role in the development of organ playing in North German regions than in southern Germany and Austria, in spite of the fact that from 1573 on, the court organist in Wolfenbüttel was promoted from the ranks of lower court servants to the elevated level of secretary.[78] The court organists in the Schleswig-Holstein ducal residence of Gottorf were ranked with the lower servants, that is, with cooks, apothecaries, and artisans—but also on the same level as dancing masters, fencers, and painters. This is recorded as early as 1573.[79] Even within the ranks of court musicians, an organist at the Gottorf court was able to progress in only one isolated case to royal treasurer and auditor (and significantly, it was not the most important organist, Franz Tunder, but his predecessor, Johannes Heckelauer), only because of his political and administrative ability, not his musical accomplishments.

As a rule, the court organist stood on a far lower income level

---

[77] Such infamous practices were exemplified, above all, by the choice of an organist at the time of J. S. Bach's candidacy at the Jakobikirche in Hamburg in 1720. See, *Bach-Dokumente*, Vol. II, ed. W. Neumann and H. J. Schulze, Leipzig and Kassel. . . 1969, p. 77 ff.

[78] M. Ruhnke, *Beiträge zur Geschichte der deutschen Hofmusikkollegien* im 16. Jahrhundert, Berlin 1963, p. 24, 27. Wolfenbüttel must be counted among the leading musical courts of northern Germany, which accounts for the prominent figures associated with it in the history of 17th-century music.

[79] L. Andresen, W. Stephan, *Beiträge zur Geschichte der Gottorfer Hof- und Staatsverwaltung 1544-1659*, Vol. II, Kiel 1928, p. 344 ff.

than the Kapellmeister and other prominent instrumentalists who, from the beginning of the 17th century, travelled from court to court and who, in the case of very accomplished performers, received most generous sums.[80]

In the course of the 17th century, court expenditures for instrumentalists rose steadily, particularly for violinists. But organists' salaries did not reach these levels, and in the case of the Gottorf court, they even declined from the time of Franz Tunder's tenure.[81] When Tunder left Gottorf for the Marienkirche in Lübeck, he was able to increase his income almost fivefold. In nearly every princely town, the municipal church organist's fixed income was greater than that of his counterpart at court, though it should be remembered that as a member of the court staff he needed to spend very little.[82] The post of palace or court organist was considered a decidedly secondary one and was frequently held by persons who were also organists at nearby municipal churches or cathedrals.[83] The court organist's secondary role is also reflected in the ranking lists at the end of the 17th century, in which he occupied a median position among the musicians and artisans.[84]

While there were isolated cases in the 17th century where North

---

[80] Tunder, upon entering his post in Gottorf in 1634, received less than a violinist engaged at the same time, and not even half the salary of the lutenist. Andresen-Stephan, loc. cit., p. 224.

[81] Similarly at the Mecklenburg court in Schwerin the organist was able, only after much effort, to raise his income to 100 thalers. — C. Meyer, Geschichte der Mecklenburg-Schweriner Hofkapelle, Schwerin 1913, p. 243.

[82] At musically active courts such as the one in Celle, the higher base salary of the municipal organist was more than compensated for during the course of the 17th century through generous grants made to the court organists for clothing and food. G. Linnemann, Celler Musikgeschichte bis zum Beginn des 19. Jahrhunderts, Celle 1935, p. 12.

[83] Examples are Ratzeburg, Landesarchiv Schleswig, Sect. 218, No. 655 ("Kirchen-visitationsprotokoll von 1614"); Glückstadt 1736, Kopenhagen, Riks-Arkivet, Patenten-Extr. 1736, p. 145, No. 1; and at times also Schleswig and Eutin.

[84] In the ranking order of the ducal court in Plön of the year 1680, the organist was placed under the municipal councilmen, pages, clerks, trumpeters, drummers, gardeners and tailors, but above the goldsmith, painter and dining-room servants. — Kinder, Urkundenbuch, p. 287. — In 1704 in Schwerin, the organist held the twentieth rank with the court painter and the gardener, behind the Kapellmeister (16th), the cantor (17th), and court musicians, trumpeter and drummer (19th). C. Meyer, loc. cit. p. 91.

German courts attempted, by means of stipends and travel leaves, to bring their organists and choirboys into contact with the best organ playing of the time, it is nevertheless undeniable that in the north, the organists found opportunities for the advancement of their art only in the larger cities. In contrast, in southern regions, it was the chamber and court organist who, to a much greater degree, were responsible for progress.[85]

XIII • THE STATUS OF ORGANISTS IN THE LATE 18TH AND 19TH CENTURIES

The social position of the organist underwent a basic change because of the general decline of church music. To be sure, things did not go quite so badly for him as for the cantor who, with the collapse of the precentorships around the end of the 18th century and the beginning of the 19th century, was essentially eliminated.[86] It was now the organist who held the congregational singing together, music which was dependent upon a harmonic foundation. The organist also had to create a solemn and reverent atmosphere, without much thought being given to the artistic quality of what passed from the organ down to the devout congregation.

The lack of interest in organ music, particularly in the second half of the 18th century, is directly related to stylistic changes which music underwent at the time. Measured against the model of orchestral sonority set up by the Mannheim School and the

---

[85] G. Frotscher, *Geschichte des Orgelspiels und der Orgelkomposition I*, p. 471. Aside from the Guelph residences of Braunschweig-Wolfenbüttel, the Hannover, Celle and Gottorf courts, "there was a lack ... of the splendor of the southern imperial and noble courts ..." F.W. Riedel, *Quellenkundliche Beiträge zur Geschichte der Musik für Tasteninstrumente in der 2. Hälfte des 17. Jahrhunderts=Schriften des Landesinstituts für Musikforschung Kiel*, Vol. 10, p. 179. Even where such princely residences actually existed, for instance that of the Bishop Elector of Lübeck in Eutin or Oldenburg, they could not approach the standards of their South German Catholic models because they lacked the material, political and religious means to do so.

[86] In 1804 there was the dissolution of the tradition-rich "Katharineums-Kantorat" [the choral school of the Katharinenkirche]. The "Johanneums-Kantorat" in Hamburg met the same fate in 1822. In most cities these institutions had long been ineffective, and the liturgy inspired by the Age of Rationalism rejected contrapuntal and choral music in the service.

keyboard style of Philipp Emanuel Bach, the organ quite naturally was thought of as a clumsy, screeching, dynamically monotonous instrumental monster, on which it was impossible to express the profound emotions demanded by the times. It also could not reproduce the strong changes of mood, or the nuances of the cantabile ideal. After the fruitless efforts of the Abbé Vogler to make the organ more flexible dynamically through the addition of various technical improvements, it was not until the Age of Romanticism that the instrument, primarily in France and Germany, was given a comprehensive repertoire which reflected its sonorities and possibilities.

The period between Bach's death and the first significant organ compositions of the Romantic Age, compositions by Mendelssohn (1837), Schumann (1845), and Liszt (1850), also marks a low point in the artistic and social position of the organist. Even the organists at important churches such as the Marienkirche in Lübeck turned to other more remunerative and artistically rewarding musical activities, and often looked upon their duties as organists as a sideline, frequently leaving them to students and substitutes. In Lübeck, as in Kiel, Flensburg, and elsewhere, organists were frequently hired as municipal music directors. This meant that they conducted the then popular amateur orchestras and choruses, organized the symphonic and oratorio music, and were the guiding and central musical figures in these cities.[87]

In smaller communities, combinations such as organist/town musician or organist/teacher were common. The amount of work assigned to such a man and the minute portion of his total time which could be devoted to organ playing can be seen from the example of the organist at the Nikolaikirche in Kiel, Georg Christian Apel. Apel also had to assume the work of vocal teacher at the municipal school, teach music at the Teachers' College, and serve as Director of Music at the University. In addition to all of this, he enriched the concert season of Kiel with at least two concerts in Harmonie Hall every winter, and presented an oratorio performance at the church with his amateur chorus. He also organized

---

[87] Examples of organists serving as leaders of bourgeois musical life were Johann Paul and Adolf Carl Kuntzen, J. W. C. von Königslow and Gottfried Herrmann of Lübeck, C.F. Paulsen of Flensburg, or Fr. Chr. A. Hundertmarck and G. Chr. Apelhund of Kiel, as well as C. Stiehl in Eutin.

concerts in Kiel for visiting artists, composed music as was required for his amateur groups, and operated an extensive dealership in music and music supplies, as well as a music lending library.[88]

From the end of the 18th century on, the organ was used as a solo instrument in public concerts. As in the field of organ building, Abbé Vogler was a pioneer here. During the course of the 19th century there was a steady increase in the number of virtuosi on the organ, both touring artists as well as those who concertized on their regular organs. There was also a corresponding growth in the literature for the instrument, despite the vehement protests of ecclesiastic authorities who viewed such use of the church as sacrilege.[89]

The organ virtuosi of the Hanseatic cities of Hamburg and Lübeck, using all of the 19th-century economic and organizational features of concert operations, continued the organ tradition of the 17th century.[90] The majority of organists in medium-sized and smaller cities, as well as those in rural areas, were schoolmasters who carried on their church-musical functions as a sideline.

As already shown, such combinations were common from the 16th century on, though in earlier times it was surely not the rule. During the course of the 18th and 19th centuries, combined positions were established in the school regulations, among the earliest of which are the Royal Regulations of the Duchy of Holstein of 1747. In these regulations, the long-range planning for combining the offices of organist, sexton, and teacher is systematically laid down in great detail. Through stricter selection procedures the

---

[88] O. Jahn, *Gesammelte Aufsätze über Musik*, Leipzig 1867, p. 1-12; *Stadtarchiv Kiel, Nikolaikirche* No. 173; *Königlich Privilegiertes Intelligenzblatt Schleswig*, 1816, p. 12 f., 31 f. "Verzeichnis der bei Apel verkäuflichen Musikalien in Berlin," *Deutsche Staatsbibliothek*, Sect. 1101.

[89] So it was, for example, for G.Chr. Apel, who had to put up with the opposition of the then well-known "Revival Movement" of proponents of Pietism, represented by such figures as the theologian Claus Harms. *Stadtarchiv-Kiel*, Nikolaikirche, No. 173.

[90] Outstanding among such virtuosi are Hermann Jimmerthal and Karl Lichtwark in Lübeck, and in Hamburg, Joh. Friedrich and Friedrich Gottlieb-Schwenke, as well as G. H. F. Armbrust and his son Carl, who was probably the most important performer in the greater Hamburg area in the 19th century.

regulations also provided the basis of higher social prestige for the teacher-organist, who became typical in the 19th century.[91]

A further important step towards a general improvement of the educational system was taken in the 18th century with the establishment of teacher-training colleges. Thus, for the first time, a standard was established with respect to a teacher's education. Naturally it was some time before schools were staffed with graduates of such institutions, but from the third decade of the 19th century on, most major obstacles had been overcome.[92]

Though organ instruction played a modest role in the curriculum, it was nevertheless acknowledged. In contrast to vocal training, organ instruction was not a required subject and was left to the more "musical" as an option.[93] Nevertheless, in the teachers' colleges certain concepts of uniform style and of minimum standards with respect to organ playing in churches were developed. This gave those who held such posts a certain stature, and admittedly, a somewhat stodgy comic dignity at times.[94]

The ideological background for the combination of church and school posts was part of the counter-revolutionary tendencies which prevailed in Europe as a reaction to the events between 1789 and 1815. In the close tie between church and state the rulers saw a basic guarantee for the preservation of the status quo. The educational institutions were viewed as an arm of the state, and their task

---

[91] E. M. Rendtorff, *Die schleswig-holsteinischen Schulordnung*, p. 106, 277. The effect of this regulation was felt relatively quickly. One can read in a church inspection report in Husum, dated 1759, that only those men who had sufficient skill (*Profectus*) to direct a large church music program could hold organists' posts in the diocese. In view of the extreme disorder, and in some cases, hair-raising conditions in the school-systems of the 17th century and the first half of the 18th century, such a requirement was a definite step forward. *Schleswig Landesarchiv*, Sect. 65.2, No. 1999.

[92] Up until that time, schools had been thought of as a haven for the care of the unfortunate or those who were no longer capable of functioning in a service. The teachers were retired officers, discharged soldiers, cooks, barbers and lackeys who had lost their positions, former students and pupils who had had to join the army because of their inability to cope with the rigors of higher study. A. Möbusz, *Hundert Jahre Lehrerbildung*, Lübeck 1907, p. 2. —H. Heppe, *Geschichte des deutschen Lehrerschulwesen*, Vol. I, Reprint, Hildesheim/New York 1971, p. 254 f.

[93] *Regulativ für das Schullehrerseminar in Bad Segeberg*, Kopenhagen 1844, p. 27, 33.

[94] A well-developed parody of the teacher-organist is given by Wilhelm Busch in *Max und Moritz* (1865) in the figure of "Lehrer Lämpel."

consisted primarily in "forming good and able citizens who were also proper Christians."[95]

In this sense, it was logical that educational authorities sought the "formation and preservation of the most important requirement (of the church): that of reverence and respect for God and His law"[96] directly in school as well as through the musical "beautification" of the sacred service.

In spite of this important function in the political sphere, it was relatively late before teachers, and thus the majority of organists, were able to attain full rights as state employeees, including civil service status. In Prussia it was not until the Teachers' Compensation Act of 1897, with the retirement amendment of 1900, that teachers were fully absorbed into the hierarchy of officialdom. Consequently, organists were relieved of the traditional problems which they had suffered in earlier times: security for their old age and their survivors.[97]

---

[95] *Allgemeine Schulordnung für die Herzogtümer Schleswig und Holstein von 1814;* H. Heppe, *Geschichte des deutschen Volksschulwesen,* Vol V, p. 207.

[96] Joh. Aug. Nebe, *Der Schullehrerberuf nach dessen gesamtem Umfange in der Schule u. Kirche,*2 Eisenach 1827, p. 402 f.

[97] When in 1784 the widow of the organist Otto Ewald in Schwabstedt requested a year's salary, which was formerly the custom for widows of church employees, a "compulsory report" was prepared by Councillor von Schönfeldt and General Director Struensee. In this document they claimed that in contrast to pastors' widows, widows of organists and sextons did not "customarily" receive such an award. Further, it was claimed that with repeated awards, there might be the danger that one would establish a precedent. *Schleswig Landesarchiv,* Sect. 65.2, No. 2020. —In contrast, a half-year payment for widows of organists and sextons was set down in the church regulations of Sonderburg-Plön in 1732. *Fürstlich Holstein-Plönsche Kirchenordnung 1732,* p. 66.

CHAPTER FOUR

On the Social Status of the *Spielmann* ("Folk Musician") in 17th and 18th Century Germany, Particularly in the Northwest

·

DIETER KRICKEBERG

G. Heilfurth has written that the problem of the *Spielmann* requires "more thorough investigation than has been accorded to it, taking in the entire scope of cultural life in recent centuries."[1] Historical sources for the professional and semi-professional folk musician prior to 1800 are difficult to come by.[2] Before the time of Herder, the literary world took relatively little notice of the "simple people." One finds detailed mention of folk musicians in records and ordinances only when they provoked offense. But such data are frequently scattered over an almost incalculable number of sources. One often comes across them in the most unexpected places, yet only a small fraction supply the investigator with anything new or valuable. The present essay does not presume to have exhausted these sources, not even those pertaining to northwest Germany. On the other hand, the attempt has been made to disclose and report extensively on such sources as council and official records, civic and church documents, as well as statute books. Beyond this, consideration was given to secondary literature on the topic itself, on local music history, city and regional histories and folklore, as well as contemporary writings on music theory and musical *belles-lettres*. The subject of the German professional and semi-professional folk musician, which is

---

[1] G. Heilfurth, *Der erzgebirgische Volkssänger Anton Günther*, 6. Aufl., Frankfurt a. M 1962, p. 32. An essay by the author, "Beobachtungen zum sozialen Selbstverständnis der deutschen Spielleute im 17. und 18. Jahrhundert" appeared in *JbfVldf* [*Jahrbuch für Volksliedforschung*] vol. 15 (1970) p. 140 ff.

[2] The most important ground work for the present essay is found in W. Salmen's *Geschichte der Musik in Westfalen*, vol. 1, Kassel 1963.

dealt with here only from the standpoint of social position, is to be pursued further at the *Staatliches Institut für Musikforschung Preussicher Kulturbesitz* in Berlin.

In what follows, the social position of the folk musician of the 18th and 19th centuries will be examined according to the method of W. Salmen,[3] that is, from the point of view of individual groups or strata of the population. A few general aspects should, however, be touched upon at the outset. The *Spielmann* under discussion is that musician who did not possess anything like regular employee status with respect to his superiors. The music which was performed by regimental oboists, or by town and court musicians at civic and rural festivities, may sometimes fit under the heading of folk music, but because of the performers' stable status this music will not be considered here. In due course, some mention will be made of the musicians of small market-towns, of whom little has been written to date, and who were far more remote from formal music than were the town musicians.

I • DISREPUTABILITY

During the Middle Ages, a large proportion of all instrumentalists were considered disreputable [*unehrlich*, cf. footnote 4]. The disreputable "were 'without rights,' that is, considered incompetent in certain legal matters: those 'without rights' could not be judge, witness, or juror. They were permitted neither to serve as guardians nor to hold civic office. As plaintiffs they had no rights to damages for homicides or normal damages; they were ineligible for land tenure and were not accepted by the trade guilds."[4] It is not surprising that this independent, unintellectual, amiable musical entertainer, often a juggler, was accorded little respect by the middle and upper classes, but rather was placed under a "mimetic taboo."[5] The aloof attitude towards him[6] was at times furthered by the fact that he satisfied the baser needs of higher circles. It was also said that

---

[3] W. Salmen, *Der fahrende Musiker im europäischen Mittelalter*, Kassel 1960.

[4] W. Danckert, *Unehrliche Leute. Die verfemten Berufe*, Bern und München 1963, p. 9.

[5] W. Salmen, *Die soziale Geltung des Musikers in der mittelalterlichen Gesellschaft*, in: *Studium Generale* XIX (1966), p. 101.

[6] Cf. K. V. Riedel, *Der Bänkelsang*, Hamburg 1963, p. 14 f.

all transcendental universal religions "are inclined to defame the profane musician."[7] In Europe, where an alien Christianity was superimposed upon traditional religions, the clergy saw the *Spielmann* as "the continuing carrier of paganism, previously considered to have been defeated."[8] The medieval European concept of ignominy was characterized by the rejection from society of certain occupational groups. W. Danckert[9] was the first to show in detail that this critical, obdurate vilification was not merely based on a combination of the reasons stated, but also on the circumstance that these professions, accorded a sacral dignity in paganism, were demonized by Christianity. The musician was the successor to the medicine man, the magician, and the singer of heroic sagas.

Though the imperial laws of 1548 and 1577 proclaimed that members of the majority of the then-disreputable professions, including pipers and trumpeters, as well as their children,[10] were eligible to become guild members, the stigma of infamy remained for a long time. This prejudice was particularly strong when it was supported by secondary causes related to the status of the musician. W. Danckert points to a reassessment of the heathen sacrament as the primary cause.

II • SPECIALIZATION

There was a distinct specialization of musicians after the period of the great migrations. Alongside those who were simultaneously jugglers or buffoons and also participated in musical performances were those who were primarily musicians. Johann Friedrich Scheid comments about those musicians who, as members of the Alsatian Piper's Guild, became respectable citizens from the late Middle Ages on: "in most recent times moreover... it was considered less appropriate that these same individuals should be included within

---

7 W. Salmen, *Der fahrende Musiker*, p. 67 f.

8 Ibid., p. 62 f.

9 W. Danckert, *Unehrliche Leute*.

10 G. Emminghaus (ed.), *Corpus iuris Germanici tam publici quam privati academicum*, vol. 1, Jena 1844, p. 406; O. Beneke, *Von unehrlichen Leuten*, Hamburg 2/1889, pp. 30 and 37.

one society along with actors, mimes, and similar people of lesser status: on which account there was established a separate brotherhood for musicians from which the others were excluded."[11] There were still traces of the comprehensive musical entertainer when the *Spielmann* struck up a song or made use of a "common juggler's trick" by covering his instrument and appearing to blow on a duck's bill, and so on.[12] An obvious constriction of his role at this time was that the musician only rarely took a mimetic part in dances and customary performances, and more often performed "from the side of the room."[13] Jugglers and the like were particularly frequent in the ranks of itinerant musicians.[14] From the end of the 16th century they were joined by the travelling actors, who also made much use of music.

III • ITINERANTS

Within the special category of travelling musicians were Bartoldt Snider and Peter Gerken, who were turned out of Bremen in the

[11] J. F. Scheid, *Dissertatio de jure in musicos, singulari, German. Dienste und Obrigkeit der Spielleut, Rappolsteinensi comitatui annexo,* Jena 1738, p. 29.

[12] In a trial over a private defamatory song which a *Spielmann* was said to have written, the accused writes in a petition on the 4th of June 1760: "...I am by profession both a mason and a musician who must know and be able to play...all sorts of songs, upon demand for the country people." He complains "that my father confessor has denied me the sacrament until this matter, in which I am totally innocent, has been resolved." (Hamburg, Staatsarchiv, Amtsarchiv Bergedorf Nr. 3984). —On the question of juggler tricks, compare F. Sieber, *Volk und volkstümliche Motivik im Festwerk des Barocks,* Berlin 1960 = Veröff. d. Inst. f. deutsche Volkskunde an d. Akad. d. Wiss. zu Berlin, vol. 21, p. 41.

[13] W. Salmen, *Geschichte der Musik in Westfalen,* vol. 1, p. 40.

[14] Compare Th. Hampe, *Die fahrenden Leute in der deutschen Vergangenheit,* Leipzig 1902. Compare also note 28 on the "Scheer-Geiger." In *Güldner Hund,* (1. Tl., Wrzeckowitz = Jena 1675, Kap. 9; 2. Tl., ebd. 1676, Kap. 1-3), W. C. Printz portrays a peddler, a quack doctor, a tightrope walker, and a *Spielmann.* The Spielmann does not only play music, but entertains his audiences with "tricks," "pranks," and "jokes." Even non-travelling musicians took part in farces, for example, the country musician in a comedy by E. Herlitz: *Musicomastix, Eine Comoedia von dem Music Feinde* (Stettin 1606, Fasc. publ. by H. Engel, Kassel 1937, page preceding fol. Hiij); this Spielmann jumps about with funny gestures *(saltat gestibus ridiculis)* while playing (page preceding fol. Iiij). According to the novel *Musicus vexatus* (1690) by W. C. Printz, the nobility made use of the *Bierfiedler* as well as "honest, upright musicians" for "court functions and dinner diversion," (H. F. Menck, *Der Musiker im Roman,* Heidelberg 1931, p. 41 f.).

middle of winter in 1593 because of their unauthorized playing at weddings.[15] According to their declarations, they had been tolerated everywhere, in "Saxonland, Braunswig, Westphalia—yes, even Hamburg, Lünenborg, Magdeburg, the state of Lyppe Schomburg and many other honorable cities." In 1624 there is again talk of itinerant players in Bremen.[16] Travelling musicians were frequently found at annual fairs. One reads in the statutes of the musicians' guild of Stettin in 1606: "although until now all sorts of foreign players have been allowed to make use of their instruments as long as they wish and according to their pleasure at annual fairs, they shall from now on be tolerated at the most for 2 or 3 days."[17] In the year 1613, on the occasion of a Dresden court festival, itinerant musicians were described as accompanying a military campaign.[18] J. Kuhnau writes of the "musical charlatan" who, wandering penniless through the land, "went into taverns and without a second thought played his guitar. Nor was he upset when one gave him, like other players, only six Pfennige; yes, he was satisfied when he could have his free drink and a meal for his attendance."[19] The town musicians of Stade complained to the council on January 20, 1750, that innkeepers were hiring then, even at performances for "respectable persons, foreign beer fiddlers and vagrants or even soldiers."[20]

Among the itinerant players could be found former farm hands, artisans, military musicians, or sometimes educated people and even women.[21] There were also those wandering musicians who, to a greater or lesser degree, worked together with gangs of thieves. They played the barrel-organ in particular, which was also much played by women in the 18th century.[22] Thieves often disguised themselves

---

[15] F. Wellmann, "Die Bremer Stadtmusikanten," in: *Jb. der Bremer Sammlung* IV, 2 (1911), p. 88 f.

[16] A. Arnheim, "Aus dem Bremer Musikleben im 17. Jh.," in *SIMG* XII (1910/11), p. 384.

[17] R. Schwartz, "Zur Geschichte der Musikantenzunft im alten Stettin," in: *Monatsblätter* (1898), p. 183.

[18] F. Sieber, *Volk und volkstümliche Motivik*, p. 70.

[19] J. Kuhnau, *Der musikalische Quacksalber*, Dresden 1700, new edition by Kurt Benndorf, Berlin 1900, p. 98.

[20] Stade, Stadtarchiv, Abt. St. V, Fach 66-67, Nr. 1.

[21] H. J. Moser, Die Musikergenossenschaften im deutschen Mittelalter, Phil. Diss. Rostock 1910, p. 100 ff.; "Fahrende Musikanten," in: *Deutsche Gaue* 36 (1935), p. 75-76.

[22] Compare K. Vogt, *Das fahrende Volk in der Pfalz*, Staatswiss. Diss. Würzburg 1921, typewritten, p. 84 ff.; Th. Hampe, *Die fahrenden Leute*, p. 101; G. Kraft, "Von Volkssängern und Wandermusikanten," in: *Musik und Gesellschaft* 9 (1959), p. 20-24.

as peddlers and musicians in order to dispose of stolen goods, to be able to survey new opportunities and possible dangers, to make new contacts, or simply to avoid search parties. The musical accomplishments of these thieves or receivers of stolen goods should not be categorically viewed as second rate, for in the first place, the temperament of an independent robber was not incompatible with that of the musician; furthermore, these questionable players were not always primarily thieves in disguise but often itinerant musicians who, through pressure of increasing governmental control, destitution, or indignation over social injustices had become outlaws. Even the robbers were not merely asocially oriented, for many of them had "good reason ... to grumble over their fate and the world around them and to view themselves simply as victims of severe social abuses."[23] The advent of the peasant wars resulted in an increase in the robber class. In connection with these wars, one repeatedly comes across reports of pipers, bagpipers or fiddlers as partisans and even as leaders of peasants.[24] Many a decree of the 18th century directed against robbers and vagabonds also makes mention of musicians, who were counted among the beggars. A charter of the Swabian regional government of 1742 identifies among the itinerants "barrel-organists, bagpipers and dulcimer players."[25] In 1746, mention is made in "the revised penal code of the ... estimable Franconian regional government of increased measures against thieves, robbers, gypsies, swindlers, the propertyless and other beggar types," including those possibly disguised as "players, drummers, fiddlers, lute players and singers of songs."[26] In contrast to southern and central German documents from the area of the peasant revolts, there are no corresponding references to musicians in documents from the Duchy of Lüneburg,[27] although after 1700 there are references to gypsies who also played music.

W. Salmen has noted a development in Westphalia beginning during the 16th century which restricted the musicians' once

---

[23] Th. Hampe, *Die fahrenden Leute*, p. 101.

[24] R. Hessen (Pseud. Eccardus), *Geschichte des niederen Volkes in Deutschland*, 1907, p. 457; G. Kraft, "Singende und kämpfende Bauern," in: *Thüringische Heimat* (1956), p. 14-26.

[25] Th. Hampe, *Die fahrenden Leute*, p. 102.

[26] A copy of this code is in the Deutsches Volksliedarchiv, Freiburg/Br.

[27] For example Stade, Niedersächsisches Staatsarchiv, Rep. 74 Hagen, Reg. 65, Nr. 1.

extensive travelling to a more limited movement within the home region.[28] Some restraints of movement had already taken place in the Middle Ages among members of the piper fraternities, where privileges were enjoyed only in their particular territory, one exception being the fraternities of Baden and Alsace, which had agreed to permit reciprocal music-making.[29] As already indicated, these musical fraternities were founded partly to escape the enmity of secular and sacred powers; they placed themselves under the protection of Christian patron saints and organized guild-like orders similar to other artisans.[30] In this way they could ward off, or at least temper, their disrepute. Territorial (*ländliche*) guilds, whose members travelled over vast areas, apparently existed only in southern Germany. Several of these survived until the end of the 18th century (Munich and Alsace).

From the middle of the 16th century on, the mountain dwellers of the border region of Saxony and Bohemia offer evidence that a stabilized group of significant size became itinerant musicians out of material need, without necessarily giving up ties to a homeland. To be sure, the mountain dwellers were later joined by poor settlers. The Bohemian musicians who travelled through the whole of north Germany were also known as *Prager Studenten.** It became clear to audiences that players from Bohemia in general, and the mountain people who performed in costume in particular, were not beggar-musicians without roots.[31] These musicians were not only popular among the people but were also extended particular toleration by

---

[28] W. Salmen, *Geschichte der Musik in Westfalen,* vol. 1, p. 81 ff. Nevertheless, a collection of farces of 1670 pretends to be based upon travels of a fiddler (*Scheer-Geiger*) through various European lands. H. F. Menck, *Der Musiker im Roman,* p. 5. Compare also R. Ritter, *Ein Menschenschlag. Erbärztliche und erbgeschichtliche Untersuchungen über die—durch 10 Geschlechterfolgen erforschten—Nachkommen von* "Vagabunden, Jaunern und Räubern," Leipzig 1937, p. 34 and 38.

[29] H. J. Moser, *Die Musikergenossenschaften.*

[30] W. Schatz, *Die Zünfte der Spielleute und die Organisation der Orchestermusiker in Deutschland,* Rechts- und staatswiss. Diss. Greifswald 1921, Teildr. Anklam 1921.

[31] L. Bär, "Erzgebirgische Bergmusikanten," in *Der Anschnitt.* Nr. 5 (1956), p. 22-24; W. Salmen, "Die fahrenden Bergmusikanten im mitteldeutschen Musikleben des 17. und 18. Jh.," in: *Der Anschnitt* 10, No. 3 (1958), pp. 11-13; K. M. Komma, *Das böhmische Musikantentum,* Kassel 1960.

*In 18th-century Germany, Bohemians were well known as musical entertainers; the so-called *Prager Studenten* were just such entertainers who dressed in folk costume, something akin to the "Tyrolean Singers" of today. *Tr. Note.*

the authorities. In 1786 one reads in the resort regulations of Kentz (Pomerania) that the music was to be supplied by town musicians. Yet it was permissible for guests "to have music made by others, particularly by *Prager Studenten* and mountain people, if they are on hand to perform."[32] Regarding all types of itinerant musicians, particularly in Lower Saxony, A. Dieck writes, "From the 18th century on, there was a significant decline in the number of wandering musicians as a growing absolutism restricted their movements."[33] This observation must be regarded as unsubstantiated, at least as far as the robber players and mountain performers are concerned.

IV • RESIDENT (NON-ITINERANT) MUSICIANS

1. *Guild musicians in the country.*—J. Raupp has written about the formation of musical guilds or charters in eastern Germany from the end of the 17th century.[34] German-speaking players were also part of this development. As with numerous piper fraternities of the Middle Ages, these were hardly guilds in the full artisan sense, considering the length of training as well as the fact that the members of some guilds only "made music as a sideline."[35] One group with considerable interest in gaining privileges of attendance and service was the Royal Hunt Piper Band of Weissenfels in Heldrungen.[36] This banding together related merely to the granting of performing rights[37] (the musicians of Guben, for example, were required to pay dues).[38]

2. *Independent Professional Musicians in the Country.* Country players alternated between music-making as a profession and as an avocation. The *Volksmusikanten* of Lübben proclaimed in 1736: "From time immemorial, there have been musicians in the

---

[32] E. Gülzow, "Prager Musikanten in Vorpommern," in: E. Gülzow, *Schrapels ut olle Tiden*, Grimmen, Waberg 1937 = Grimmer Heimatbücherei 4, p. 20.

[33] A. Dieck, *Die Wandermusikanten von Salzgitter*, Göttingen 1962, p. 20.

[34] J. Raupp, *Sorbische Volksmusikanten und Musikinstrumente*, Bautzen 1963 = Schriftenreihe des Instituts für sorbische Volksforschung 17.

[35] J. Raupp, *Sorbische Volksmusikanten*, p. 101.

[36] A. Werner, *Freie Musikgemeinschaften im mitteldeutschen Raum*, Wolfenbüttel und Berlin 1940, p. 24.

[37] Compare section V.

[38] J. Raupp, *Sorbische Volksmusikanten*, p. 98.

villages, poor stall-keepers who don't possess an acre of land and who have been available to help the farmer during threshing and harvest time for a minimum daily wage."[39] Such a musician might have been the subject of a complaint made by the Town Musicians of Stade on November 11, 1714, when "Clauss Budde, who resides in Deinst under the jurisdiction of the magistrate, presumed to play with us for the bride* [wedding] . . ."[40] Budde played the "violin." According to the proceedings of a hearing in 1768, a wedding in Wiepenkaten had been attended "by a musician who had come from Gröpel" (in the vicinity of Stade).[41] On October 27, 1785, a ship's captain requested the Council of Stade, on behalf of a sailor, "graciously to permit the peasant musicians residing in Kehdingen to perform at this wedding."[42] In a petition dated September 11, 1696, by the town musicians of Stade concerning the musicians residing "in the countryside" around Freiburg and Horneburg (Bremen-Verden), it is stated "that they are helping at weddings with music and entertainment."[43]

3. *Music as an Avocation in the Country.* Born in 1752, Peter Claussen of Ostenfeld (Schleswig-Holstein)[44] was an "Inste" (small landholder with minimal livestock) and a musician, who named his farm *Speelmanns.*[45] A shoemaker and a mason were referred to as village musicians in the area of Ulm in the 18th century, as were sailors and farm-hands in the *Alten Land* near Stade.[46] The instrumentalists of the central German *Adjuvanten-*

[39] Ibid., p. 89.
[40] Stade, Niedersächs. Staatsarchiv, Rep. 74, Harsfeld VIII, Fach 18a, Nr. 4.
[41] Stade, Niedersächs. Staatsarchiv, Rep. 80 G, Gewerbe, Tit. 208, Nr. 1.
[42] Ibid.
[43] Stade, Niedersächs. Staatsarchiv, Rep. 5 a, Fach 330. Nr. 108; also see Section V, under Licensing.
[44] Personal correspondence from Dr. K. S. Feddersen, Ostenfeld.
[45] Compare, K. S. Feddersen, "Die Hofnamen im Westen Mittelschleswigs," in: *Die Heimat* (Neumünster) 66 (1959), p. 6 ff.
[46] W. Hölzle, "Von alten Dorfmusikanten und ihrem Spiel," in: *Aus dem Ulmer Winkel* 30 (1937), p. 6. Stade, Niedersächs. Staatsarch., Rep. 80 G, Gewerbe, Tit. 208, Nr. 1, Schreiben vom 29.9. 1767. Concerning a mason as musician in Bergedorf, compare fn. 12.

*The German here reads: 'Braut über feldt gespielet . . .' which presumably refers to the fact that the musician led a wedding procession, perhaps from one village to the next or from church to farm. Tr. Note.

vereine,* among whose members there were numerous village artisans, also performed as musicians. In 1768 near Stade, the "school-master of Wiepenktan" gave performances, while in Prussia, the village school teachers were prohibited by the General School Regulations of August 12, 1763, from playing the violin at dances.[47] Often the sexton, or even on occasion the parson, played music.[48]

4. *Guild Musicians in Cities.* Those players residing in cities and small towns also played in the countryside, as did the regular town musicians. Considerable study has been devoted to the municipal musicians' guilds.[49] Some, as in Hamburg and Lübeck, resembled the craft guilds; the sexton and choral fraternity of Lübeck generally required an apprenticeship period of six years with a guild musician. The members of this particular guild could, under certain circumstances, rise to the ranks of town musicians, whom they were required to assist at church services. Similar to the village "musical instrument" players,[50] they were closely linked to formal music, though in Hamburg there were, in addition, the so-called *Rollbrüder*, the musicians of the *Grünrolle* who were actually folk musicians in the strict sense. They were also given the designation of *Bierfiedler* and "asked the chamber of deputies for permission to play at dances in the surrounding countryside, and also to

---

[47] A. Werner, *Freie Musikgemeinschaften*, p. 22 ff.; Stade, Niedersächs. Staatsarch., Rep. 80 G, Gewerbe, Tit. 208, Nr. 1; S. B. Carstedt, *Atzendorfer Chronik*, Magdeburg 1928 = Geschichtsquellen der Prov. Sachsen und des Freistaates Anhalt N. R. 6, p. 131.

[48] Ibid. Carstedt; E. Stoltze, "Unehrliche Leute," in: *Zs. für Kulturgeschichte* NF 2 (1873), p. 255.

[49] R. Schwartz, "Zur Geschichte der Musikantenzunft im alten Stettin," in: *Monatsblätter* (1898), pp. 180-185; H. Engel, *Spielleute und Hofmusiker im alten Stettin zu Anfang des 17. Jh.*, Greifswald 1932 = Musik in Pommern, Heft 1; C. Stiehl, *Geschichte der Instrumentalmusik in Lübeck* 1885; J. Hennings, *Musikgeschichte Lübecks*, vol. 1 (Weltliche Musik), Kassel 1951; J. Sittard, *Geschichte des Musik-und Concertwesens in Hamburg*, Altona und Leipzig 1890; W. Gurlitt, "Die Hamburger Grünrolle vom Jahre 1691," in: *SIMG* 14 (1912/13), pp. 210-217. See also A. Loft.

[50] See page 104.

*The *Adjuvantenvereine* were organizations which promoted religious music. *Tr. Note.*

appropriate an annual 150 Thaler* for whenever the school children of the city had an excursion into the country or performed a comedy.** They were designated as *Grün-* or *Pantaleonsmusikanten* because they had exclusive rights to play at open-air and summer festivals."[51] Their regulations of 1691 gave them the attributes of an artisan guild;[52] they must thereafter have had civil rights. In 1693 their number decreased from fifty to thirty. The majority of them were artisans by profession.[53]

5. *Independent Professional Musicians in Cities.* As an example, Christoph Winsser and Johann Brüggemann, citizens of Bremen, are cited. They complained in 1624 about the competition from regular town musicians, for it was claimed that they were forced to rely on musical performances to maintain themselves and their families, since they had learned no other skills.[54]

6. *Music as an Avocation of Independent Players in Cities.* After the peace of 1648, numerous players "had settled in Celle and strove to improve their income by playing at weddings.... Since they had their 'bourgeois nourishment' and were consequently not dependent on musical performances alone, they could be more modest in their demands. Thus, they were often given preference over the *Turmmann*."[55] In 1680 in Stade, the "quartered soldiers" were cited as competition for the town musicians.[56] In the 18th century in Atzendorf (Magdeburger Börde), perfor-

---

[51] J. Sittard, *Geschichte des Musik- und Concertwesens in Hamburg,* p. 6.

[52] W. Gurlitt, *Die Hamburger Grünrolle.*

[53] L. Krüger, *Die hamburgische Musikorganisation im XVII. Jh.,* Strassburg 1933 = Sammlung musikwiss. Abh. 12, p. 188.

[54] A. Arnheim, *Aus dem Bremer Musikleben,* p. 385; also compare C. Sachs, "Archivalische Studien zur norddeutschen Musikgeschichte," in: *ZfMw* 2 (1919/20), p. 270 f.; H. P. Detlefsen, *Musikgeschichte der Stadt Flensburg bis zum Jahre 1850*= Schriften d. Landesinst. f. Musikforschung Kiel XI, Kassel 1961, p. 86 ff.

[55] G. Linemann, *Celler Musikgeschichte bis zum Beginn des 19. Jh.,* Celle 1935, p. 4.

[56] Stade, Niedersächs, Staatarch., Rep. 5 a, Fach 330, Nr. 108.

*The original employs the symbol: $\mathcal{Y}$, designating varying denominations of the Thaler. *Tr. Note.*

**The reference here is to a school holiday for the Venetian Patron Saint. *Tr. Note.*

mances were given by "soldiers designated as 'chevron musicians.'"[57]* During the period of the Thirty Years' War, players in Bremen were reported to be also instrument makers or "had taverns." One served as constable for the city.[58]

V • LICENSING AND TAXATION

In the 18th century, the authorities with increasing frequency licensed to musicians the right to be sole performers in a given territory or on the occasion of various festivals. Here was a certain gradual convergence with the system of guilds. Even the piper fraternities founded in the Middle Ages brought their patrons certain financial advantages and also gave their members privileges in exchange for money. The granting of rights or privileges was, however, not always based upon musical auditions or proof of training but, on occasion, depended upon the musician's need or his popularity. Music-making was thus not necessarily advanced through the granting of such rights. In 1720 in Prussia, an "edict on sustenance monies to be deposited by musicians and players with the taxation treasury" was simply a provision for the taxation of musicians living in cities and "on the flat lands."[59] Thus there existed for the population a certain degree of freedom of choice of musicians. Soon thereafter there were efforts towards a more formal licensing arrangement.[60] In the county of Lippe, every citizen had to apply to the appropriate licensing official whenever he "required music for entertainment or for dances at weddings, christenings, consecrations of houses, festive meals and similar honorable gatherings."[61] Only qualified "guilded" persons were permitted to serve as licensees.

[57] S. B. Carstedt, *Atzendorfer Chronik*, p. 131.
[58] F. Wellmann, *Die Bremer Stadtmusikanten*, p. 91.
[59] C. Sachs, *Musikgeschichte der Stadt Berlin bis zum Jahre 1800*, Berlin 1908, p. 23 f.
[60] F. Uhlenbruch, *Herforder Musikleben bis zur Mitte des 18. Jh.*, Phil. Diss. Münster 1926, p. 9 ff.
[61] W. Schramm, "Die lippische Musikerorganisation," in: *Mitt. aus der lippischen Geschichte und Landeskunde* 14, Detmold 1933, p. 157. The town musician of Oldenburg (in Holstein) was awarded the privilege (to supply the music) at weddings and bird shootings. The town musician of Eutin leased out his rights, in turn, for

*These musicians are also called *Winkelmusikanten* and are soldiers who doubled as musicians. *Tr. Note.*

One should mention here a development observed in Bremen-Verden. In 1690, a local musician, Johan Meyer, made a request as "loyal servant" to the governmental authority in Stade for the exclusive right to supply music at weddings and in taverns in a certain district around Horneburg. He spoke of the fact "that others have such a privilege" (for example, the *Dommusikanten* of Bremen) and wished to submit such "Recognition" to the royal house. He promised to serve "with musical instruments." His application was denied.[62]

On February 14, 1718, a magistrate (?) wrote from Wehl to the government of Stade: "Recently a resident under local jurisdiction here by the name of Cordt Eytzen made application to me, requesting exclusive attendance rights for music in the vicinity of Mulsum and Bargstedt... and asking whether said Cordt Eytzen (who, as a poor subject, would benefit thereby)... could in return for an annual fee of 10 Reichstaler be granted such exclusive rights?"[63] A town musician of Stade petitioned the local government on December 15, 1719, for the granting of an exclusive music license "in the Freiburg district of Kehdingen" and noted that in "our most gracious King's and Lord's other lands there are here and there some privileged musicians to be found, who maintain their own apprentices and journeymen," but "there are no exclusively licensed musicians in the area of Bemelt." In the government reply on January 10, 1720, "because the granting of such an exclusive license has not been customary or previously introduced in this district," the petitioner was asked to supply an attestation "that would substantiate the demand of an exclusively licensed status on his behalf."[64] The exclusive license was obviously not granted.

In 1737, an inquiry was addressed to the magistrate to "ascertain if the exclusive license for private attendance with music at weddings" in the district of Buxtehude had been granted by the royal chamber. The answer, dated March 6 of the same year, states that "up to that time no one had been granted such a concession and that

---

attendance at "lesser public festivals" to village fiddlers (secondary leasing). W. Hahn, "Musikanten in Neustadt, Oldenburg und im Amt Cismar," in: *Jb. für Heimatkunde im Kreis Oldenburg, Holstein* 7 (1963), p. 146, p. 155 f.

[62] Stade, Niedersächs, Staatsarch., Rep. 5 a, Fach 330, Nr. 108.

[63] Stade, Niedersächs. Staatsarch., Rep. 74, Harsefeld VIII, Fach 18 a, Nr. 4.

[64] Stade, Niedersächs. Staatsarch., Rep. 80 G. Gewerbe, Tit. 208, Nr. 1.

subjects had full freedom of choice."[65] In contrast, the town musicians of Stade issued a complaint on October 11, 1738, to the effect that a former colleague had been granted a music license by appointment of the chamber. The magistrate in Alt-Closter received a communication from the electoral chamber in Hannover on April 28, 1750, which cites "the legal action pending since 1737 involving a number of parties respecting the granting of music privileges," maintaining that the issue "had been resolved by the royal and electoral superior appellate court at Celle by a decision handed down on June 7—that such music privilege is not a right per se, but the prerogative of those whose seniority and service have established this. Such is the report of the secretary (in Stade). It should also be stated at the same time that as far as the Marsch districts are concerned, similar evidence cannot be produced. Hence, in that area (as well as in the sandy uplands) it is hoped that licensing privileges will cease from this time forth."[66] It was requested that the magistrate see to "the maintenance of justice on behalf of the sovereign authority. . ."[67]

Finally, on the 11th of September 1758, the governing authority of Stade made it known that "in view of the fact that frequent disputes have arisen in the countryside because of the granting of music privileges which have resulted in extensive law suits, and in view of the fact that the royal chamber and its deputies have ruled on the abolition of the granting of such privileges, be it ordered . . . that from this time forth, said privileges shall not be granted for musicians in the countryside, and similarly in the royal domains of the duchy of Bremen (from which the districts of Blumenthal and Neukirchen are exempt by necessity) and other royal hereditary courts." Previous privilege contracts were to expire, and those granted after November 1, 1756, were to be nullified immediately. Music-making was now to be "free to anyone" to carry out.[68]

The interests of rulers and ruling classes in profiting from the activities of musicians thus interfered with the activities of players from the lower classes, in that privileges were perhaps predominant-

[65] See fn. 63.
[66] See fn. 64.
[67] See fn. 63.
[68] As in fn. 63. Concerning the privileged status of country musicians in Vierlanden (1767), see Hamburg, Staatsarchiv. Amtsarchiv Bergedorf No. 3965. This privilege already existed in 1745.

ly granted to the more accomplished musical performers; yet here too, there was only a limited granting of these privileges.

VI • PROPERTY

As resident taxpayers, musical performers could no longer be considered disreputable. It is questionable, however, whether they were granted social recognition as a result of their ownership of property.[69] Many folk songs deal with the "poor musician,"[70] and the information uncovered to date only confirms this fact. Numerous references to the poverty of musicians have already been made above.[71] According to G. Kittler, the independent musicians were "in their primary trade simple artisans or farm laborers."[72] J. Raupp sums it up with respect to Wendian folk musicians; they were mostly "poor cottagers."[73] The Hessian personnel register of 1639[74] frequently contains family names such as Fiedeler, Piper, or Spilman, almost all descendants of musicians, some perhaps musicians yet, who, judging from their possessions, belonged to the lower strata of the villages' population of the time.

VII • MUSICAL ACCOMPLISHMENTS

There has been unfavorable criticism from time to time of the musical accomplishments of the German instrumental folk musician of the 17th and 18th centuries. E. W. Böhme writes, for example;

---

[69] S. B. Carstedt, *Atzendorfer Chronik*, p. 127, and G. Linemann, *Celler Musikgeschichte*, p. 78, report that players received approx. 100 Reichstaler at a wedding in the 18th century.

[70] A saying attributed to the principalities of Göttingen and Grubenhagen goes as follows: "Young musicians, *àle Baddellüe* [old beggars] (*Deutsches Sprichwörterlexikon*, ed. K. F. W. Wander, 1863/80, under the heading "Musikant").

[71] See page 100 ff.

[72] G. Kittler, *Musikgeschichte der Stadt Köslin*, Greifswald 1939 = Pommernforschung Reihe 5 (Studien zur Musik in Pommern), Heft 3, p. 28.

[73] J. Raupp, *Sorbische Volksmusikanten*, p. 81 ff.; the same author, *Sorbische Musik*, Bautzen 1966, p. 15.

[74] H. Milbradt, *Das hessische Mannschaftsregister von 1639*, Frankfurt a.M. 1959 = Forschungen zur hess. Familien- und Heimatkunde 26.

"their music was characterized by the bagpipe. They carried out their reprehensible, dilettantish activities not only in the country, but often even ventured into the cities. . . ."[75] There is, however, little reason to assume that the accomplishments of the *Bierfiedler* were any less than those of folk musicians of the hinterlands in more recent times. To be sure, the musicians of the 17th and 18th centuries made judgments similar to that of E. W. Böhme; yet their invectives such as "faker" and "bungler" signify first and foremost that the art in question was not executed according to the rules of a guild, that is, in the manner of formally learned music. There was an emphasis on the technical terminology of the crafts.[76] More will be said concerning the enmity among groups of musicians.[77] The stimuli that the performers received in the 17th and 18th centuries were less international than during the Middle Ages because of the curtailment of travel. Influences from the cities were more important, particularly in places where teachers' associations served as mediators between formal music and folk music. On the other hand, folk musicians found sufficient support[78] among their audiences to enable them to preserve or develop particular styles. There was a broad middle group between the extremes of guild-educated musicians and the archaic, folkloristic *Spielmann*.

VIII • PROFESSIONAL DESIGNATIONS

In the course of the 17th and 18th centuries, the designation *Spielmann* gave way to the appellative *Musikant*. A *Spielmann* was first and foremost a secular instrumentalist, a player of dance music,[79] and as late as the second half of the 17th century, the town musician was often so designated whenever he played at dances.[80] In

---

[75] E. W. Böhme, "Soziale Schichtung Thüringer Musiker im Jahrhundert des Barock," in: *Thüringen* 6 (1930/31), p. 95.

[76] E. J. Kulenkamp, *Das Recht der Handwerker und Zünfte*, Marburg 1807, p. 202.

[77] Compare page 119 (section XI).

[78] Compare page 119 ff. (section XI).

[79] See D. Krickeberg, *Das protestantische Kantorat im 17. h.*, Berlin 1965 = Berliner Studien zur Musikwiss. 6, p. 112.

[80] See Dotter, *Das Collegium musicum zu Alsfeld*, in: .itt. des Geschichts- und Altertumsver. der Stadt Alsfeld 11 (1907), p. 8 ff.

the comedy play *Hanenreyerey* (Hamburg 1618)[81] the old affiliation *Spielmann* = "juggler" (*Gaukler*) was still maintained. The abbot's fool is called *Körtken Speelman*. In northwest Germany from 1600 on, the designation *Stadtspielmann* gave way to *Stadt-(Rats-)musikant*, and around the middle of the 18th century, when town musicians were already called *Musici*, there is also mention in the records of Bremen-Verden of *Bauern-musicanten* ("peasant musicians"). A frequently used, semi-official but derogatory designation for the instrumental folk musician was that of *Bierfiedler*.

IX • PEASANT AND *SPIELMANN*

As mentioned above, the strongest denunciations of musical players came from the church. At the time of the *Sachsenspiegel* (13th century) when the disparagement of secular musicians had reached a high point, the Christianization of northwest Germany had already been accomplished. This does not, however, signify that the peasants' lives were completely pervaded by the spirit of Christianity. On the North Frisian Islands Christianity was not fully accepted until about the end of the 14th century.[82] "Heathen elements seemed to . . . have maintained themselves for some time in Schleswig-Holstein. As late as the 17th century, old people still told of virgins dancing in the New Year in the churchyard."[83] Here, unlike most other German lands, the drum processions were not, by way of astrological interpretation, transformed into celebrations of Epiphany or Twelfth Night (cf. fn. 83). In northern Europe the *Spielmann* was still regarded "as a symbol for the mythical prestige of 'Näck' "[*84] On the other hand, even in northern Germany, from the height of the Middle Ages on, the church gave the peasants a biblical picture[85] of

---

[81] New Edition in: *Niederdeutsche Schauspiele älterer Zeit*, ed. by Johann Bolte and Wilhelm Seelmann, Leipzig 1895 = Drucke des Ver. für niederdeutsche Sprachforschung.

[82] C. P. Hansen, *Chronik der Friesischen Uthlande*, Garding 1877.

[83] W. Wittrock, "Volkslieder in Schleswig-Holstein," in: "Norddeutsche und nordeurop." *Musik*, Kassel 1965 = Kieler Schriften zur Musikwiss. Vol. 16, p. 105.

[84] W. Danckert, *Unehrliche Leute*, p. 243.

[85] E. Feddersen, *Kirchengeschichte Schleswig-Holsteins* Vol. 2: 1517-1721, Kiel 1938.

*Näck—Swedish mythological water-god. *Tr. Note.*

the world mixed with superstitious heathen concepts which stubbornly persisted.[86] The medieval *Spielmann* saw himself "in many a sense still active as 'magician,' 'soothsayer,' or 'sorcerer' . . . and besought to conduct rituals of priestly origin."[87] He might well, therefore, have found work to do, especially among the peasants, who exhibited that mixture of timid respect and aversion which W. Danckert[88]mentions, and which E. G. Wolters shows to be an after-effect of the witchcraft trials in the peasant areas of Bremen-Verden.[89] Executioners, gravediggers and shepherds (who were frequently *Spielleute*), itinerants in general, and even the clerics themselves were held to be knowledgeable in witchcraft.[90] Seldom, however, were they specifically musicians, except perhaps in legends.

Nevertheless, one often encounters the *Spielmann* in the records of witchcraft trials in the 16th and early 17th centuries. The witch craze obsessed all strata of society, and the *Spielmann* was involved through the witches' dances. In a witch trial in Essen in 1581 it is said of a *Spielmann* by the name of Heine from Holtbeckh: "Heine was able to produce a sound as though one were beating on a kettle."[91] In Attendorn (Westphalia) in 1594 a bagpiper was thrown into prison along with others because of witchcraft.[92] In 1649 the witch trials were prohibited in Bremen-Verden by order of the Swedish regional government.[93] Since the pipers had been freed from disrepute by the imperial laws in the 16th century, the "demonic" powers formerly attributed to the *Spielmann* became increasingly a matter for legend

---

[86] E. G. Wolters, "Kirchliche und sittliche Zustände in den Herzogtümern Bremen und Verden 1650-1725, dargestellt auf Grund der Generalvisitationsakten," III, in: *Zs. der Ges. für niedersächs. Kirchengeschichte* XXI (1916), p. 126.

[87] W. Salmen, *Der fahrende Musiker,* p. 33.

[88] W. Danckert, *Unehrliche Leute.*

[89] E. G. Wolters, *Kirchliche und sittliche Zustände,* III, p. 130. (The reference here, however, is not to the *Spielmann.*)

[90] G. Fischer, *Die Einzelgänger, Struktur, Weltbild und Lebensform sozialer Gruppen im Gefüge der alten Volksordnung,* in der Sammlung von Aufsätzen Fischers: *Volk und Geschichte, Studien und Quellen zur Sozialgeschichte und historischen Volkskunde,* Kulmbach 1962, p. 259 ff.; W. Danckert, *Unehrliche Leute,* p. 17; P. Zaunert, *Rheinland Sagen,* Vol. 2, Jena 1924, p. 174.

[91] F. Feldens, *Musik und Musiker in der Stadt Essen,* Essen 1936, p. 65.

[92] W. Salmen, *Geschichte der Musik in Westfalen,* Vol. I, p. 237.

[93] H. Poppe, *Vom Lande Kehdingen. Ein Beitrag zu seiner Geschichte und Kultur* Freiburg a.d. Elbe 1924, p. 158.

and fairy tale. The musician does not appear here primarily in a threatening role, like the Pied Piper of Hamlin. In legends about witches he often "does not take direct part in the sorcery of the witches; he is identified as the assistant who carries their equipment to the places of their dances."[94] In Christian times legend made Wodan into a *Spielmann* whose magical music-making compelled the listener to dance (cf. fn. 94). According to other legends, it was said that the devil preferred the guise of *Spielmann* because boys and girls were often seduced while dancing. (cf. fn. 94). The dishonorable burial of musicians outside the churchyards led to a harvest-time expression which persisted even into the 19th century: whenever the reapers came upon large ant or mole hills it was said, "There a musician lies buried."[95] In a Rhenish legend the peasants and magistrate protected the *Spielmann* from the clergy. In 1615 a musician arriving in Monheim was said to have waded across the Rhine, fiddling, upon which the Dominican monks demanded that the magistrate initiate action to put him on trial as a master sorcerer. The magistrate claimed, however, that one could wade across the Rhine without the devil's help and sentenced the *Spielmann* only for an act of mischievous wantonness; the peasants sent him food in prison.[96]

Nevertheless, there were sound reasons for peasants to regard musicians with disdain. Villagers mistrusted all itinerants and feared that a beggar *Spielmann*, if dissatisfied with wages paid him, would set their houses on fire and then disappear forever. When a musician was a resident, a small amount of property could at least earn for him a low position in the village hierarchy.[97] Although the *Spielmann* of the 18th century rarely still held a priestly office, he participated in the customary services and ceremonies, not only as a

---

[94] *Handwörterbuch des deutschen Aberglaubens,* Vol. IX, Berlin 1938, Stichwort [heading] "Spielmann."

[95] R. Andree, *Braunschweiger Volkskunde,* Braunschweig 1901, p. 364.

[96] P. Zaunert, *Rheinland Sagen,* p. 172 ff.

[97] Concerning the peasants' pride of ownership, the pastor of Atzendorf (Magdeburger Börde) writes in the 18th century: "Only the judge is referred to as 'sir.' Since the peasants consider the designation *Bauer* as something sound and substantial, referring to a citizen with property of 5, 6, or 7 acres of land, one can't 'call them fools' when one hears that they are disdainful of titles." S. B. Carstedt, *Atzendorfer Chronik,* p. 89. Also compare G. Gerdts, *Hadler Bauernleben und Hadler Bauernwirtschaft in verflossenen Jahrhunderten,* in: Jahrbuch der Manner vom Morgenstern 29 (1939), p. 27.

musical extra but also in an active role,[98] which represented a retrogressive tendency.

The customs themselves became more "enlightened," at least insofar as aspects of the Enlightenment were inherent in Protestantism from the very start.[99] E. G. Wolters speaks of the fertile areas of Bremen-Verden as "enlightened marshes."[100]* Through custom, dance became primarily a form of entertainment[101] or an erotic end in itself. Insofar as music was still part of custom and ceremony, it was not necessarily performed by professionals. In the wedding procession the *Spielmann* no longer bore the priestly role of driving away demons, but instead appeared as a servant hired to highlight the rank of his employer in the village community. His way of earning money, at best artisanal, was far removed from the peasant mentality. Even the village artisans who were musicians by avocation enjoyed little respect.[102]

This attitude of disdain towards the *Spielmann* was, however, ameliorated by another factor. His occasional and secondary role as a sorcerer had always been an ambivalent one; his participation in this role reflected remnants of an intrinsic sensibility to magic. Even in a legal sense, the *Spielmann* was at times indispensable during the Middle Ages and the beginning of more recent times. The landowner was required to provide music for the peasants who served him.[103] At weddings the *Spielmann* was required to participate in the church procession as well as in the following "festivities," which served the purpose of testifying to the legality of the marriage before a large assemblage of witnesses.[103a] The original (spiritually reconciling,

---

[98] Compare F. M. Böhme, *Geschichte des Tanzes in Deutschland,* Leipzig 1886, p. 150 ff.

[99] Insofar as peasants owned books, these were predominantly religious. H. Poppe, *Vom Lande Kehdingen,* p. 155; G. Gerdts, *Hadler Bauernleben,* p. 24.

[100] E. G. Wolters, *Kirchliche und sittliche Zustände,* III, p. 134.

[101] R. Andree, *Braunschweiger Volkskunde.*

[102] M. Rumpf, *Deutsches Bauernleben,* Stuttgart 1936 = Das gemeine Volk, Vol. I, p. 495.

[103] W. Salmen, *Der fahrende Musiker,* p. 120.

[103a] W. Salmen, as above; E. Drägert, "Recht und Brauch in Ehe und Hochzeit im hamburgischen Amt Ritzebüttel nach der Reformation," in: *Jahrbuch der Manner vom Morgenstern* 43 [1962].

*The German *aufgeklärten Marschen* refers to the enlightened populations of these marshes, enlightened in the sense that they had given up their heathen ways and come under Christian influence. *Tr. Note.*

legally symbolic) role of the *Spielmann* on such occasions has scarcely been investigated to date. After 1600 the *Spielmann*'s role at special services was primarily limited to entertainment. At weddings he was no longer present specifically to fulfill a legal function.

Between the itinerant musician and the poorer country population there existed in certain cases a solidarity of the less fortunate. The resident *Spielmann,* in spite of everything, was frequently a small landholder, or at least displayed a peasant-like striving towards that end.[104] Then too, in the peasant conflict with the city-dweller[105] there proved to be common spiritual factors. The peasants objected to the fact that the town musicians had the privilege of serving in the countryside, not only because the town musicians were more expensive, but also because their manners and "artistic" music were foreign to them. Independent players of Bremen playing in and around the city alleged, in opposing the town musicians in 1617, "Although we have not been schooled in music as thoroughly as Mr. Hauss Knop and his associates, the common man nevertheless, ignorant of such matters, would rather be served by us, who can perform for less than the officially licensed musicians."[106]

Hessian players argued in opposition to the town musician of Wetter, claiming that he did not possess the instruments demanded by the peasants.[107] The town musicians of Stade lodged a complaint with the governmental authority in 1768, claiming that at a wedding in Wiepenkaten the peasants had pounded on the tables and finally driven them away. The bridegroom stated before the authorities that "he had not noticed that tables had been knocked over, and if it had happened, such a thing could easily occur at peasant dances."[108] The elders and residents of Agathenburg argued in opposition to town musicians of Stade in 1779: "Whenever country musicians come they are regarded as wedding guests themselves in that, like others, they give their offering and possess nothing other than what they earn with their music-making."[109]

---

[104] Compare E. Herlitz, *Musicomastix, Eine Comoedia von dem Music Feinde,* Stettin 1606, Facs. publ. by Hans Engel, Kassel, 1937, fol. Biij.

[105] E. G. Wolters, *Kirchliche und sittliche Zustände,* III, p. 147 f.

[106] A. Arnheim, *Aus dem Bremer Musikleben,* p. 381. Compare also E. Herlitz, *Musicomastix,* Act I, Sc. 1, especially fol. Biiij.

[107] E. Gutbier, "Hessische Musikanten," in: *Zeitschr. des Ver. für hessische Geschichte und Landeskunde* 14 (1963), p. 122.

[108] Stade, Niedersächsisches Staatsarchiv, Rep. 80 G, Gewerbe, Tit. 208, Nr. 1.

[109] Ibid.

X • ARTISAN AND *SPIELMANN*

The artisans, who in a special sense represented popular propriety[110] and within the guilds attached great importance to a "sense of honor," were in practice the strongest spokesmen against the dishonesty and impropriety of certain professions.[111] W. Danckert[112] points to evidence from the late 18th century with respect to secular musicians (instrumentalists). After 1652 in the duchy of Braunschweig the baptismal certificate required for acceptance into a craft guild omitted the remark that the applicant was not the son of a piper. It still appears, however, in birth certificates in Hildesheim in 1681.[113] It was a tailor who around 1660 attacked a town piper "on the occasion of a *convivio* ('dinner party') with coarse words against his honor," and who thus induced the founding of the Instrumental Collegium of Upper and Lower Saxony, whose members were town musicians.[114]

The extra-religious motives which in the Middle Ages had already strengthened the contempt of citizens for musicians persisted. The itinerant was regarded as outside society *(eine gebrochene bürgerliche Existenz)*,[115] and was disdained all the more perhaps because he was secretly envied. Among resident musicians not even the regular town musician was always respected. Even less recognition was given to such guild members as the *Lübecker Köstenbrüder,* not to mention the non-guild players in the city and countryside. The musician, after all, produced nothing tangible and appeared primarily as a vehicle for display and symbolic representation, or as a dinner or dance entertainer. Even discounting the contempt of artisans, the peasant musician became the victim of the sharply defined class distinction of the time. At most, the numerous

---

110 M. Rumpf, *Deutsches Handwerkerleben,* Stuttgart 1955, p. 69.

111 G. Fischer, *Die Einzelgänger,* p. 243.

112 W. Danckert, *Unehrliche Leute,* p. 227 f.

113 E. Stoltze, *Unehrliche Leute,* p. 256; W. Danckert, as above, p. 11.

114 H. J. Moser, *Die Musikergenossenschaften,* p. 88.

115 W. Salmen, *Der fahrende Musiker,* p. 82 ff.; H. F. Menck, *Der Musiker im Roman,* p. 40. According to the official dress regulations of Strassburg of 1660, "players who perform at dances" were placed on the same level as "common artisans." (D. Krickeberg, *Das protestantische Kantorat,* p. 112). In Freiberg/Sa. the town piper was counted among the more "elevated" workers (Dress Regulation of 1673) (ibid. p. 94 f.).

musicians who were not artisans by profession enjoyed minimal social recognition from other artisans.

The condition of at least minimum social prestige is borne out by the fact that folk musicians were often preferred over town musicians, even by the artisans. The reason cannot be based solely on the fact that they were less expensive, for the town musicians complained in 1750: "though we offer our services at the same prices as those who make music in public inns and taverns ... they stick fast to their beerfiddlers and soldiers."[116] Obviously, the folk musicians' music corresponded to the uneducated tastes of the artisans. Yet one cannot deduce a value judgment from this. There was rather a continuing dichotomy in the artisan between his mistrust of the elemental and indispensable power of music as contrasted with his own carefully guild-regulated existence.

XI • TRAINED MUSICIAN, SCHOLAR AND *SPIELMANN*

The educated musician differentiated himself most decisively from the *Spielmann*. This was particularly true of the town musician who felt called upon to defend his "moral uprightness," newly achieved in the 16th century. This "uprightness of calling" was based primarily upon his assimilation into a craft guild which repeatedly referred to the *Spielmann* as *Bönhase* and *Pfuscher* ("bungler and faker") in order to emphasize the *Spielmann*'s status outside the guild organization.[117] Whenever the town musicians speak of *Bierfiedler* they contrast themselves as "artistic" church musicians. Because they had to compete with folk musicians at weddings in town and country, they were particularly critical of them. Such proximity to the *Spielmann* necessitated a particularly hard line to emphasize their professional and social superiority. The musicians who were not involved in playing for peasants' dances were a little more objective in their judgments. In spite of prevailing disdain on the part of the general population, composers have always derived inspiration from

---

[116] Stade, Stadtarchiv, Abt. St. V, Fach 66-67, 1. Compare also page 100-101 Section III), Bremen musicians.

[117] Compare page 111, Section VI.

folk customs and forms.[118] German music theoreticians nevertheless predominantly represented the learned, civic-artisan point of view[119] which was supported by the other intellectuals as a whole.

XII • THE AUTHORITIES AND THE *SPIELMANN*

According to J. Fr. Scheid[120] it was *"nemini turpitudini ... musicen addiscere"* (no disgrace for anyone to learn music). Nevertheless, there was reflected in the directives of the authorities something like fear, certainly insofar as the Protestant church had anything to say about it. This fear was based upon and maintained by the association of music with heathen customs. Protestantism distrusted and isolated itself from Christian musical folk customs with their external forms of piety, reflecting the joy of the senses. Around 1760 rationalism asserted itself with the clergy of Bremen-Verden.[121] The animosity towards the *Spielmann* (who was regarded as a seductive ambassador of the devil) now was based primarily upon motives of inner asceticism. Though dancing was permitted, it was supposed to be "discreet." That would, however, have subdued the desire to dance and diminished the income of musicians.[122] Yet wild dancing was a danger to sexual morals. Music kept the guest in the tavern and led to more drinking, often inciting crimes and fights. Here religious motivations merged with secular considerations. Over and above this, the governments wanted to curb dancing because, with particular respect to the concepts of mercantilism, they feared for

---

118 W. Wiora, *Europäische Volksmusik und abendländische Tonkunst,* Kassel 1957 = Die Musik im alten und neuen Europa I, p. 94 ff.

119 There have been numerous comparative studies of the trained musician and the folk musician. See, for example, I. Otto, *Deutsche Musikanschauung im 17. Jh.,* Phil. Diss. Berlin 1937; W. Wiora, *Europäische Volksmusik;* R. Dammann, *Der Musikbegriff im deutschen Barock,* Köln 1967, p. 433 ff.; Additional references are to be found in the writings of Johann Beer, Johann Kuhnau and Wolfgang Caspar Printz (cited by H. F. Menck, *Der Musiker im Roman*).

120 J. F. Scheid, *Dissertatio,* p. 30.

121 E. G. Wolters, "Kirchliche und sittliche Zustände," I, in: *Zs. der Ges. für niedersächs. Kirchengesch.* 19 (1914), p. 24. With respect to the position of the church also see fn. 12.

122 Compare the description of a large wedding by S. B. Carstedt, *Atzendorfer Chronik,* p. 121 ff.

the work ethic, as well as for the purses of their tax-paying subjects.[123]

Only two examples will be cited here. On the 17th of December 1734, the elector of Hannover published an edict "on the abolition of Christmas Matins (early morning services), Midsummernight festivals, Pentecost-Beer drinking, Easter and Midsummernight blazes, and other superstitious and vexatious abuses." It was furthermore claimed that "in some places a so-called Midsummer-night festival was celebrated by young people of both sexes the whole night through, with music and drinking, after they had been recruited by a house to house invitation," and that such "part-papist, part-heathen abuses" should be abolished.[124] In a mandate of July 9, 1771, it is stated that "on the day of the King of Estebrügge's hunt the night revelry among the young got more and more out of hand, for which the inn-keepers, through joint efforts and the hiring of musicians, were largely responsible. . ." The servants were said to be unfit for work the following day.[125] The animus of the authorities was, of course, particularly directed at the itinerants who evaded police control, as well as taxes (except for consumption taxes).

Privately though, the nobility allowed the folk musician to play for them. They maintained a certain degree of freedom from the erudition of the "pedants" and were not obliged to share the same views. The landed nobility even felt a certain ancient solidarity with the life of the peasant. J. Kuhnaù writes of one lady of the landed gentry: "Oh, she likes very well to strike up a dance and permit herself a turn to and fro."[126] Whenever folk musicians and peasant dancers appeared at great court festivals, it was regarded as a welcome enrichment of the ceremonial forms of court life. In court festival processions the populace was often "boorish" or demonstrated a "lively boisterousness" and, as in the late Middle Ages, enjoyment of the art of the folk musician coexisted with social disdain, based upon feudalism.[127]

---

123 Compare F. M. Böhme, *Geschichte des Tanzes*, p. 91 ff.

124 *Chur-Braunschweig-Lüneburgische Landesordnungen und Gesetze*, Vol. I, Göttingen 1739.

125 Stade, Niedersächs. Staatsarch., Rep. 74 Jork, Fach 165, Nr. 1.

126 J. Kuhnau, *Der musikalische Quacksalber*, p. 100. Compare also E. Herlitz, *Musicomastix*.

127 F. Sieber, *Volk und volkstümliche Motivik*, p. VII.

Thus the folk musicians of the 17th and 18th centuries—with the exception of the itinerants—were no longer such social outcasts as the minstrels of the Middle Ages. The "clearing of the spiritual horizon" (A. Weber), an increasingly settled life, as well as numerous bourgeois callings and, in some instances, mercantile interests, furthered their integration. Yet even when folk musicians became members of the society, they were little respected. The servant nature of their calling as members of the lowest strata of the established social order their unlearned, secular art, not geared to material needs, which at the same time loosened uncontrollable vitalities, contributed to the maintenance of their low status in the eyes of the established order. In view of the many differences among them, one cannot speak of a true class of folk musicians.

CHAPTER FIVE

The "Hautboist;" an Outline of Evolving Careers and Functions

·

WERNER BRAUN

A fluctuating and at times seemingly contradictory state of affairs exists among the old professional and official appointment designations, as well as within musical terminology in general. An extreme example of this is the theme of this essay. An *Hautboist* or *Hoboist,* in the first half of the 18th century, was accomplished on the oboe, but was also able to perform on other instruments. Approximately a century later, when the word was used as a general description of a military musician, he could rarely perform on the oboe. These contradictory definitions point up a fundamental change in the history of military music. In place of numerous small ensembles consisting primarily of woodwinds, there appeared in France, as early as 1789 when the *Garde Nationale* was founded,[1] massive performing groups made up mostly of brass instruments. A similar development took place in Germany from about the time of the Wars of Liberation (1812-1814) on. The following discussion is dedicated to the early period, when the first definition of "Hautboist" was still applicable. However, in an examination of conditions after the beginning of the 19th century, it would be more appropriate to use the term "military musician."

Yet even this concept can lead to misunderstanding if one means it only as the act of giving signals and commands. In all countries actual military engagements were always conducted by the lowest service ranks only. Furthermore, these actual military obligations were overshadowed by growing artistic duties. Statistical studies of

---

[1] R. F. Goldman, *The Wind Band. Its Literature and Technique,* Boston, 1961, p. 20.

the last third of the 19th century verify the existence of military musicians without military obligations, as well as regimental bands under the direction of uniformed civilians.[2] The only things military about such musicians were their uniforms, their superiors and their provisioning. The military aspects become even less significant when one realizes that in earlier times many other professions and classes were identified by a uniform, and that many civilian occupational relationships were based upon command and obedience.

It is particularly difficult to describe the German hautboist because the documents referring to his existence—employment records like those often found for town pipers, cantors, organists, court musicians, trumpeters and drummers—are not usually available. One must search laboriously for the names of military musicians in rosters, discharge records, and roll books of individual regiments.[3] Hautboists turn up in civilian files principally when their activities interfered in some way with those of other musicians. In the main, official records deal with controversial matters and very frequently there is merely a parenthetical mention of the hautboist. Given the large number of such controversies in which the fundamental concern is with legal questions and the interpretation of performing privileges rather than with music per se, the profession of hautboist emerges in a somewhat distorted light. Consequently the historian, seeing himself forced into the role of judge after the fact, soon loses any pleasure in the work. This explains why, although there has been an almost incalculable number of references to hautboists, a monograph devoted to them has not yet been written.[4]

The problematic situation regarding source materials is so faithfully reflected in the literature that merely tying together related but separately transmitted facts could be considered a

[2] A. Kalkbrenner, *Die Organisation der Militärmusikchöre aller Länder,* Hannover 1884, p. 5 f., 13 and passim.

[3] H. Schieckel, "Die Oboisten im oldenburgischen Infanteriekorps 1783-1800," in: *Genealogie* IX, 17, 1968, pp. 377-9.

[4] Contemporary discussions are found in encyclopedia articles under "Hoboist(en)" by H. Chr. Koch, *Musikalisches Lexikon,* Frankfurt/M. 1802, p. 759 and by G. Schilling, *Encyklopädie der gesamten musikalischen Wissenschaften,* vol. III, Stuttgart 1835, p. 598. Some more recent articles deal with the wind ensemble, such as R. F. Goldman in various places and B. Husted, *The Brass Ensemble,* Diss. Rochester (N.Y.) 1955, Ms.

126

scholarly accomplishment. Under such circumstances an historical, comprehensive sociological study of the hautboist seems improbable. The preliminary work must first be done. This would have to include the checking of paradigmatic cases and an attempt to define and classify the hautboist. The term is found in diverse connections, but above all refers to garrison musicians (regimental hautboists) and to members of town militias and privileged *independent* town music associations (town hautboists). In addition, it is used to describe members of royal hunting groups (hunt hautboists) and beyond that, in connection with brass bands in mining districts (mountain hautboists).[5] Finally, mention should be made of the respected court hautboist, who was an employee of a resident court with special status and assignments. There is also the oboe player of the more recent orchestra, the orchestra or chamber hautboist. The correlation between the first five groups, not yet adequately defined, is characterized by a concentration on woodwinds which performed in *Chöre* as ensembles[6] or were grouped together in *Banden.*[7] There were also militarily inspired, pragmatically organized groups without traditional guild-like rules, which had a preference for three-part music like the famous march of the Frankfurter Piper Tribunal, mentioned by Goethe.[8] As a rule, these were groups of six or twelve hautboists. Although numbers not divisible by three were permissible, the consistent feature was a three-part setting ($4 = 2+1+1$),[9] which after about 1750, and considerably earlier at the courts, gave way to a desire for richer sonorities.[10]

---

[5] Mentioned by, among others, Chr. G. Thomas, *Unpartheiische Kritik*, Leipzig 1798, p. 157.

[6] This French term meaning wind bands was used in Vienna and in Germany after about 1780; see below, p. 153.

[7] Concerning the history of this word *Bande*, originally west germanic, *Trübners deutsches Wörterbuch*, ed. by A. Götze, I, Berlin 1939, p. 223 f. reports that because of the pejorative nature (= disreputable company) of the word, the expression was looked down upon by German musicians from about the end of the 18th century on. On the other hand, "band" has the meaning of an ensemble of wind players in Anglo-Saxon countries without any deprecatory connotation. In this borrowed form such a meaning is also possible in German (for ex. "Jazzband").

[8] C. Valentin, *Geschichte der Musik in Frankfurt a.M.*, Frankfurt a.M. 1906, p. 46-49. Fasc. edition in *MGG* I, 1949-51, Sp. 1913 f.

[9] P. Panoff, *Militärmusik in Geschichte und Gegenwart*, Berlin 1938. p. 60; J. Reschke, *Studien zur Geschichte der brandenburgisch-preussischen Heeresmusik*, Diss. Berlin 1935, p. 11. Cf. also fn. 139.

[10] P. Panoff, *Militärmusik*, p. 87 and 102.

I • COURT HAUTBOIST

At what period do we find the earliest references to a class of musicians designated as hautboists? The answer to this question necessitates a kind of definition: at a period when the playing of a strong woodwind instrument, an *hautbois,* was first considered something unique. Reference must also be made to the development of *haute musique,* played in large rooms or at festivals in the open air, in contrast to the softer *basse musique* of the late Middle Ages. The first hautboists thus might have been respected players of the *Schalmei* and the *Bomhart,* like the trumpeters *Alta* of the Burgundian court,[11] described by Johannes Tinctoris, who were still of importance in later French music practice. In any case, Thoinot Arbeau (Jean Tabourot) in 1589 characterized the playing together of oboes and trombones *(hautbois et saqueboutes)* as the norm at dances, even in the case of the common man who was said to have still been satisfied with pipe and drum as late as 1530.[12] When, instead of the trombone, the *courtand (Kortholt),* meaning short wood, or a similar bass instrument was used, the oboe ensemble could be said to have been clearly defined. It quickly reached England,[13] where generic names such as *Passomezzo de haultbois* (from 1569 on)[14] testify to a type of sound quite obviously widespread in France in the 16th century.

From this time until the *grands hautbois de l'écurie ou même de la chambre** of the 18th century,[15] there appears to have been an uninterrupted tradition of courtly oboe playing in France. This tradition is also apparent in the three-part woodwind compositions of Jean Baptiste Lully. Shortly after 1600[16] mention is made of a

---

[11] H. Besseler, *MGG* I, 1949/51, Sp. 378 f.

[12] R. Sommer, ibid, Sp. 603.

[13] H. G. Farmer, *A History of Music in Scotland,* London 1947, p. 69; W. Salmen, *Der Fahrende Musiker im europäischen Mittelalter,* Kassel 1960, p. 165.

[14] H. M. Brown, *Instrumental Music Printed Before 1600. A Bibliography,* Cambridge/Mass., p. 241 and 311.

[15] See among others, J. Ecorcheville, "Quelques Documents sur la musique de la Grande Ecurie du Roi," *SIMG* II (1900/01), p. 625-629.

[16] F. Lesure, "La naissance de l'orchestre en France au début du XVIIe siècle," in *Histoire de la Musique,* Encyclopédie de la Pléiade I, 1960, p. 1564; N. Broder, "The Beginnings of the Orchestra," *JAMS* XIII (1960), p. 180.

*The reference here is to the staffing of the large ensemble as well as that of smaller chamber groups of the royal court. *Trans. Note.*

standard group of twelve musicians. They were admired because of their *chant élevé,* careful improvisations, well-sounding *tremblements* and proper and correct diminutions.[17] From the last third of the 17th century, oboes of a new type[18] were available, which made their way rapidly from France to England, Scandinavia and Germany.[19] Plate 12 shows an ensemble of ten oboes and two bassoons on the occasion of the coronation of Louis XV at Reims on October 25, 1722.[20]

That this export was not restricted to the instrument is evidenced by French names among the membership rosters of German bands, for example in those of Celle (1681), Bonn (1697 f.) and Dresden (François le Riche, after 1699).[21] The French hautboists in residence at the court of the Elector of Brandenburg in Berlin from December 22, 1681 on, drew the same salaries as other court musicians and were given equal status.[22] In such a prosperous city, extensively influenced by the military, there must have been something like a training and exchange center for German court hautboists.

On July 21, 1698, the occasion of the birthday dinner for Duke Friedrich Heinrich of Saxony-Zeitz in Zeitz castle, "a musician of the elector of Brandenburg by the name of La Puisier, together with his six students, performed on oboes and flutes."[23] On the 24th and 25th of July this group also performed at the central German royal residence.[24] This is proof that the name *Lubuissière* or *La Bassire* in the Berlin files from 1693 until his departure in the year 1700 was that of an hautboist and that he was the director of a band with

---

[17] Such was the judgment of the Abbé des Pures in J. Ecorcheville, *Vingt suites d'orchestre,* Paris 1906, I, p. 92.

[18] E. Halfpenny, "The French Hautboy I," in: *The Galpin Society Journal* VI (1953), p. 23. H. Becker, *MGG* IX, 1961, Sp. 1781-1813.

[19] E. Halfpenny, "The English Debut of the French Hautboy," *MMR* 79 (1949), pp. 149-153. At Swedish court festivals there often were groups of eight hautboists. T. Norlind and E. Trobäck, *kungliga hovkapellets historia* Stockholm 1926, p. 59. For information on the Swedish literature, I am indebted to F. Bohlin.

[20] Reproduction of the entire picture in F. Lesure, *Musik und Gesellschaft im Bild,* Kassel 1966, ill. 80.

[21] G. Linnemann, *Celler Musikgeschichte bis zum Beginn des 19. Jahrhunderts,* Celle 1935, p. 59; A. W. Thayer, *L. van Beethovens Leben,* Vol. I., Leipzig 3/1917, p. 16 f.; M. Fürstenau, *Zur Geschichte der Musik und des Theaters am Hofe zu Dresden,* Vol. II, Dresden 1862, p. 66.

[22] C. Sachs, *Musik und Oper am kurbrandenburgischen Hof,* Berlin 1910, p. 172.

[23] Blockflöten [recorder]; fletuse = flûte douce.

[24] Hofdiarium Zeitz, LHA Dresden, Loc. 8699, Jg. 1698, Bl. 73.

which he went on concert tours.[25] Similarly, Gottfried Pepusch can be considered an hautboist even though he was active as first violinist at the Prussian court chapel (1693-1708, 1710-1713).[26] Three facts substantiate this: his appearance in public with seven wind players in London (April 4, 1704);[27] the summoning of six hautboists from Berlin to Hannover, 1701/02, who were instructed and engaged after a period of training and probation in 1705;[28] and finally, the well-known appointment of Pepusch to the post of staff musician of King Friedrich Wilhelm I. The number of his students must have been considerable[29] and the ensembles trained by Pepusch were highly praised and well paid. When Johann Mattheson visited Hannover on June 5, 1706, he took particular note of "the most select group of hautboists" among the virtuosi there.[29a] And in the same year, in the Prussian capital, six wind players of the royal guard attained the rank of court musician, on a par with string players,[30] after they had been instructed in composition for a period of two years by none other than Johann Theile.[31]

Similar training institutions also existed in other areas of Germany towards the end of the 17th century. In 1697, for example, the *Passauer Hubuisten* of Bavaria taught two young musicians from the seminary at Kremsmünster to play oboe and bassoon.[32] Around 1700 almost every court of consequence possessed the "new" instrument and maintained bands of hautboists, e.g., Stuttgart (from 1680),[33] Weissenfels (from 1695),[34] Dresden and Gotha (from 1697),[35]

---

[25] C. Sachs, *Musik und Oper*, p. 182.

[26] Ibid. p. 181.

[27] Cl. Cutworth, *MGG* X, 1962 Sp.. 1030.

[28] H. Sievers, *Die Musik in Hannover*, Hannover 1969, p. 58.

[29] In 1703 five hautboists came to Berlin from Ansbach, most probably for the purpose of training. Compare also G. Schmidt, *Die Musik am Hofe der Markgrafen von Brandenburg-Ansbach*, Kassel 1956, p. 72.

[29a] J. Mattheson, *Grundlage einer Ehrenpforte*, Hamburg 1740 (new ed. by M. Schneider, Berlin 1910), p. 195.

[30] C. Sachs, *Musik und Oper*, p. 183 f.

[31] M. Geck, *MGG* XIII, 1966, Sp. 278.

[32] A. Kellner, *Musikgeschichte des Stiftes Kremsmünster*, Kassel 1956 p. 285.

[33] J. Sittard, *Zur Geschichte der Musik und des Theaters am Württembergischen Hofe*, Vol. II, Stuttgart 1891, p. 13.

[34] M. Seiffert; Vorwort to DDT 54/54, Leipzig 1916, p. XIX; A Werner, *Städtische und fürstliche Musikpflege in Weissenfels*, Leipzig 1911, p. 95.

[35] A. Werner, *Vier Jahrhunderte im Dienste der Kirchenmusik*, Leipzig (1933), p. 246/48.

and Gottorf (around 1699).[36] There is still a tendency to use the term "court-hautboist," even though the decentralized nature of German musical life forced the musician to perform many other functions.

Second only to trumpeters and drummers, the hautboists are the most frequently mentioned musical groups in the court publications of the central German *Sekundogenituren** of Saxony-Weissenfels and Saxony-Zeitz.[37] Their incorporation into court life was accomplished in two stages:

1. There was occasional recruitment of outside wind ensembles for performances at dinners and dances. Such was the case with twelve shawm** players (Weissenfels 1676)[38] and twelve court pipers from Eisenberg (Zeitz 1686/89) who were also dubbed The Apostles because of their number.[39] As was the case with all court groups, they also had to be capable of playing violins. In Zeitz there were pipers of the guard (1681), dragoon pipers (1687/88), and eight regimental pipers (1690) in addition to others not specifically identified. From August 16, 1690 on, the *hopoen* were heard here.

2. Hautboists were engaged as the second, or if one counts the trumpeters as a separate group, as the third court musical ensemble.[40] In March, 1690, the *Zeitzer Diarium* speaks of the "local piper." The *Fourierzettel* (Quartermaster Record) of 1693 through 1715 mentions six hautboists. These instrumentalists also served as lackeys in Zeitz (March 9, 1697) and in Weissenfels.[41] According to the description of the Zeitzer *Heimführung* in July, 1689, the *Musikanten* ("pipers and trumpeters") ate their meals at their respective tables. One may assume that this practice persisted.

---

[36] B. Engelke, *Musik und Musiker am Gottorfer Hofe,* Vol. II, Manuscript in the Kiel University Library.

[37] LHA Dresden, Loc. 8698 and Loc. 8699.

[38] Not according to E. Wennig, *Chronik des musikalischen Lebens der Stadt Jena bis 1750,* Jena 1937. See also fn. 110 and 126.

[39] A. Werner, *Weissenfels,* p. 96.

[40] The Pay Regulations of Weissenfels confirm this order. Compare also A. Werner, *Weissenfels,* p. 57 ff., 88, 96, and A. Schmiedecke, *Zur Geschichte der Weissenfelser Hofkapelle,* Mf XIV (1961), p. 416 f. and 418 f.

[41] A. Schmiedecke, *Weissenfelser Hofkapelle,* p. 418.

*The smaller secondary courts of the land. Tr. Note.
*See below, p. 136. Tr. note.

The string players or, after 1688, the trumpeters who played two-part compositions (*Bicinia*), as well as the oftmentioned recorder players, along with their apprentices[42] and the shawm player or hautboist competed with one another to supply the ordinary midday and evening musical services. Often *fletussen* (recorders; see note 23, p. 129), violins and, after 1703, French horns were also used. The offerings of the court band, the *Capell Music,* possessed something more of an official character. After January 6, 1693, this term was replaced by the expression *grosse Musik,* perhaps because the hautboists were thereafter used as members of the ripieno section of the court band.[43] A preference for alternation between various sonorities continued, while the range of court music (especially in dinner concerts) went from robust folk music to the virtuoso accomplishments of foreign instrumentalists and castrati singers. The hautboists were the constant element in this colorful range. In Zeitz they accompanied their sovereign on journeys, led the processions of the court on either oboes or violins, played violins for an hour before the evening meal outside the rooms of the Duchess (Jan. 17, 1692), carried sauerkraut and bratwurst to the hunt (Oct. 14, 1698), played to the good health of a court official at his wedding, played minuets along with other pieces at a dance (Feb. 21, 1693), and played a courante for the performance of a tightrope walker and his wife (Aug. 15, 1696). From a socio-historical point of view, the hautboist can be placed somewhere between the peasant musician and the real court musician. Johann Stadermann, mentioned in Zeitz as a dulcimer player (*Hackebretierer*), was also described as an accomplished player of the French oboe (1694) and as an oboist (1680).[44] For him *usus* and *ars* were still of equal importance.

The increased accomplishments and recognition of hautboists after 1700 is evidenced by the mention of individual members of the *Banden* (see fn. 7) in publications, where formerly there was only a collective reference (Zeitz, Dec. 30, 1716: the hiring of Adam Friedrich Schumann), as well as by the indication of solo playing (Zeitz, Dec. 1, 1705: appearance of a "foreign Hautboist;" or Feb. 2,

---

[42] Such a group was also to be found at the Württemberg court. J. Sittard, *Zur Geschichte,* p. 12 f.

[43] The opposite concept, *kleine Music,* is mentioned only ,nce, with respect to the performance of the Kapelldirektor Christian Heinrich Aschenbrenner in Zeitz on the 27th of July 1698. Hautboists most likely did not participate.

[44] A. Werner, *Städtische und fürstliche Musikpflege zu Zeitz,* Leipzig 1922, p. 90.

1717: *Grosse Musik* "at which an hautboist by the name of Carl Beversdorff was heard upon the *Fagotte* [bassoon]").

In contrast to the ordinary regimental hautboists, paid from the general revenues and subject to military discipline, the court hautboists, as members of a personal guard or as members of what in some other way was designated an elite group, were paid from the court budget and placed administratively under the Lord Chamberlain.[45] Unlike the court musician proper, they were more "naturally inclined" to play wind instruments. They were paid out of a special budget, receiving a bonus for playing with the regular court ensemble, or sometimes merely with the *Expektanz* ["hope"] that they might eventually be able to fill a vacated permanent position there. This differentiation between the two types of court musicians was not equally established in all places and there were a number of disputes over status. The simplest situation was one in which the court musicians were "delegated" hautboists because they were the only ones available. This natural kind of arrangement was still to be found in and outside of Europe at the end of the 19th century.[46] Unlike the actual court musicians, the *Bandisten* ["band members"] were required, in the manner of lackeys, to be on hand at all times, even when outside the residence.[47] Their grouping into *Gesellen* ["apprentices"] and *Meister* ["masters"] was based upon military arrangements, or as with some folk music groups, more or less by loose understandings rather than detailed contracts. Only during joint appearances with the band in church,[48] at dinner, and

---

[45] A. Werner, *Vier Jahrhunderte*, p. 246-248; J. Sittard, *Zur Geschichte*, vol. II, p. 14; the arrest of Zeitzer hautboists on the 18th of Nov. 1697 because of disobedience towards the Hofmarschall.

[46] A. Kalkbrenner, *Die Organisation*, p. 3, 13, 142.

[47] An undated regulation from Stuttgart emphasized that hautboists were employed "not only at the court, but also upon the wish of his royal highness, in the countryside. (J. Sittard, *Zur Geschichte*, Vol. II, p. 173).

[48] The above-quoted Stuttgart regulation specifically includes church service duties for the hautboists. The significance of their participation for central Germany is reflected in the obligato woodwind parts of Cantatas written around 1700. Compare G. Thomas, *F. W. Zachow*, Regensburg 1966, p. 222 f.

somewhat later at the theater[49] did they follow the instructions of the court conductor.[50] When band hautboists were at the same time court musicians,[51] or if they occupied such a position exclusively, their particular group status was lost completely. The expression "court hautboist"* nevertheless persisted for a considerable period of time.[52]

By and large, these arrangements were applicable to the entire 18th century, although the observation should be made that solo wind players did not always come from the ranks of the hautboists but sometimes developed in the manner of other orchestral musicians.[53] To a certain extent, hautboists formed a kind of "advance guard" in many newly formed court orchestras. They supplied new blood and served in special cases as reinforcements.[54]

---

[49] Hautboists played an important role in the history of music for the theater. A relatively early record from Altenburg, dated the 18th of October 1738; registers the expenditure of 12 Taler for musicians of the prince's own regiment "for the services rendered... at the recent *Comödien und Bals"* (E. W. Böhme, "Zur Vorgeschichte der Barockoper in Altenburg," in: *Jahrbuch der Vereinigung der Theaterfreunde für Altenburg,* 1931, p. 27).

[50] J. Sittard, *Zur Geschichte,* Vol. II, p. 173.

[51] So it was in Schwerin in 1701: Cl. Meyer, *Geschichte der Mecklenburg-Schweriner Hofkapelle,* Schwerin 1913, p. 38 and 44 f.; the hautboists of Berlin elevated to the rank of court musicians in 1706 received 100 Taler over and above their military pay: C. Sachs, *Musik und Oper,* p. 66.

[52] For example in Würzburg: *Artistisch-literarische Blätter für Franken,* ed. by J. B. v. Siebold, Vol. I, 1808, p. 39.

[53] How long the association of *hautboist* and *oboist* or *Oboer* remained is shown by the example of the family of musicians by the name of Braun, which produced many well known wind players (cf. H. Erdmann, "Die Musikerfamilie Braun," *Mf* XII [1959], p. 184 ff.) and their progenitor Anton Braun, who was an hautboist prior to his employment as court musician in Kassel (1st violin March 31, 1760) H. Kummer, *Beiträge zur Geschichte der Hofmusik... in Kassel,* Diss. Frankfurt 1922, Ms., p. 13. — The origins of oboe virtuosi around 1710 and later have not been systematically researched to date.

[54] D. Rouvel, *Zur Geschichte der Musik am Fürstl. Waldeckschen Hof zu Arolsen* (Kölner Beiträge zur Musikforschung XXII) Regensburg 1962, p. 10 f.; L. Schiedermair, "Die Oper an den badischen Höfen des 17. und 18. Jahrhunderts," *SIMG* XIV (1912/13), p. 371 f. In his suggestions for the reorganisation of the 'Eisenacher Kapelle' Johann Ernst Bach also considered "persons... in the hautboist-ensemble of Weimar as members of the Eisenach ensemble as well." (H. Becker, *MGG* X, 1962, Sp. 183). — The French practice of strengthening the strings by means of

*Retaining instrumental identification as opposed to the regular court musician (*Hofmusiker*). Tr. Note.

Thanks to their participation, older court orchestras, made up in equal part of vocalists and string players (*Violinisten*), were transformed into strong-sounding instrumental ensembles. Even Johann Sebastian Bach was familiar with such an ensemble in Weimar in 1702.[55] The ready availability of dismissed musicians made it possible for even minor nobles to maintain an orchestra. At no other time did so many court orchestras exist as in the 18th century. It is said that around 1780 some 400 musicians were employed in the service of the nobility in Vienna.[56] If one calculates a *Bande* [see fn. 7, p. 127] at six men, one arrives at a total of almost 70 groups of players.

Mattheson, who observed and commented on the growth of music-making, saw only its negative aspects. He noted that the corruption of "true music" was being aided by

> empty fashion and that almost every *Grand Seigneur en diminutif* and every little village chieftain wants to have at his disposal a few *violons, hautbois, cors de chasse*, etc., and in such a manner that they be immediately equipped with all-season uniforms, polished shoes, powdered wigs, and that they stand in attendance behind the coach, to enjoy a lackey's accommodations and pay, when better, professionally trained musicians ought to be performing than all these pipers. One wonders how much such servants really know . . .[57]

A resident ensemble of this type was maintained in 1767 by General Ernst Heinrich von Czettritz, consisting of a viola-playing* concertmaster who was also a valet; a thorough-bass player from Bohemia by the name of Veronika; a servant who could play violin and flute, as well as some hautboists. In eager initation of the royal

---

unison oboe playing is observed by H. Botstiber in two suites in the collection of André Philidor (1647-1730): *Geschichte der Ouvertüre* (*Kleine Handbücher der Musikgeschichte IX*), Leipzig 1913, p. 43.

[55] H. Becker, *MGG* X, Sp. 174.

[56] C. F. Cramer, *Magazin der Musik*, Vol. II, Hamburg 1784, p. 112. With respect to the Viennese *Harmonien* more recently also U. Sirker, *Die Entwicklung des Bläserquintetts in der ersten Hälfte des 19. Jahrhunderts* (*Kölner Beiträge zur Musikforschung* L), Regensburg 1968, p. 6 f.

[57] J. Mattheson, *Critica musica*, Vol. II, Hamburg 1725, p. 169 f.

*In the 18th century the German word *viola* may have referred to a viola da gamba. *Tr. Note.*

model, the general himself played along on the flute. Symphonies of Georg Christoph Wagenseil and *Singspiele* were performed.[58]

The concept of court music[59] is as diversified as the concept of court. It encompasses primarily popular offerings by bagpipe players, vagrants, dulcimer players, Jews and mountain people, virtuoso performances by famous singers and instrumentalists, as well as more or less appropriate performances of contemporary works. If court-hautboists took part in all these concerts, then negative evidence would seem to indicate that as a class, hautboists were markedly without profile or unique characteristics in comparison to other music groups. More positively expressed, they could be described as extremely adaptable to whatever demands were made of them.

II • REGIMENTAL HAUTBOISTS

In pre-Enlightenment society, where status symbols were a basic fact of life, military music occupied a firm place, particularly with the establishment of "standing armies" from the middle of the 17th century on. Drums and pipes were the mark of the infantry, trumpets and drums of the cavalry.

In the dragoons, a group of mounted infantry that came into existence during the Thirty Years** war, the characteristic instruments were double reeds and tympani. They initially made use of the older and shrill sounding *"Schalmei"* (Plate 13 shows early double reed of the oboe family, also known as shawm). The dragoons of Brandenburg had four such players after 1646 as well as four drums (*Tambours*),[60] and later they also used the oboe, which was capable of producing softer sounds and greater dynamic variation. In view of the strong French influence on military things (e.g., the terms

---

[58] G. Kerber, "Musikalisches aus dem Nachlasse des Generals C. H. v. Czettritz," *MfM* 32, p. 164.

[59] Also see M. Ruhnke, *Beiträge zu einer Geschichte der deutschen Hofmusikkollegien im 16. Jahrhundert,* Berlin 1963, p. 10.

[60] J. Reschke, *Heeresmusik,* p. 11.

*A combination of spoken dialogue and music; a forerunner of opera, e.g., *The Abduction from the Seraglio* by W. A. Mozart (1782). *Tr. Note.*

**(1618-48). *Tr. Note.*

Bataillon, Kompanie, Füsilier, Tambour), one need hardly point out the "French" characteristics of the German dragoon music. Once we have acknowledged this fact, we can better understand Johann Georg Kastner's observation that the oboe was first used in military ensembles in France only after the French had become acquainted with the use of the shawm in German music; in turn, the oboe gradually replaced the shawm in German dragoon group.[61] In France, however, court-hautboists were first and foremost civil servants. Consequently, in Germany, French oboists played less often in military than in civilian ensembles,[62] and the old shawm continued to be used for a time.[63] It was undoubtedly the better instrument for signaling because of its loud, penetrating tone, while the oboe lent itself more to sociability and entertainment.

Both instruments were considered social symbols and esteemed accordingly. The lowly position of the shawm as it is reflected in a statement of Burkhard Grossmann[64] was still manifest in Lübeck at the end of the 17th century.[65] On the other hand, the fact that in 1702[66] the newly organized wind ensemble in Halle was allowed to use oboes alone is a reflection of the high esteem in which the instrument was held as a result of its association with the court. The Halle regulation, however, was naturally even less effective than the

---

[61] J. G. Kastner, *Manuel général de musique militaire*, Paris 1848, p. 105 f.; also cited by P. Panoff, *Militärmusik*, p. 110.

[62] Compare also J. Reschke, *Heeresmusik*, p. 11.

[63] P. Panoff, *Militärmusik*, p. 63.

[64] *"Jetzt seynds Sackpfeiffer und Schalmeyer, oder wenns hoch kömpt drey Geiger."* Quoted among other places in: Heinrich-Albert-Festschrift, ed. by G. Kraft, Weimar 1954, p. 79. (For important occasions fiddles are preferred over shawms and bagpipes.)

[65] "Konkurrenzstreitigkeiten der Chor- und Kostenbrüder mit den Hautboisten wegen der Musik in den Krügen vor den Toren, Lachswehr, Fischerbuden,"* pp. 1726-49, Sign. 2 Musik Konv. 7. Microfilm in the Stadtarchiv Lübeck, document dated Nov. 4, 1696 (copy dated August 31, 1726): It was decided, "that shawm players must refrain from playing string instruments in all social gatherings. They may, however, play their shawms or hautbois for entertaining the common soldiers . . ." cf. also E. Preussner, *Die bürgerliche Musikkultur*, Kassel 2/1950, p. 146, note 3.

[66] W. Serauky, *Musikgeschichte der Stadt Halle*, Vol. II, 1, Halle-Berlin 1939, p. 417.

*The German terms *Lachswehr* and *Fischerbuden* might also refer to the places where the fishermen's nets were strung, or possibly even to such a specific place in Lübeck. *Tr. Note.*

well-known mandates for the protection of the trumpet, after which it was modeled. Around 1750 the town pipers had taken up the oboe with special enthusiasm[67] because it could replace the cornets, which required greater effort to blow,[68] and also in order to defend themselves against the competition of other oboists.[69] Yet Johann Joachim Quantz, coming from a background of municipal pipers and holding the position.of first violinist at the court of Bernburg, considered it unreasonable when he was offered the post of hautboist at another court.[70]

The military character of the regimental hautboists is documented in a variety of ways. Their basic musical training was often obtained in town bands, that is, civilian institutions. Johann Joachim Bode (1730-1793) was accepted as an apprentice at age 13 or 14 by the town musician Kroll in Braunschweig and was supported by his uncle, who paid the tuition. Scarcely had he been elevated to journeyman when he joined the regiment of Weihe at Braunschweig as an hautboist.[71] Appointment was based, as it was in other cases, on accomplishment as a player as well as valid diplomas and recommendations. Since the bands were subsidized or even sometimes maintained solely by donations from the officers,[72] there seems to have been an unusual concern over the abilities of the candidates. Public vacancy notices reached many interested persons. At the beginning of October, 1763, a newspaper in Kassel published:

> The laudable Hessian *Leib-Dragoner-Regiment* requires an hautboist who can play hautbois, transverse flute and clarinet and who possesses good references. The applicant should contact the above regiment at Kirchhayn.[73]

---

[67] A. Schering, "Die Leipziger Ratsmusik von 1650-1775," *AfMw* II (1921), p. 44 f.

[68] O. Spreckelsen, *Die Stader Ratsmusikanten,* in: Stader Archiv, NF H. 14, Stade 1924, p. 34 f. (comments from the year 1765).

[69] C.-A. Moberg, *Fran kyrko- och hovmusik till offentlig konsert,* Uppsala 1942, p. 110 ff.

[70] Autobiography in: F. W. Marpurg, *Historisch-kritische Beyträge zur Aufnahme der Musik,* Vol. I, 5, Berlin 1755, p. 206.

[71] F. v. Schlichtegroll, *Musiker-Nekrologe,* New Edition by R. Schaal, Kassel 1954, p. 42; G. Linnemann, *Celler Musikgeschichte,* p. 91.

[72] R. F. Goldman, *The Wind Band,* p. 25.

[73] *Casselische Polizey- und Commercien-Zeitung,* 1763, p. 407. In a similar advertisement at the beginning of the year 1766 (p. 19), only proficiency "in der Hautbois" is asked for. The *Leibdragoner* were in existence from 1751 to 1806 (Hess. Staatsarchiv Marburg, January 31, 1969).

PLATE 12. French court hautboists (see p. 129f.) Detail from "The coronation of Louis XV in Reims, 25 October 1722." (Anonymous engraving in the Bibliothèque Nationale, Paris)

PLATE 13. Georg Philipp Rugendaes (1666–1742): Mounted hautboist (dragoon). (See p. 136.)(Drawing in the Staatlichen Kunstsammlungen der Veste Coburg)

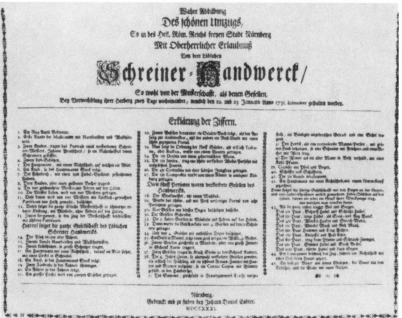

PLATES 14. and 15. Parade of the Nüremberg Joiners with three "bands" (Nos. 2, 15, and 41). Nüremberg 1731. (See p. 146.) (Germanisches Nationalmuseum Nürnberg)

PLATE 16. Procession of a hautboists' corps. Intarsia on a guild chest of 1754 in the Landesmuseum Schleswig. (See p. 000.) The related opposite panel (not shown) depicts a drummer, four soldiers with guns on their shoulders, and a leader with a lance.

PLATE 17. Meal-time music (*Tafelmusic*) of Prince Kraft Ernst of Oettingen. (See p. 000.) Silhouette on a gilt background, ca. 1791, in the Fürstlich-Oettingen-Wallersteinschen Bibliothek in Maihingen. Frantz Anton Rössler (Rosetti) wrote "Parthien" for wind instruments there.

In order to become proficient on other instruments, hautboists, as well as other members of court orchestras, sought the help of well-known specialists at their own expense. The above-mentioned Bode was granted a year's leave from the regiment in order to perfect himself on the bassoon under the chamber musician Stolze in Helmstedt. He supported himself by teaching music during this period.[74]

The frequent use of the regimental hautboist in peace time has a long history. In the preface to *Lustigen Feld-Musik*, which appeared in 1704, Johann Philipp Krieger states that the purpose of such music was "the entertainment of music lovers and then also for the use of those hautboists who were at the courts and in the field." It was all-purpose music which could be performed by winds or strings, for marching or for entertainment.[75]

In a picture from around 1700,[76] six musicians are playing shawms, standing before a tent where officers are dining. One of the musicians is singing or conducting. In a book which is most informative concerning the history of the hautboists, *Der vollkommene Soldat* by H. von Fleming (Leipzig 1726), one can read:

> Every morning the hautboists perform a little morning piece in front of the officers' quarters, a march which is pleasing to them, a little *Entrée* and a few minuets, for which the commander has a special liking. This is also repeated in the evenings or whenever the commander has guests or entertains. Then they like to hear violins and viols, as well as the recorder and other instruments . . .[77]

To the degree that military music conformed to an artistic rather than a military standard, it forfeited a certain socio-historical clarity. An example of just such blurring is the founding of shawm and hautboist *Banden* within the infantry troops.[78] In the Saxon-Polish army in 1723 two French horn players participated in hautbois music for purely aesthetic reasons ("they cause a very pleasing harmo-

---

[74] F. v. Schlichtegroll, *Musiker-Nekrologe*, p. 42.
[75] M. Seiffert, *DDT* 54/55, p. LXXIV.
[76] P. Panoff, *Militärmusik*, illustration 41.
[77] Cited from P. Panoff, *Militärmusik*, p. 60.
[78] Ibid.

ny").[79] The precedent had long been established at the courts, but there such participation, in connection with the numerous hunts, had a concrete social function. Of greater importance was the introduction of a "standing trumpeter" into the hautboist ensemble of the Prussian-Brandenburgian regiment,[80] for it intruded upon the privileges of the trumpeters' and tympanists' guilds. Yet here was a development which, once begun, could no longer be held back.

In addition to the open-air music, which was their domain by tradition and profession, the hautboists were active as string players or wind players in civilian orchestras, as were their colleagues at the courts. With the increase of public concerts from about 1750, one may observe a development comparable to the founding of the great court orchestras fifty years previously. The hautboists joined existing musical organizations in the garrison towns in which they were stationed. Such organizations were composed of town musicians and amateurs as a rule, and the hautboists served as *Ripienisten* ("supporting players") or even took the initiative themselves,[81] encouraging the civilian musicians.[82]

The differences between the court and the regimental hautboist should certainly not be overlooked. The latter had numerous military obligations such as participation in campaigns,[83] regular parades, drills, military funerals and mourning ceremonies, and later on, public open air concerts.[84] Both military and artistic aspects were determining factors for the generally rising social status of the hautboist which, corresponding to the status of the mounted infantry, lay somewhere between the piper and the trumpeter. The low esteem in which the *Feldpfeifer* ("field piper") was held in the last third of the 17th century and the stubborn persistence of medieval prejudices with respect to the *Spielmann*[85]* are revealed in a court

---

[79] H. v. Fleming in P. Panoff, *Militärmusik.*

[80] Ibid.

[81] In Halle they organized the first public concert. W. Serauky, *Halle,* p. 547.

[82] These aspects of public concerts, as well as the performance of music for the theater by military musicians, have been examined in various scholarly works, including O. Schreiber's *Orchester und Orchesterpraxis in Deutschland zwischen 1780 und 1850,* Berlin 1938, p. 36-50.

[83] Cf. the curriculum vitae of Bernhard Hupfeld below, p. 152.

[84] As for ex. in Lippe 1803/04. W. Salmen, *Geschichte der Musik in Westfalen,* Vol. II, Kassel 1967, p. 192.

[85] Collected and interpreted by W. Salmen, *Der fahrende Musiker,* pp. 61-68.

*Folk or itinerant musician. See Chapter IV; D. Krickeberg. *Tr. Note.*

action in Hildesheim in 1674.[86] The drummer was also ranked equally with the field piper. Each of the ten companies which made up a regiment in the Prussia of Friedrich Wilhelm I had three such musicians. The wind players belonged to the headquarters, while the regimental drummer and the six hautboists were part of the *Leibkompanie* ["first company of the regiment"]. The Prussian pay regulations which were in effect between 1726 and 1788 reflect this social division. Accordingly, the tambour and piper received a monthly wage of three Taler, the regimental drummer five, while the hautboists were given six Taler.[87] In Saxony-Poland similar conditions prevailed:

> While marching they (the hautboists) precede the regiment; they possess the rank of a corporal and are part of the staff.[88]

III • TOWN HAUTBOISTS

Although originally established for protection, the battalions of troops,[89] maintained by the free imperial cities, were used more and more frequently for display and ceremony. The players assigned to such contingents in the 17th century were shawm players, pipers and drummers,[90] and from around 1750 were known as "town hautboists."[91] Their number varied from place to place and even

---

[86] Protests and a (futile) law suit of the shoemakers' guild against one of their masters whose father-in-law had been observed as "a fieldpiper playing before the regiment." J. H. Gebauer, *Die "Unechten" und "Unehrlichen" in der Stadt Hildesheim*, Archiv für Kulturgeschichte XXXII (1944), Anm. 62.

[87] All of this in J. Reschke, *Heeresmusik*, p. 31. Concerning the conditions at a Southwest German resident court: E. F. Schmidt, *Dienerbuch des Herzogtums Pfalz-Zweibrücken 1724*, Ludwigshafen 1969, p. 15.

[88] H. v. Fleming in P. Panoff, *Militärmusik*, p. 60.

[89] Compare the retrospective description of a Kölner hautboist of July 1816 in: K. W. Niemöller, *Kirchenmusik und reichsstädtische Musikpflege im Köln des 18. Jahrhunderts (Beiträge zur rheinischen Musikgeschichte XXXIX)*, Köln 1960, p. 171.

[90] So it was in Hamburg in 1625. In Augsburg, after 1603, three members of the *guardia* participated in performances. H. Engel, *Musik und Gesellschaft, Beiträge zu einer Musiksoziologie*, Berlin-Halensee 1960, p. 212 and 225.

[91] Lübeck 1738: "*Konkurrenzstreitigkeiten*"; Köln 1759: K. W. Niemöller, *Köln*, p. 77.

within a given community.[92] In general, however, one could count on six players,[93] who were indispensable for festive processions through the city.

On the occasion of the archduke of Austria's birth, the artillery (*Stücke*) fired a salute in Frankfurt a.M. on August 10, 1716,

> at which event the hautbois preceded the troops in their neat uniforms, playing in honor of the Frankfurter artillery . . . the march by Telemann.[94]

For the seven church festival days, it was the custom of the town hautboists of Cologne to participate "in their municipal uniforms in the processional group."[95] In the year 1731, three *Banden,* each with three oboes, two horns and a bassoon, took part in the cabinet-maker's procession in Nürnberg. (cf. Plates 14 and 15)[96]

In sober Lübeck the military and public assignments of the town hautboists were basically limited to "posting the guard," or the morning parade.[97] For this they received a salary corresponding to the wages of a common drummer or musketeer.[98] As with other members of the military who practiced another profession, the hautboists were dependent on earning additional income in their leisure time. They were, however, not satisfied with the exclusive performing privileges they were given, which enabled them to play at some of the taverns outside of the city gates, in the *Fischerbuden* and *Lachswehr.** They turned up also at artisans' festivals and merchant associations' bird hunts, and took part in boat trips as well as musical activities which were the domain of the choir and sexton fraternities. Thus there resulted a series of suits and countersuits.[99]

---

[92] In Köln (Cologne) in the 18th century there were five to eight town-hautboists. K. W. Niemöller, *Köln,* p. 77-79. In Lübeck in 1738 there were, according to the records just cited above, five.

[93] For example, in Aachen. A. Fritz, "Theater und Musik in Aachen zur Zeit der französischen Herrschaft" in: *Zeischrift des Aachener Geschichtsvereins* XXIII (1901), p. 159.

[94] C. Valentin, *Frankfurt,* p. 240.

[95] 1759. K. W. Niemöller, *Köln,* p. 77.

[96] Both illustrations were kindly supplied by Dr. Heinrich W. Schwab of Kiel.

[97] *"Konkurrenzstreitigkeiten"* and *"Beschwerde der Hautboisten gegen eine Marstallentscheidung,"* Non-titled records 1660-1804, Musik 4, 1803-04, microfilm in the Stadtarchiv Lübeck.

[98] Eleven *nss* per week. *"Konkurrenzstreitigkeiten."* In addition, non-titled records 1660-1804, Musik 9, microfilm in the Stadtarchiv Lübeck.

[99] E. Preussner, *Musikkultur,* p. 146-149.

*See note p. 137 after fn. 65. *Tr. Note.*

146

Under the heading of "town-hautboist" one must also include those *Banden* which, in certain cities, were granted the right to perform specific public duties and were officially recognized. These were groups of musicians of varied origins, but primarily retired regimental hautboists, veterans of five or ten years service, or discharged after the conclusion of peace treaties.[100] Many military musicians had to leave the service for reasons of health and they demanded appropriate provisions for accommodation in a civilian post. Often there was no work for these musicians and letters of recommendation from the highest places caused the city fathers to have a troubled conscience.[101] Whenever they could place the unemployed hautboists in available posts such as town pipers or organists, their social acceptance was relatively easy. The existing structure was thus preserved and even strengthened.

The idea of an hautboist playing the organ should not be surprising, for employment as an organist was often combined with many extra-musical professions and activities. Hautboist organists were found in such places as Weissenfels (David Heinrich Garthoff, from 1702),[102] Berlin (Gottfried Dümler, from 1704),[103] and Köslin (D. S. Arsandt, from 1735).[104] Battalus, the hero of a novel by Wolfgang Caspar Printz (1691), had led a restless life as a shawm player, prior to his appointment as an organist.[105] Similarly, as early as the first half of the 18th century hautboists competed for positions as town pipers.[106] This professional overlapping was natural, for a large number of the hautboists actually came from the ranks of town piper groups.[107] One gets the impression that the ability of an individual military musician could raise the stature of

---

[100] For example, in 1749 the *Banden* in all imperial regiments were dissolved. C. F. Cramer, *Magazin*, Vol. I, 2, Hamburg 1783, p. 760.

[101] G. Kittler, *Musikgeschichte der Stadt Köslin bis Ende des 18. Jahrhunderts,* in: *Musik in Pommern*, H. 6 (1936), p. 81, 89 f.

[102] A. Werner, *Weissenfels*, p. 74 f.

[103] C. Sachs, *Musik und Oper*, p. 183.

[104] G. Kittler, *Köslin*, p. 81.

[105] H. Riedel, *Musik und Musikerlebnis in der erzählenden deutschen Dichtung* (Aphandlungen zur Kunst-, Musik- und Literaturwissenschaft XII), Bonn 1959 p. 520.

[106] C.-A. Moberg calls the one time *musikant och oboist*, Christian Wenster, a *Stadtmusikant* (town musician) in Landskrona (Sweden). In Delitzsch in 1729 a petition by a former hautboist was denied. A. Werner, "Zur Musikgeschichte von Delitzsch," *AfMw* (1918/19), p. 60.

[107] See fn. 71.

this position, which from about 1750 on had not been very attractive.[108] In southern Germany and Austria, the possibility of becoming a paid member of a parish choir or even the choirmaster still existed.[109] On the other hand, appointment to a Lutheran organist post was generally unavailable to the hautboist.

There were vehement protests, however, when an "independent" musical group came into conflict with one officially recognized by the authorities. The hard-won social position of town piper, recognized by civic authorities, was thus again called into question. From about 1570 on, the town piper's post had been based upon three principles in Germany, namely, service to the town council (sounding retreat), to the church (participation in polyphonic music), and to individual citizens (performance at private functions). Encroachment (by "independent" musical groups) upon the last-named, particularly lucrative area had always been a threat. From the 17th century on, however, it had become an acute danger.

One must keep in mind the growing power of the courts in an age of absolutism. Groups of popular musicians were in great demand to provide varied dinner entertainment for court officials.[110] In return, the performers were granted rights and privileges to perform privately, thereby guaranteeing their basic livelihood. The cities were forced to search for ways and means for both the older and newer musical groups to co-exist.

Again, the solution appeared to be the demarcation of areas of competence. From here, the granting of privileges to hautboists was only a small step. What occurred was that this group, which could no longer be ignored and still had to be accommodated, was assimilated into an existing, often already dissolving group, and assumed its attendant "rights" and "duties:" the performance of music at a specific church.

In Halle, as early as 1676, there were twelve green-frocked shawm players who (as mentioned above in the example of the residence at Zeitz) were in attendance at the princely evening meals without

---

108 Compare the examination report from Greifswald of 1777. H. Engel, *Musik und Musikleben in Greifswalds Vergangenheit*, Greifswald 1930, p. 18.

109 W. Senn, *Musik und Theater am Hof zu Innsbruck*, Innsbruck 1954, p. 321.

110 "Heinrich Röder und Caspar Lossa zu Jena und den Haussmann daselbst, die aufwartung bey denen Hoffdienern und sonsten betr. Aō: 1688," *LHA* Weimar B. 6169.

having a permanent position, and who therefore called themselves *Hof-Schalmey-Pfeiffer* ["Court-Shawm-Pipers"]. At the beginning of the 18th century, they assumed the inheritance of the *Kunstgeiger* ["trained violinists"] of Halle, which included the right to play in outlying villages and at the court chapel.[111] Similar adjustments are known to have taken place in Leipzig[112] and in Cologne, where hautboists had functioned as town musicians since 1723 and where they assisted in the cathedral orchestra.[113]

Even the issuance of a license limited to the country districts of Saxony-Thuringia contained as a condition that assistance be given with church music.[114] The spread of music-making in the circles of the nobility corresponds to a blossoming of sacred music in villages from the late 17th century on. In both areas the hautboists played a decisive role.[115]

With the gradual dissolution of the traditional structures from about 1750 on, the age of the municipally privileged hautboist ensembles also came to an end. The civic family fest, the main source of income for the musician, had long ceased to play the same role as it had a hundred years before. Town pipers of Magdeburg complained, for example, of weddings "where only a cup of coffee was served."[116] The circle of persons who could order music according to their own choice increased noticeably. In general, these people were the so-called *Eximierten* ["exempt class"] who were not subject to municipal law.[117] In Prussia from 1766 on, this included officers, government officials, councillors and professors.[118] In the place of lavish private fests there came new social celebrations, not (or only rarely) protected by musical privilege—balls, concerts, and theater performances. Basically they were open for competition, in growing measure, to all musicians; a development that has continued up to the present time.

---

[111] W. Serauky, *Halle*, p. 423 ff.

[112] A. Schering, *Leipziger Ratsmusik*, p. 46 ff.

[113] K. W. Niemöller, *Köln*, p. 77 f., 113.

[114] A particularly good source for this are the central German police records.

[115] More below (p. 151) about two German cantata composers coming from the ranks of the hautboists.

[116] O. Riemer, *Musik und Musiker in Magdeburg*, Magdeburg 1937, p. 61.

[117] Jena 1688 (note 110), Altenburg 1739 (K. Gabler, "Ein Musikstreit vor 200 Jahren," in: *Altenburger Heimatblätter*, 3. Jg. 1934, p. 55).

[118] O. Reimer, *Magdeburg*, p. 60.

IV • THE SOCIAL RECOGNITION OF THE HAUTBOIST

In due course, it has become apparent, through the use of such catch-words and concepts as "lackey," "band," "corporal," "sideline," "suburban," and "villages," that there remained a discrepancy between the relatively low social status of the German hautboists and their musical-historical significance as omni-present court musicians, as inexpensive performers for entertainments, and as the backbone of civic concerts.[119] Recognition is a consequence of achievement. Yet is it possible to conceive of the advancement of hautboists to the status of court musician and their consequent court or municipal "privilege-status" as recognition of a "class"? Was such recognition not primarily due to the possibility for individual success? One could say that in German-speaking areas the profession of hautboist was a transition, an opportunity to learn and prove oneself for other more respected and better paying activities.

The availability of hautboists provided the non-musician, intent on the elevation of his life-style, with the desired opportunity to hear full orchestral sonorities to which he was unaccustomed, and to maintain a small private ensemble, all for a modest sum. It allowed him to hear music in almost all places and on every possible occasion. The number of hautboists from the period of the late 17th century cannot even be approximated. Lavish courts had their origins in the period of absolutism. Great armies document the might of ambitious nations: France, Prussia, England and the long, bloody struggle with the Turks, the Spanish Wars of Succession, the Seven Years War—all threw the continent into confusion. And over all of this sounded the playing of the hautboists, both regularly employed and free-lance, glorifying the enterprises of the powerful and veiling the misery of their own existence, ruled by unrest and uncertainty. Only relatively few musicians were able to make the transition to a secure post. The majority exchanged one insecurity for another after serving their time, or after early discharge, and most likely the new uncertainty was even more oppressive. Under such an interpretation the phenomenon of the hautboist points to a great artistic reservoir which provided new blood for almost all branches of the musical professions. On the other hand, it points to a

---

[119] Compare W. Salmen, *Der fahrende Musiker,* p. 61.

large number of disappointed human beings who were more or less deceived in their life expectations.

The situation in the sphere of the French court culture was different. Here "hautboist" designated a respected and sought after post, one which also presupposed more than practical experience. Jean d'Estrée, who from before 1559 until his death (in 1576 or the beginning of 1577) was a member of the royal orchestra in Paris,[120] stands as the composer of four volumes of dance music at the head of the list of important French hautboists. In the 18th century they are represented above all by the bass-viol/bassoon player and flute teacher Jacques Martin Hotteterre, who was also active in the music of the Grand Ecurie. In addition there was the arranger of music for musettes, Nicolas Chédeville le jeune (1705-1782).[121]

Yet the leaders of German *Banden* possessed, as a rule, some theoretical knowledge, prior to the introduction of such official titles as *Musikmeister* (1823),[122] *Premier, Kapellmeister,* or *Hoboistenmeister.* H. v. Fleming says about them: "The *Premier* must understand composition in order thus to be better able to control the music."[123] "Heinrich Simon, former oboist with the (Saxon) bodyguard" wrote for his own ensemble, for example, "many small individual pieces, which became well-known." This was probably true for the aforementioned Berlin musician Pepusch, as well as Steinmetz, identified as an hautboist with the Hunting Band in Dresden in 1714.[124]

Two German hautboists achieved modest fame as composers of cantatas: Garthoff, who had written sacred vocal music even before a mouth injury forced him into service as an organist (1702), and a Thuringian who became famous under the name of Liebhold. Johann Gottfried Walther has given us a pretty dismal picture of the latter's character. Liebhold was "a coarse person who kept to the villages, never entered a church and did not receive the sacrament." He is said to have frozen to death.[125] It is also conjectured that he originally had another name and that he had served as hautboist in

---

[120] F. Lesure, *MGG* III, 1954, Sp. 1579 ff.

[121] A selection of his duets in: *Duos galants pour deux musettes* in: *Hortus musicus* 81, Kassel 1951.

[122] J. Reschke, *Heeresmusik*, p. 41.

[123] P. Panoff, *Militärmusik*, p. 60.

[124] J. A. Hiller, *Wöchentliche Nachrichten die Musik betreffend*, 4. Stück, Leipzig 1766, p. 28.

[125] Cf., by the author, "Die alten Musikbibliotheken der Stadt Freyburg (Unstrut)," *Mf* XV (1962), p. 143.

Hungary for a time. "He also played the violin and French horn and even wrote the majority of his own texts for his compositions."[126] In this description there is much which characterizes the profession: the anonymity of the members of the *Banden*, the lack of a permanent base, the reference to the two auxiliary instruments, and the stay during military engagements in Hungary. Even Prince Battalus (1691) participated in the campaign against the Turks as a shawm player.[127] It is reported that Johann Graf, later court musician in Mainz and Bamberg, served as *Hoboistenmeister* for six years in Hungary.[128]

Of particular interest in this connection is the *vitae* of Bernhard Hupfeld of Kassel. After a period of time as a composition student and service as music director of a small court orchestra, he became, in 1740, regimental *"Capellmeister* of the imperial nobleman Waldeckischen."[129] His job consisted of conducting

> the (eleven or) twelve hautboists[130] and occasionally to write compositions for them. In 1741 he led a convoy from Arolsen to the regiment in Hungary and also returned a released Turk to Turkey. He took part in eight campaigns . . . until the peace in 1748.

As a university musician and concertmaster in Marburg, he was among those musicians who achieved the breakthrough. Significantly, though, he is reproved in the same report for the weak foundation of his musical and artistic education.[131] An even more illustrious career was destined for the previously mentioned former hautboist

---

126 Ders., *MGG* VIII, 1960, Sp. 745. — As Prof. Günther Kraft of Weimar has kindly informed me, there is a reference to a *jänischen Liebhold* ("Liebhold of Jena") in the records in Zeitz. Perhaps this points to a possible connection between this musician and the Jena musical organizations discussed in the present essay (see fn. 110).

127 H. Riedel, *Musik und Musikerlebnis*, p. 520.

128 P. Gülke, *Musik und Musiker in Rudolstadt*, Rudolstadt 1963, p. 14 f.; compare also the song: *"Frisch auf, wohl in das Ungerland, ist manchn Soldaten wohlbekannt."** W. Rogge, *Das Quodlibet in Deutschland bis M. Franck*, Wolfenbüttel 1965, p. 113.

129 Particulars on the composition of the Hautboist Band of Waldecken in D. Rouvel, *Arolsen*, p. 102-109.

130 The number "eleven" is mentioned in the records (D. Rouvel, *Arolsen*, p. 103 and 108). Hupfeld, on the other hand, speaks of twelve players.

131 C. F. Cramer, *Magazin*, Vol. I, 2, p. 762.

*" 'Arise, the call to Hungary' is well-known to many a soldier." *Tr. Note.*

Joachim Christoph Bode, who later became friend and collaborator of Lessing.[132]

V • HAUTBOIST MUSIC

In evaluating the specialized aspects of a musical profession and its traditional association with a specific set of duties, one must also consider how this specialization is reflected in the resultant work of art. There has been mention of the music of organists and cantors.[133] The analogous designation, music of hautboists, refers to the repertoire available to the members of the bands, the manner of its performance and composition. The underlying question, however, is: Are there typical, clearly unique characteristics in this music which for a long time distinguished it from other music?

One characteristic of hautboist ensembles between 1680 and 1750 was their sonority, a feature from which they derived their name. Around 1700 the combination of oboe, *Taille* (meaning here normal oboe, perhaps one a third lower, of the *da caccia* type)[134] and bassoon was typical of this group.

The illustration of an hautboist quartet, based on the formula mentioned at the outset: (4 = 2 [*"Dessus"* or *"Trebles"*] + 1 [*Taille*] + 1 [*Fagott*]) can be seen on the bell of an instrument of the 17th century.[135] In French four-part playing,[136] as in Krieger's *Lustiger Feld-Musik*,[137] the middle voices were divided into Taille 1 and 2. Compositions written solely for oboe ensembles are repeatedly attested to. The title of a forgotten work of Friedrich Erhardt Niedt: *Der teutsche Frantzose* (Copenhagen, 1708)[138] demonstrates an awareness of its western origins. Most probably the same music was used for the softer, more chamber-music-like playing of the recorder, for

---

[132] E. L. Gerber, *Neues . . . Lexikon der Tonkünstler,* Vol. I, Leipzig 1812, Sp. 437-442.

[133] M. Geck, *Die Vokalmusik D. Buxtehudes und der frühe Pietismus* (*Kieler Schriften zur Musikwissenschaft* XV), Kassel 1965, p. 60-68 passim.

[134] G. Thomas, *Zachow,* p. 223.

[135] E. Halfpenny, "A 17th-Century Oboe-Consort," in: *The Galpin Society Journal,* Vol. X (1957), ill. next to p. 62.

[136] Compare the 22 *"Airs des Hautbois"* from the collection of A. Philidor in G. Kastner, *Manuel.* appendix. Also see ref. to *"drey Geiger"* in fn. 64.

[137] G. Thomas, *Zachow,* p. 223.

[138] Suites for three oboes with thorough-bass.

both instruments shared the same, or very similar, finger technique. From about 1730 the Saxon-variant dominated the hautboist ensembles, with the combination of 2 oboes, 2 horns and 2 bassoons (Plate 16).[139] Some 30 years later clarinets, and still later, flutes, were added and in this final form one could hear, at the beginning of the 19th century, the "genuine" hautbois music.[140]

With respect to the quality of performance of hautbois music there were, as in all areas of art, widely varying levels of accomplishment.[141] Weak groups such as the *Militärmusiker* (Berlin, 1728)[142] existed alongside exceptional ensembles like the one in Hannover in 1706 or the 8-member *Kaiserlich-Königliche Harmonie* in Vienna (1780). It was the judgment of the town pipers that the hautboists of the neighboring garrison in Stade at the end of the 17th century "had not learned or properly understood music."[143] This points to the defects inherent in the guild-like education, yet affirms a consciousness of levels of competence within the profession.

To what degree the sound of the oboe, described by Mattheson as *"gleichsam redende"* [like the voice , almost capable of speech];[144] characterized the music of the first half of the 18th century is discernable in part from the diverse uses of this instrument in the works of Johann Sebastian Bach.[145] Antonio Vivaldi seems to have been among the first to use the oboe as a solo instrument.[146] Ensemble oboe playing in churches can be traced from the late 17th century into the last third of the 18th century.[147] When, in a central

---

[139] I am grateful to Prof. Salmen in Kiel for sharing his knowledge of Illus. 5. An example for the kind of instrumentation depicted here is the "Dragoons March" of 1729 for oboe 1 and 2, horn 1 and 2 and bassoon, in R. Eitner, "Tänze des 15. bis 17. Jahrhunderts," Supplement to *MfM* VII (1875), p. 151. The basic 3-part structure is here expanded through the use of the horns to a five-voiced composition.

[140] Town pipers could also avail themselves of the above 5-part playing. One might assume that such adaptations were considered imitative playing.

[141] C. F. Cramer, *Magazin*, Vol. I, 2, p. 1400, Anm. 190; cf. in this chapter pp. 126-7, 155-7.

[142] J. Reschke, *Heeresmusik*, p. 27.

[143] O. Spreckelsen, *Stader Ratsmusikanten*, p. 32.

[144] *Das Neu-eröffnete Orchestre,* Hamburg 1713, p. 268.

[145] J. Hadamowsky, *Die Oboe bei J. S. Bach*, Diss. Wien 1930, Ms. On Bach's association with individual oboists see the chapter by R. Petzold in this volume.

[146] Compare also, E. Preussner, *Die musikalischen Reisen des Herrn v. Uffenbach,* Kassel 1949, p. 70.

[147] F. Krummacher, "Über daz Spätstadium des geistlichen Solokonzerts in Norddeutschland," *AfMw* XXV (1968), p. 286.

German liturgical Passion, violins are mentioned six times, recorders seven times and oboes eight times as choral accompaniment,[148] it is evidence of a technique of alternating sonorities familiar to the *"Banden."** Leopold Mozart praised the Salzburger *Hautboisten-Mass* of 1777 by Michael Haydn because in it the oboes and bassoons were used to approximate the human voice.[149] This moving, sensitive similarity of timbre and the subsequent early romantic transfiguration of open air music helped to give wind music a new lease on life.

> Music at the festive midnight hour in the month of May, under the gentle shimmer of the triste moon, enveloped by the thrilling horns of Spandau and Nissle, the silvery oboes of Fischer and le Brun, the singing bassoons of Schubart and Schwarzer—God!—whereto might not the soul, drunk with bliss, soar![150]

Among non-military secular musical activities, dinner music had been of greatest importance for many years. Every professional musician, even cantors and organists, took part in it. Nevertheless, it appears that the genre was influenced in a special way by hautboists because of their numerical superiority. If the dinner music prior to 1670 was differentiated by class distinctions—performances of court ensembles at the residences[151] and *Bierfiedler* or *Gebratensgeiger*** in modest taverns—it appears that afterwards the distinctions were to be measured more by the different abilities of the individual hautboists. Their role at the courts (Plate 17) was alluded to previously. In an often reprinted account Charles Burney reports on dinner music with "French horns, clarinets, oboes and bassoons" on a very low artistic level in the Vienna of 1773.[152] Mozart chose the

---

[148] W. Braun, *Die mitteldeutsche Choralpassion im 18. Jahrhundert*, Berlin 1960, p. 197.

[149] W. A. Mozart, *Briefe und Aufzeichnungen*, Vol. II Kassel 1962, p. 95 f.

[150] (C. L. Junker?), *Musikalischer Almanach auf das Jahr 1782*, p. 93. The biographies of the virtuosi mentioned by E. L. Gerber, *Historisch-biographisches Lexikon und Neues. . . Lexikon*, Leipzig 1790 and 1812-1814.

[151] They had, however, always contained folk-like music.

[152] C. Burney's . . . *Tagebuch seiner Musikalischen Reisen*, Vol. II (Übersetzung von C. D. Ebeling und J. Chr. Bode) Hamburg 1773, p. 246.

*Unscored oboe and bassoon parts, like unscored trumpet and drum parts, are thought to be common in some types of early 18th-century orchestral music. *Tr. Note.*

**Gebraten* ("roasted or baked"); *Geiger* ("violin"); hence, a musician who played in taverns and eating places. *Tr. Note.*

same instrumentation for the three dinner concerts depicted on the stage in the last act of *Don Giovanni* and thereby confirms a format that was in use, at least in the Austrian capital.[153] The hautboists portrayed by Mozart performed popular operatic melodies. Such arrangements may very likely have been played by small orchestras in Vienna, after a fashion,[154] before it was pronounced artistically legitimate by the Imperial and Royal *Harmonie* around 1780, and long before the frightful arrangements of the 19th century.[155] But this characterizes only one side of hautbois music. Of earlier vintage are the more or less original utilitarian pieces for winds, the dances and marches, on which the literary sources report[156] and of which there are many extant examples. Thus, for example, the archives of the princes of Thurn and Taxis at Regensburg have preserved numerous suite-like pieces of ten or more movements for wind instruments.[157] In such *Partien* an older tradition, already well developed by men like Krieger in 1704,[158] was continued at a time when the Suite stood in the shadow of other musical forms. With the social changes of the 18th century, dinner and entertainment music also outlived its baroque high point and became available to everyone without special ceremony or reason. Hautbois music

---

153 Compare H. H. Eggebrecht, "Tafelmusik" in: *Riemann-Lexikon, Sachteil,* Mainz 1967, p. 933. On the music of hautboists in the "coffee-gardens" of Leipzig: Chr. G. Thomas, *Kritik,* p. 103 ff.—One could here mention the illustration of the enticing Venusberg music in R. Wagner's *Tannhäuser* (1845).

154 Compare also the report in a Viennese theater almanac of 1794: *Nachtmusiken* consist of *Terzetten* and *Quartetten,* mostly taken from operas." (K. Strom, *Beiträge zur Entwicklungsgeschichte des Marsches in der Kunstmusik bis Beethoven,* Diss. München 1926, Druck: Suhl p. 57). There are also valuable references to matters concerning arrangements in U. Sirker, *Bläserquintett,* p. 10 f.

155 In this connection one should consider the Vivaldi arrangements of the Parisian hautboist, M. Chedeville.

156 The hautboists of Zeitz played *Menuette und Courante(n).* H. v. Fleming mentions in 1726 the *March, Entree* and *Menuette* as serenade music (*Ständchenmusik*). The three shawm players who were with the Brandenburg Occupation in 1682/83, played a Polish dance in addition to the native dances. (O.v.d. Gröben, *Guineische Reise-Beschreibung,* Marienwerder 1694, p. 42).

157 R. Hess, *Serenade, Cassation, Notturno und Divertimento bei M. Haydn,* Diss. Mainz 1963, p. 164.

158 New Edition of No. 3 of *Lustigen Feld-Musik* with the movements Ouverture, Entree, Menuett, Passacaglia, Fantasia, Menuett, Gavotte, Menuett, Gigue, Menuett, in: *Organum* III, 9 by M. Seiffert. Overture-Suites for wind orchestra were also composed by, among others, Johann Mattheson and Georg Philipp Telemann.

appears to have been intimately associated with popular forms which, around 1780, were suites and arrangements (*Sekundäre*). Primary art forms (*Primäre*), such as motets, sacred concerts and cantatas, were created by cantors and organists. The derivative nature of hautbois music and its unchanging, functional quality[159] might explain why many composers hesitated to deal directly with it, and then only with caution.

In addition to Krieger, regular collections of wind music[160] were written by Georg Philipp Telemann (*Neue auserlesene Arien, Menueten und Märsche; Musique Héroique ou XII marches* for two oboes or violins and bass, 1728),[161] Carl Philipp Emanuel Bach (*VI Piccole Sonate*) and Joseph Haydn (*Feld-Parthien*). Individual contributions were made by Leopold and W. A. Mozart, Michael Haydn, Carl Ditters v. Dittersdorf, Ludwig van Beethoven and Felix Mendelssohn (1826), among others.[162] In general, marches, suites and arrangements remained in the hands of lesser masters. Here only limited technical ability was required and utility went before originality.[163] The march was a familiar composition to hautboist composers and noble dilettants alike (Anna Amalie of Prussia 1767 f., 1777; Count Ludwig IX of Hessen-Darmstadt, 1719-1790; A. H. Baron v. Eschstruth, 1783). When the concertmaster Franz Benda (1709-1786) was asked by his friend, head of the Dragoon Regiment, to compose a march, he acceded to the request only on condition that the hautboists not learn the name of the composer. Benda felt no inclination to be looked upon as a specialist in march music.[164]

In a more indirect way, yet very intensively, hautbois music entered the classic repertory as the representative of popular forms and has been preserved as such. The oft-mentioned serenade as it is portrayed in Act II, Scene 4 of *Cosi fan tutte* by a *banda di stromenti* (two each of clarinets, horns, bassoons and later also flutes) makes

---

[159] In this connection, R. F. Goldman speaks of a functional, popular type of music which always remained somewhat foreign to orchestral music (*The Wind Band*, p. 7).

[160] Cited by, among others, R. F. Goldman, *The Wind Band*, p. 205-216 and U. Sirker, *Bläserquintett*, p. 9-11. See also G. Karstädt, "Blasmusik" in *MGG* I, 1949/1951, Sp. 1910 ff.

[161] Compare C. Valentin, *Frankfurt*, p. 240; *MGG* XIII, 1966, Sp. 194.

[162] Sources in K. Strom, *Entwicklungsgeschichte des Marsches*.

[163] It is said of the compositions of the former *Hautboisten-Meister*, Hupfeld, that they contain too many similar patterns. C. F. Cramer, *Magazin*, Vol. I, 2, p. 762.

[164] G. Kerber, *Musikalisches*, p. 161.

itself immediately accessible to the listener, relaxes him, and puts him into a cheerful mood. The minuets and marches, which were casually interjected into the serenades, cassations, and divertimenti, point as a socio-historical source to the milieu in which these genres were originally found, the playing and compositions of the German and Austrian hautboists.

Beethoven's wind music—for example, the Octet op. 103[165] must also be seen from the perspective of this background. Here there are singing lyrical passages, episodes reminiscent of ensemble scenes, hints of marches and popular tunes of the day. Yet the lightly ironical cadence points to the beginning of a new era in the history of wind music, one whose naive-popular phase was coming to an end. The Parisian music of François-Joseph Gossec and Charles-Simon Catel gives forth a revolutionary pathos and patriotic seriousness.[166] Of the manifold possible combinations of wind instruments, the quintet of flute, oboe, clarinet, horn and bassoon developed into the norm for chamber music.[167] The arrangements for the new promenade concerts had their counterpart in the ingenious pianistic transcriptions of Franz Liszt, which are really re-instrumentations. In contrast to musical development between 1680 and 1780, individual cities (Vienna, Paris, Berlin) and individual personalities (Bernard Sarrette, Anton Reicha, Adolphe Sax, Wilhelm Friedrich Wieprecht) became, one hundred years later, more significant for wind music. Music for winds presented itself visibly as art *sui generis,* music for Everyman, free from narrow social significance, yet somewhat uniform, a price which had to be paid for its technical perfection.

---

[165] On the important *Harmonien* in Bonn between 1780 and 1790 see: A. W. Thayer, *Beethovens Leben,* Vol. I. p. 64, 98, 186, 248, 268, 283, 299f., 342.

[166] R. F. Goldman characterizes them as the first masterpieces of original band music (*The Wind Band,* p. 26).

[167] G. Karstädt, *MGG* I, Sp. 1913; U. Sirker, *Bläserquintett,* p. 12 f. passim.

CHAPTER SIX

The Economic Conditions of
the 18th-Century Musician*

.

RICHARD PETZOLDT †

*This essay is based upon research done at the Karl-Marx University in Leipzig.

Man does not live by bread alone. This biblical quotation has been frequently expanded in popular usage, but the fact remains that bread is a most basic food, at least on this continent. In times of war and need this has been proven over and over again, and for this reason economists suggest that in comparing social position within various professions, one consider the buying power of money with respect to bread as a fundamental element. Formerly, when people still ground their own flour and baked their own bread, one would consider the price of grain and flour in making such comparisons. Today one can most easily ascertain the true value of income in various countries by calculating how many pounds of bread are earned in a given period of time, or in other words, how long someone must work in order to be able to buy a given quantity of bread.

Naturally, in our contemporary civilization, the price of bread is not the only relevant factor in determining the standard of living. Even for earlier epochs a great number of additional factors must be taken into consideration, such as the cost of other foods, clothing, shelter, etc. There could be instances where the price of bread in two countries would be comparable, but expenses for other necessities such as rent, clothing, transportation, etc., would be radically different. Thus the cost of daily necessities must also be itemized and compared. Unfortunately, one encounters almost insurmountable difficulties in following this procedure for past centuries.[1]

---

[1] Some of the studies done in this manner are G. Schmoller, *Umrisse und*

Even the most elementary attempts to compare older currencies to one another can be complicated. We may begin, simply enough, with an enumeration of coins: at the bottom of the scale, the *Pfennig* (from Lat. *pondus* = little pound) and *Heller* (named after the town of Hall, in the Tirol); in the intermediate denominations, the *Groschen* (from Lat. *grossus* = thick), with their various types and values (e.g., "good" *Groschen* [ggr.], to be differentiated from the less valuable *Silbergroschen*), and the *Schilling* (from Lat. *solidus* = genuine, hard). In addition, there was the *Gulden*, which from the middle of the 17th century on was no longer made of gold but was a silver coin of widely differing value within the innumerable small states of the German Empire. The *Florin* was named after the city of Florence, and the *Taler* was named after the *Joachimsthal* coin (the word is still evident in "dollar"). The *Taler* was also available in various values such as *Konventionstaler, Speciestaler, Couranttaler, Reichstaler*, etc. Gold coins were called *Dukaten*.[2] Merely listing the coins points out the immediate difficulties encountered in investigating the economic state of the 18th-century musician in Germany.[3]

In those "good old days" people lived from hand to mouth. Prices often fluctuated radically whenever there was a poor harvest and the money lenders and profiteers were active. In the famine year of 1740 the price of wheat and rye in Leipzig almost doubled, returning to normal in 1741. Around 1800 in Prussia ration cards were issued to the poor so that they could obtain cheap army bread.

Not only were the values of coins extremely variable, but weights

Untersuchungen zur Verfassungs-, Verwaltungs- und Wirtschaftsgeschichte Deutschlands, Leipzig 1898; W. Abel, *Agrarkrisen und Agrarkonjunkturen in Mitteleuropa,* Berlin 1935; M. J. Elsas, *Umriss einer Geschichte der Preise und Löhne in Deutschland,* 2 vols., Leiden 1940 and 1949; E. Waschinski, *Währung, Preisentwicklung und Kaufkraft des Geldes in Schleswig-Holstein,* Neumünster 1952.

2 Also see H. Gebhart, *Die deutschen Münzen des Mittelalters und der Neuzeit,* Berlin 1930.

3 Up to now, only a few very limited investigations have been done for the period of Bach-Telemann and for the time of Schütz. Among others, see R. Petzoldt, "Zur sozialen Lage des Musikers der Schütz-Zeit," in: *Festschrift zur Ehrung von Heinrich Schütz,*" ed. by Günter Kraft, Weimar 1954; R. Petzoldt *Zur sozialen Stellung des Musikers im 17. Jahrhundert,* in: Kongr. Ber. Köln 1958, Kassel 1959; U. Hain, *Johann Sebastian Bach als Leipziger Bürger,* Staatsexamensarbeit der Fachrichtung Musikererziehung der Karl-Marx Universität, Leipzig 1961; A. Otten, *Die soziale Stellung Bachs in Leipzig,* Staatsexamensarbeit der Fachrichtung Musikerziehung der Karl-Marx Universität, Leipzig 1967; R. Petzoldt, *Georg Philipp Telemann,* Leipzig 1967.

and measures were not standardized either. Thus, for example, in Hildburghausen in the winter one *Malter* equaled 212.4 liters of grain in contrast to the summer, when it equaled 252.4 liters. One therefore made a distinction between the summer and winter price of grain, according to the moisture content. In the neighboring town of Meiningen one *Malter* was equal to only 167.1 liters, while in Munich it was measured at 222.[4]

As a consequence of varying silver content, the relationship between *Taler* and *Gulden* also fluctuated. In the Leipzig of Bach's time, and in Saxony and the smaller states of Thuringia in general,[5] the *Taler* was worth 24 *Groschen* and the *Gulden*, 21—a ratio of 8 to 7. On the other hand, in Hamburg the ratio was 2 to 3. There the *Mark* was equal to ½ *Taler* and the *Scheidemünze* to 16 *Schillinge*; each was equal to 12 *Pfennige*.[6]

An additional complication arose from the fact that the coinage contracts, initiated by the various cities or individual German rulers as well as by the Empire, were not carried out according to strictly uniform standards. Examples demonstrating this are the coinage regulations in Esslingen (1524) and Augsburg (1551); Leipzig's agreement with the Elector of Saxony and with Braunschweig (1690); the *Zwölftalerfuss* in Leipzig (1738) which decreed that from one Mark of fine silver—preferably the *Kölner Mark* equal to 234 grams of silver—12 *Taler* should be coined; or the Prussian coinage regulations of 1751, by which a ratio of 14 *Reichstaler* or 21 *Gulden* to the Mark was established. The 18th-century German rulers promoted inflationary tendencies by granting coinage rights to dishonest entrepreneurs who, by means of *Kipper und Wipper* (*kippen* = cutting off, *wippen* = flinging into the scale), radically pared down coinage values. Thus, in 1621, in the time of Heinrich Schütz, it took 7 or 8 new *Taler* to equal one old *Taler*, and by 1623 the rate had risen to 16 to 20. Especially inglorious were the actions of Frederick II of Prussia. Not only did he coin 14 *Taler* from the same quantity of silver as had previously been used for 12, but during the unlawful occupation of Saxony he had inferior money coined from the Saxon-

---

[4] Compare R. Jauernig, *Die im alten Thüringen gebräuchlichen Masse und ihre Umwandlung*, Gotha 1929; and M. J. Elsas, *Umriss einer Geschichte.*

[5] Also see the treasury reports and pay rosters in the State Archives of Weimar, Gotha and Meiningen.

[6] F. Engel, "Tabellen alter Masse, Gewichte und Münzen," in: *Methodisches Handbuch für Heimatforschung in Niedersachsen*, ed. by Helmut Jäger, Hildesheim 1965.

Polish dies, which citizens were then required to accept at full value.[7] Making calculations even more difficult is the fact that in the 17th and 18th centuries the *Reichstaler,* equated at 24 *Groschen,* was actually just an arithmetic concept; the *Taler* which was coined, the *Speciestaler (species* = face, i.e., coin with head or bust), was calculated at 32 *Groschen.* Thus one really had to pay more *Groschen* in order to obtain a *Taler* coin.[8]

These remarks should suffice to characterize the situation which confronts a musicologist when he reads in Bach's famous letter to his one-time fellow student:

> In Thüringen I can make out better with 400 *Courant-Thaler* than in this place with twice as much, because of the very high cost of living. (Leipzig, Oct. 28, 1730)

Similarly, one can read that when Frau Telemann abandoned her husband, she left behind a debt of 3000 *Taler.* Were these men poor, members of a comfortable middle class, or well-to-do people? Further, what was their socio-economic status with respect to their neighbors?

The Age of Absolutism, oriented towards strict etiquette, categorized subjects rigidly according to rank. This is borne out by the allocation of tiers in theaters, for example. Next to the rulers who governed by divine right, the aristocracy and nobility held the highest positions. They in turn were divided into higher and lower ranks, as were the members of the not very highly respected merchant nobility. Even the various levels of city dwellers were differentiated according to their rights and obligations. They, of course, were brought up to look with disdain upon the peasants. In the ranks of court officials, the position of music director (*Kapellmeister*) was, for conditions at that time, not a particularly lowly one, though he could never rank with Italian prima donnas or castrati singers. In Köthen, Johann Sebastian Bach's position was salaried like that of the *Hofmarschall,* the second highest official of the province of Anhalt. In the order of precedence of the court of Halle-Weissenfels, the *Kapellmeister* held the third position, on a par with court secretaries and magistrates. In the year 1765, Georg Benda, music director in Gotha, was advanced to tenth rank in the

---

[7] Compare H. Gebhart, *Die deutschen Münzen.*
[8] Compare W. Haupt, *Tabellen zur sächsischen Münzkunde,* Berlin 1963.

court, while on the other hand the *Kapellmeister* in Schwerin in 1704 only held fifteenth place, after the thirteenth position of the ducal valet and fourteenth place of the personal servant of the duchess. Nevertheless, he was one of the prince's personal servants and above the *Kantor* ("vocal music director") who held the sixteenth position, or the court drummers and trumpeters and other musicians who were eighteenth.[9] Similarly, an employment contract dated 1703 for the *Pagen-Informator und Hofkantor* ("page tutor and vocal music director") Johann Ludwig Bach in Meiningen indicates that he should "hold a rank immediately ahead of the personal servants."[10]

One was also required to observe precedence at table. Telemann reports with some pride on his activities in Eisenach and states that he was given "the title of *Secretar* as well as a place at the *Marschall*'s table," a position which he had already been given once before in Sorau. Finally he achieved a rank "close to the Councillors."[11] From 1713 on, the chief steward (*Pagen-Hofmeister*) and chamber musician (*Kammermusikus*) at the court of Weissenfels, Adam Emanuel Weldig, was given free lodging as well as meals at the table of the royal children, in addition to cash and produce (including a daily ration of 1 measure of wine, 3 of beer and two rolls).[12*] Almost three quarters of a century later W. A. Mozart complained that from the standpoint of the rights of the artist in a new era he should not be required to eat at the same table with personal servants, bakers and cooks,[13] a view not shared by the Archbishop of Salzburg.

For the musician of the Bach-Händel-Telemann epoch, there existed only two main professional spheres: service at a court as singer, *Kapellmeister*, court musician (*Hofmusikus*), or organist; and in the municipal-church sphere as school music director (*Schulkantor*), organist or town musician. Occasionally there was some

[9] H. Engel, "Musiker" (C) in: *MGG* Vol. IX, Col. 1092-1105.

[10] Chr. Mühlfeld, *Die hersogliche Hofkapelle in Meiningen*, Meiningen 1910.

[11] See "G. Ph. Telemann's Autobiographies," ed. by M. Schneider in preface to *DDT*, Vol. 28 (1907), p. VI-XVII and W. Kahl, *Selbstbiographien deutscher Musiker des XVIII. Jahrhunderts*, Köln, 1948.

[12] A. Werner, *Städtische und fürstliche Musikpflege in Weissenfels*, Leipzig, 1911.

[13] Letter to his father, dated March 17, 1781 in: *Mozart, W. A. Briefe und Aufzeichnungen*, ed. by W. A. Bauer and O. E. Deutsch, Vol. III, Kassel and Leipzig 1963.

*Weldig was an acquaintance of J. S. Bach; his Christian name indicates that he was godfather to Carl Philipp Emanuel Bach. J. S. Bach reciprocated by assuming a similar role for Weldig's son Johann Friedrich. *Tr. Note.*

overlapping. At first outside the cities and later within them as well, there existed musicians on the periphery who, in today's terms, would be called free-lance dance and entertainment musicians. They were looked upon with contempt by the steadily employed musicians who called them *Bratengeiger* and *Bierfiedler** because they often played at festive meals. By the 19th century there developed, with individual differences reflecting political-economic considerations in different countries, the prototype of the artist virtuoso or composer, who would from then on be dependent on agents and publishers.

What were the economic facts of the court musician's relatively high status in the court? The payroll records in the district of Saxony-Thuringia are fairly good indicators, though admittedly there is still much research to be done here. Nevertheless, a relatively clear picture of the existing court structure emerges when one compares the various ranks of court officials in relation to one another.

As has already been mentioned, German instrumental musicians could not in any way compare their positions with those of their Italian colleagues, especially with singers. Some statistics from the records in Dresden substantiate this.[14] In a volume entitled *Die Operisten, Musicos, Sänger und andere zur Opera gehörige Personen betr. ao 1717, 18, 19, 20* one reads under the date Nov. 29, 1717, a "specification of what personnel belonging to the Italian opera should receive according to the stipulations of their contracts." The specification begins with the "Capellm. Antonio Lotti and his wife Santa Stella as first singer . . . with an annual 10,500 Thlr." Next the famous castrato Senesino with 7,000 Taler, various male and female singers at 4,500, 4,000 or 3,000 Taler, and finally an Italian instrumentalist by the name of Personelli and the poet, Abbate Luchini, each with 1,000. It is added that they were all entitled to free lodging or received a housing allowance. Further it is stated under the date of February 1, 1719, "that a rented carriage be maintained for the *Operisten* Senesino and Berselli." For Senesino, who came and went between Dresden and Venice during the court festivals of the Elector of Saxony in 1719, it was even allowed that "he be paid the

---

[14] Dresen, Staatsarchiv, among others especially Vol. 383, 907 I and II.

Braten—roast; *Bier*—beer; *Geiger* and *Fiedler*—violin(ist). *Tr. Note.*

first and third installments in Venice, the second and fourth in Dresden."

The records in Dresden also give us comparable information for the non-Italian musicians during these years. A list of names dated December 1, 1711, itemizes as follows:

Thlr:

1200   Johann Christoph Schmidt, Der Capellmeister

1200   Jean Baptiste Woulmyer [also Volumier], Maistre des Concerts

400   Christian Pezold, Camer Componist und Organist

400   Petrus Cosmovsky, Kirchen Componist und Organist

400   N. N. [sic] Pissendel, Violist und Camer Musicus

350   Thismar Selencka [sic], Contre Basse . . .

Further down the list there are musicians with an annual salary of 300, 250, 240 and a mere 100 Taler for a violist (*Bracciste*). The instrument inspector was allocated 100 Taler, a copyist 50, and another 100 for the "organ builder, Gräbner . . . for the purpose of tuning and maintaining the keyboard instruments." In another undated list the name of Johann Christoph Schmidt, who was active in Dresden from 1664 to 1728 and appointed head music director (*Oberkapellmeister*) in 1717 follows the names of "Capell-Meister Davit [sic] Heinichen" and "Compositeur de la Chambre, Francesco Maria Veracini," each with a salary of 1200 Taler. Receiving the same amount was Pantaleon Hebenstreit who had gained fame through his invention of the *Pantalon*.* The salary of Johann Georg Pisendel, today considered one of the most important violinists of his time, had in the meantime been raised to 500 and that of the court organist Pezold to 450. Similarly, the name of a Czechoslovakian, Jan Dismas Zelenka, today highly regarded as a composer, appears frequently in the Dresden records. He had come to Dresden as a bass player in the court orchestra in 1710, tried his luck in other places in 1715, but from 1729 on remained in Dresden as director of church music, and after 1735, as a composer of sacred music.

---

*The Pantaleon or Pantalon was an enlarged dulcimer invented around 1690 by Hebenstreit. It had a total of 185 strings and was played with two small hammers. Towards the end of the 18th century the name was also used for a number of different types of pianoforte in which the hammers struck from above. *Tr. Note.*

These entries also give evidence of a nasty chapter in the financial policy of Saxony, i.e., the custom of delaying the payment of musicians' (and most probably other court employees') wages, perhaps for years. On November 18, 1733, Jan Dismas Zelenka requested that the post of *Kapellmeister*, vacated by the death of Johann David Heinichen, be given to him and that he be awarded a salary supplement "in one installment." He asked, too, that he might further receive a bonus because of additional expenses incurred. He claimed that without reimbursement he had composed and conducted music for the church as well as the court, first working with Heinichen and, after his death, continuing alone. He had had to "use almost half of the salary paid him to date in order to have parts copied." The appeal begins with the obsequious words, "At the feet of your most revered royal majesty bows your most humble servant in deepest submission because he is in dire need. . . ." To this the answer of the Elector-King was, "Should be patient. Cracau, February 12, 1734."

This phrase "should be patient" or others, such as "to be set aside because funds already disposed of," appear with tiresome regularity under such appeals. The totality of these documents reflects the pitiful conditions of German musicians which had changed little since the time of Heinrich Schütz. Thus, a court violinist Augustin Uhlig writes on November 7, 1733, that he had served for fifteen years performing sacred music with the Catholic Court Orchestra, the first four years without pay. Now he was asking for an increase, "for it is difficult to live on 200 Thl. in this area because everything is so expensive." On the 12th of April 1733, the violinist and contra-bass player George Friedrich Kästner writes: "because for the last eighteen years I have not had more than a yearly income of 200 Thl., things have been most difficult . . ." In the following year, Kästner calls attention to the fact that during the course of his nineteen years of service he had been required to fill the post of the deceased first violinist for six years without receiving additional compensation.

These conditions changed very little during the course of the 18th century. Saxony's ruinous wars also emptied the treasury and those first to bear the burden, as always, were the court employees. In August 1765, the musician Götzel was jailed because of debts. He made an appeal that he be paid the seven months back pay due him, for he had accumulated a total of 4,350 Taler in debts, dating from

1756. Similar appeals were filed by singers, dancers and actors. After the Seven Years' War, which had caused great misfortune in Saxony, an austerity decree was issued by Minister von Einsiedel in February 1764, for the purpose of "rebuilding the disorganized electoral finances," and on March 1st of that year a new ruling took effect which allocated "for the annual budget for theater and music" only 32,232 Taler instead of the previously allocated 51,982 Taler and 15 Groschen. Even the leading artists were affected by this action. On June 11, 1734, the annual sum of 6,000 Taler plus 500 in travel expenses had been awarded to the "contracted *Capellmeister* Hasse and his wife, retroactive to December 1, 1733." After the death of the Elector Friedrich August II in October 1763, Johann Adolf Hasse and Faustina Hasse-Bordoni, who had retired from the stage some time previously, were dismissed without pension.[15] An "Extract" dated April 30, 1764,[16] shows that Hasse was awarded a sum of 1,000 Taler since he had performed services in November and December. Not mentioned, however, was the fact that the couple was still owed 30,000 Taler by the court treasury—five years' wages! For better or worse, the Hasses settled for a sum of 12,000 Taler in order at least to recover something.[17]

The considerable contrasts in wages between the 10,500 Taler received by the married couple Lotti in 1717, the 7,000 of the castrato Senesino, or the 6,000 received by Hasse and his wife from 1733 on, and the German conductors or chamber musicians, whose salaries ranged from 100 to 1200 Taler, points to a significant variation among the ranks of court musicians. Yet one cannot judge with certainty what proportion of the total income of these musicians is represented by the wages indicated in the Dresden records. It was customary to give gifts on special occasions, either in the form of cash, or articles of value. We also do not know about extra allowances in kind, a custom in other districts. Nevertheless, one can arrive at a certain judgment in relation to other professional groups. In Dresden for example, which in the year 1728 had a population of 46,572 in the old city, 19,000 in the new part of the city, and some 16,000 in the suburbs,[18] a mason received, during the construction of

15 C. Mennicke, "J. A. Hasse," in *SIMG* V (1903).
16 Dresden, Staatsarchiv, Acta. Das Chor Fürstl: Orchestre und dessen Unterhaltung . . . betr. Anno 1764-1768.
17 Compare C. Mennicke, "J. A. Hasse."
18 Records of the Museum of the City of Dresden.

the *Frauenkirche* in the years 1733-1735, a daily winter salary of 6 Groschen, for a weekly total of 1 Taler and 12 Groschen. In the summer it was 7 Groschen per day, or 1 Taler and 18 Groschen per week. A supervisor (*Pollir**) received 8 Groschen per day, while his helper had to be satisfied with 3 Groschen and 3 Pfennige. Among the carpenters, the foreman received 7 Groschen, the others 6 Groschen per day. During the construction of the Town Hall some years later, the mason foreman's wage was raised to 9 Groschen daily "in May"—for the other masons it was raised to 8 Groschen.[19] Some 100 years earlier in 1625, a mason journeyman had received a daily wage of 4 Groschen and 4 Pfennige and a helper 3 Groschen and 6 Pfennige. But in the interim, prices had risen considerably. At that time, a *Scheffel* of grain (about 100 liters) cost 2 Taler while in 1719, a year of great drought, one had to pay 4 Taler in late summer and 4½ Taler in October. There was an enormous contrast between the amount of money at the disposal of the average citizen and the wasteful extravagances of the average court. This is particularly obvious when one considers that even in that year of famine a sum of 6,000 Taler was spent on gilding the bridal carriage for the celebration of the prince's wedding,[20] and that the privy councillor Count Vitzthum von Eckstedt was allowed "the sum of 10,000 Taler for carrying out his responsibility in outfitting the Polish and Saxon livery," as well as for obtaining carriages, swords, ammunition cases, etc.[21] During this time an average worker had less than 100 Taler annual income.

Great differences in wages among musical artists were also the rule at the Prussian Court. A listing for 1742-43 entitled *Königlichen Capell Bedienten*,[22] from which excerpts are given below, gives us some idea of the range:

> For the Capellmeister
> [Carl Heinrich] Graun   2,000 Taler

---

[19] Construction records for the Frauenkirche and the Town Hall in The Stadtarchiv in Dresden.

[20] J. Chr. Hasche, *Diplomatische Geschichte Dresdens*, 4. Teil, Dresden 1819.

[21] Dresden, Staatsarchiv, 907 Vol. I.

[22] Formerly the brandenburgisch-preussisches Hausarchiv, now in the Deutschen Zentralarchiv, Abt. Merseburg, Sign. Rep. XIX Theater E No. 1.

*In modern German also spelled "Polier," meaning a superior foreman or supervisor. *Tr. Note.*

For the Concert Meister	
[Johann Gottlieb] Graun	1,200
For [Franz] Benda Senior	600
George Benda	225
For the new orchestra personnel hired in 1741:	
For Gasparini [female singer]	1,700
For [Philipp Emanuel] Bach	300
For new orchestra personnel hired in 1742:	
For Quantz	2,000
For the poet, Bottarelli	400
For the piano tuner	30
Ballet Master Potiers	1,625
Mad.selle Roland, premier [*sic*]	
Danseuse	1,354 T. 4 gr.

It is also interesting to contrast expenditures dating from the same time for other Prussian Court employees from a list entitled *Hoff-Staats und Fourage-Etat.*[23] One can assume that those who came from upper class backgrounds had supplementary income from personally owned properties. In the case of some of the others, there was a considerable supplement in the form of free room and board at the palace. A sampling is given below:

Field Marshall Graf von Schwerin	2,000 Taler
Colonel v. Wurmb	1,000
Chamberlain v. Wilckenitz	1,000
Chamberlain Marshall v. Bierberstein	
	500
Valet de chambre Tilde	500
The Moor, Friedrich Wilhelm, Quartermst.	
	130
Personal Physician, Council Eller	1,332
[+ supplies for 168 Taler,	
other physicians at 600, 500,	
and 200 Taler]	
Gardner, Müller in Ruppin	400
Midwife, Mehlitzen	120

---

[23] Ibid. Hausarchiv Rep. II B No. 10.

Royal wood bearer to his Majesty	60
Keeper of the Wine Cellar, Alberdhal	300
Assistant to the Keeper, Creutz	52

On an expenditure roster[24] dated ten years later, the Graun brothers are still awarded 2000 and 1200 respectively, while the King's favorite, Quantz, is now listed in third place, once again with 2000 Taler. Although some musicians had received salary increases in the interim, Philipp Emanuel Bach is still listed with the small sum of 300 Taler. It is no wonder that he made efforts to leave the court during this time and applied for municipal service (1750, Cantor post at the Thomaskirche in Leipzig and 1753 in Zittau). Yet according to this list, Christoph Nichelmann, employed as second cembalist, received 500 Taler and Johann Friedrich Agricola, also of the school of Johann Sebastian Bach, was awarded 400 Taler as *Compositeur*! Not until the fiscal year 1756/57, the year of his departure from the Prussian Court, did Philipp Emanuel Bach's annual wage reach 500 Taler, still a modest sum in comparison to the salaries of other members of the court orchestra. In fact, a separate listing is devoted to Italian singers in the cited roster of 1752/53, where some are listed with salaries of 4752 and 4440 Taler and others with 1800 or 1500. Nevertheless, the differences in relation to some of their German colleagues are not as extreme here as they were in Dresden.

The conditions for musicians in the small German principalities were scarcely different from those in relatively large residences, though there were, to use a present-day term, *Ortsklassen,** in the musical life of larger and smaller cities. The court of Sachsen Halle-Weissenfels provides a good example.[25] With the reorganization of the orchestra in 1677, the conductor David Pohle was awarded 500 Taler in cash plus 104 Taler for expenses as well as 32 Taler for a lodging supplement. A violinist received 230 Taler and an additional 65 Taler for expenses so "that he might be utilized on such other

---

[24] Ibid. Rep. XIX Theater E No. 1. The comment about Ph.E. Bach's raise in salary in: Hausarchiv, Rep. XIX E No. 1 Kapellrechnungen.

[25] Compare A. Werner, *Städt. u. fürstl. Musikpflege.*

*These are regional groupings which dictate modification of base salaries, depending upon local cost of living index in German cities. *Tr. Note.*

instruments on which he was proficient." The court organist drew 200 Taler and likewise 65 Taler for expenses "in the event he might have to be used as a singer." It may be safely assumed that these figures remained applicable for quite some time. It may likewise be assumed that the court's unwillingness to deny itself any worldly pleasures frequently emptied the ducal treasury. Under the rule of the Dukes Johann Georg (reign 1697-1712) and Christian (reign 1712-1726), one sumptuous court festival followed another. In order to defray the relatively high cost for such a small duchy, they incurred debts among rich citizens and occasionally even pledged jewelry with Jewish bankers in Vienna. Finally, in 1727, an imperial decree was proclaimed so that some order might be achieved in the country. Christian's successor, Duke Johann Adolph II (reign 1736-1746), rid himself of the accumulated debts to the court musicians by abruptly and arbitrarily dismissing the orchestra. The heirs of the court Kapellmeister Johann Philipp Krieger, who died in 1725, were still owed no less than 2,885 Taler, 18 gr., and 5 1/2 pf. in back pay belonging to their deceased father. In addition, his treasury owed the son, Johann Gotthelf Krieger, who succeeded to the post of Kapellmeister, an additional 535 Taler. The director of church music, Johann Augustin Kobelius, was owed 3,278 Taler, 8 gr., 1 1/3 pf. plus 234 Taler in interest! Even a singer, Pauline Keller, hired in 1710 at the relatively high wage of 500 Taler, who had been offered the use of a ducal carriage for her *"plaisir,"* was owed the sum of 1629 Taler, 19 gr., 6 pf. in 1726, sixteen years later.

Wherever one looks it is the same tale, the same travail. Johann Ludwig Bach of the Meiningen branch of the family, who was highly esteemed by Johann Sebastian Bach, was hired in 1703 as instructor to the pages and as court vocal music director (*Hofkantor*). In addition to his base salary, he was given free room and board. This arrangement was altered to the extent that he now received only an annual rental allowance of 16 Taler and fifty pounds each of carp and venison. On the 15th of September 1725 he sent a petition to Duke Anton Ulrich von Sachsen-Meiningen indicating that he had not received his extra allowance since 1715:

> This allowance, most graciously granted me, which is nevertheless scarcely sufficient, is now in arrears to the sum of 405 Taler, 7 ggr. . . . The losses and damages caused me in these ten years, even though I have labored

honestly and industriously, have elicited many a sigh and groan from me and have caused bitter hours.

He requested back payment of the rent allowance and retroactive delivery of the fish, meat and candles due to him, at least from 1719 on, and called attention to the fact that he was, after all, providing lodging for the choristers and that he "must do without these rooms which could otherwise bring in funds through their rental." His initial salary was a meager 100 Taler and was made up of payments from various different funds and sources, from the royal treasury (*Fürstlichen Cammer*), the royal church treasury (*Hof-Kirchenkasten*), and the income of the duke from Grimmenthal near Meiningen (*Grimmenthaler-Kasten*).[26] The court music director (*Hofkapellmeister*) in Meiningen from 1702 to 1706 was Georg Caspar Schürmann, who received an annual salary of 240 Taler. It is not clear whether Johann Ludwig Bach, in his later capacity as *Kapelldirektor*, ever received a commensurate salary.[27] Study of the court records in Meiningen is complicated by the fact that bookkeeping and payments involve several accounts.[28] Nevertheless, Johann Ludwig Bach's reminders seem to have borne fruit, for in the *Records on Income and Expenditures from 1724 to 1726* his name again appears next to the sum of 55 Taler and 4 gr. allowance for wheat, corn, barley, beech and pine lumber.

In general, the records in Meiningen provide a good overall insight into the structure of a court orchestra. The five trumpeters, drummer, court vocal music director (*Hofkantor*), one or two chamber musicians (*Kammermusici*) and a singer are listed as a separate group, while the remaining musicians are always found under the heading of *Laquey und Hoboist*, implying that they most probably also performed duties not connected with music. The leading court officals received more substantial salaries than musicians. Here one finds a "privy councillor and magistrate" with

---

26 Chr. Mühlfeld, *Die herzogliche Hofkapelle.*

27 Finance records provide evidence that Schürmann was active in Meiningen for a period of "18½ weeks" from the end of July 1702 and not later, as is reported in Gerhard Croll's article, "Schürmann" in: *MGG* Vol. XII, Sp. 195-201. Johann Gottfried Walther's encyclopedia entry is thus correct. From Michaelmas [day] 1706 Schürmann's name no longer appears in the "Grimmenthals Kasten-Rechnung."

28 Meiningen, Staatsarchiv, Kammer-Rechnungen, "Grimmenthals Kasten-Rechnungen," personnel files, etc.

a salary of 1,283 Taler, 1 gr, 9 pf., and another "privy councillor and marshall" earning 518 Taler, 15 gr., 2 1/2 pf. These entries for allowances down to a twelfth of a Pfennig, as well as a price list appended to the records of 1728-29, provide us with some point of reference to how things might have looked in a musician's household of that time. Nevertheless, one immediately perceives the difficulties in converting weights and measures in entries such as: "1 *Malter* of Salzunger corn and oats equals 1 *Malter* and 3 *Metzen* in the Meiningen measure . . . 1 Wasung *Malter* of corn and oats equals 1 *Malter* and 3/4 *Metzen* in Meiningen measure . . ." A housewife paid 2 Taler for a   Meiningen *Malter* of wheat (almost 170 Liter), 5 Groschen for one goose, 2 Groschen for "1 old chicken," and 1 Groschen for a young chicken. Three-score eggs cost 5 Groschen, and the court kitchen reported that it spent 34 Taler, 13 gr., 7 pf. "for 8 3/4 hundred weight of carp." A pig is priced at 5 Taler, 2 horses are entered at 81 Taler, 4 Taler were spent "for a pair of leather boots for the mail boy," and 83 Taler, 2 gr. for "3 large bookcases for the library."

In view of the conditions described above, which entailed considerable economic insecurity for the court musician, it is easy to understand why many artists played with the idea of exchanging a court career for a somewhat more secure municipal position. One can even deduce that it was not only financial insecurity which led to such a change in service, but that in a century of spiritual enlightenment and sporadic revolutionary uprisings, there was an early conscious or unconscious recognition by the middle-class citizens (*Bürger*) that the feudal system as a whole had become shaky. This is suggested, for example, by G. Ph. Telemann's departure from the court of Eisenach (Autobiography of 1739) to go to the free imperial city of Frankfurt: ". . . but this I do know having heard at that time: Whosoever wants a secure post for life should settle in a republic."[29] In Sorau he had discovered that the favor of the court could change from one day to the next. Court servants were dismissed summarily, naturally without pension. Although G. Ph. Telemann in his 1739 Autobiography camouflages the actual motivation for making the change, he had already made it very clear in his Memoirs of 1718 that he recognized the social consequences of

---

[29] "G. Ph. Telemanns Selbstbiographien," in *DDT* 28 (1907), Vorwort, p. VI-XVII.

such fluctuations in royal mood. In a French verse he speaks of the atmosphere of the court:

> *Qu'au matin l'air pour nous est tranquielle et sérain,*
> *mais sombre vers le soir et de nuages plein.*
> (That in the morning the weather seems calm and cheery,
> but in the evening clouded and dreary.)

Exactly one hundred years earlier another great musician, Claudio Monteverdi, experienced a similar situation. After twenty years of service in Mantua, the composer of *Orfeo* and *Arianna* was abruptly dismissed with 21 scudi in his pockets, less than a month's wages. Monteverdi also made the move to a patrician republic, Venice, where new and better opportunities were open to him in a more cultivated and enlightened social structure.

In addition to G. Ph. Telemann, other musicians remarked on the changes which took place during that century. The librarian and chamber musician of Weissenfels, Johann Beer (1665-1700), known as a writer on music as well as a composer, already conceived of a new type of independent artist. He called the eighth chapter of his *Musicalischen Discurse,* first printed in 1719: "On the Advantages Republics offer over Courts in Holding on to Good Musicians." J. Beer considered, for example that

> . . .there are numerous courts which at the least disruption reduce their state or merely dismiss their servants so that the court structure is dissolved *vel sua* (by itself). Therefore, there are many court musicians who are desirous of going to the cities, and who would immediately go there if the municipalities paid as well as the courts.

Yet Beer was not only concerned with money:

> While it is easier to adjust to one master than to many, so on the other hand is it easier to fall out of favor with one than many.

He describes the hectic nature of court employment:

> With the court it is one day here, the next day off to someplace else. There is no difference made between day and night. Today one must perform at church, tomorrow

at dinner, the next day at the theater. In comparison to this, things are a little calmer in the cities.

Beer further exposed royalty, saying that they often prevented their artists' further development:

> The better he (the musician) is, the more he is required to remain in the post in which he was originally hired. They pluck the feathers from his wings so that he may not soar higher.

The treatment of Christoph Graupner, *Hofkappelmeister* in Darmstadt, who was prevented from accepting the *Thomaskantorat* in Leipzig, or J. S. Bach, who left his post in Weimar (in order to go to Köthen) despite a "testimonial of unfavorable dismissal" are examples of such attitudes among feudal lords.

In addition, the policy that the compositions of a musician became the property of his employer as part of his obligation to serve the court corresponded to long antiquated concepts of justice, and was rejected by musicians who were developing greater consciousness of themselves as artists. Yet Joseph Haydn, according to his employment contract under Prince Esterhazy, dating from 1761, was still required to assign all rights of authorship over to his employer. As time went on, the composer quietly freed himself from this bondage which, in an age of middle-class emancipation, was certainly undignified. G. Ph. Telemann had also agreed to a similar stipulation in his contract with the Eisenach court. It is evident, however, from the correspondence on the Frankfurt Cantatas with the Eisenach court, to whom he was contractually obliged as non-resident *Kapellmeister* to supply with music, that he had long ceased to take seriously the exclusive rights of the Saxon duke. Telemann in particular was one of the most progressive of German composers with respect to this concept of musical copyright.[30]

Events on the death of *Hofkapellmeister* Christoph Graupner in 1760 in Darmstadt evidence the growing support for the legal rights of the aspiring middle class. In spite of protests by his heirs and in opposition to his own advisory council, the Count of Hesse had expropriated all of the deceased Graupner's manuscripts. But the

---

[30] Compare H. Pohlmann, *Die Frühgeschichte des musikalischen Urheberrechts*, Kassel 1962; also R. Petzoldt, *Georg Philipp Telemann*, Leipzig 1967.

councillors did not agree to this and obtained an opinion from the *Hofkapellmeister* in Gotha, Georg Benda. Only upon Benda's declaration that, according to the deceased's contract, the rights to his works passed to his heirs, did the heirs of Graupner in Darmstadt obtain a settlement for the confiscated musical compositions, accepting a pension, which most likely from fear of the count's anger was taken not as a matter of right, but merely as a "merciful gratuity."[31]

In the cities, the life of a musician was not a bed of roses either. The school organists and cantors were in a particularly poor situation from a financial point of view. Like the court musicians, whose feudal masters often owed them wages for years, one can assume that many town musicians had to supplement their income. In the case of towns whose economic life was dominated by agriculture, this often meant working in the fields and raising animals. The wages indicated in the records may well have also been supplemented through various donations, including those from the proceeds of the church collections. This is ascertained from the very detailed council and church records in Leipzig. A pathetic aspect in the careers of teachers and cantors was the necessity of their directing itinerant boys' choirs and funeral singing for additional income. The meager income of organists in particular was most insufficient. In 1725 in Weissenfels, for example, they earned only 80 Taler, and so it is easy to understand why musicians' petitions speak of the "atrocious organists' pay."[32] As late as 1806, in a consistorial decree concerning a petition by the organist at the Nicolaikirche in Zeitz, Johann Gottlob Dreyhaupt, who was also a teacher at the girls' school, it is stated that his income is assessed at an annual 70 Taler and 15 Groschen with an additional 11 bushels of corn and 3 of wheat. In view of the fact that the grain was consumed by himself and his family, Dreyhaupt claimed that a conversion into currency was meaningless, even if the figure were thus claimed to be 143 Taler. He claimed that "incidental income from weddings hardly brought in any cash" and since the organist had to spend 18 Taler of his income on rent, very little remained for the necessities:

> Thus it is self-evident that income from his service was very limited and not sufficient for himself and his family, particularly in the city.

---

[31] Compare H. Pohlmann, *Die Frühgeschichte.*
[32] Compare A. Werner, *Städt. u. fürstl. Musikpflege.*

The Consistory (Lutheran Church Council) decided that the organist Dreyhaupt was to receive an extra allowance for wood, "partly *in kind* and partly in cash...but in total 5 Taler per year...from church funds."[33]

There is extant from the same year the record of a consistorial council at the castle church in Zeitz concerning the petition of Gottlob Bachmann, an organist. His compensation from the collegiate church fund came to an annual 122 Taler and 12 Groschen, with an additional 6 Taler coming from the treasury of the castle church. He claimed that only insignificant sums were forthcoming from organ playing at weddings and baptisms, and that he received neither free lodging nor payment in kind. As far as music lessons were concerned, "there was much competition and little compensation." Bachmann asked for 4 bushels of grain per year in view of the fact that there was

> a great rise in prices, and that with a monthly salary of 10 Taler and 5 Groschen he was required to buy bread, wood and clothing, in addition to paying rent at a time when 1 bushel of grain was priced at 10 Taler.[34]

Such conditions appear to have been particularly typical for the church musician of earlier times. Long before Bachmann, the *Schlosskantor* Georg Christian Schemelli, well known from the life of J. S. Bach, asked the authorities of Zeitz in 1727 for free lodging and some grain, as well as a cash supplement to his pay of 30 Gulden. His petition was denied.[35]

In the Leipzig of Bach's time, the records of 1724/25[36] indicate that the organist of the Nicolaikirche, Johann Gottlieb Görner, received an annual cash wage of 61 Taler and 6 Groschen from the municpal treasury in addition to 40 Taler in rental allowance. The organist of the Thomaskirche, Christian Gräbner, received 87 Taler and 12 Groschen. Incidentally, this is the same basic salary that J. S. Bach received as cantor of the Thomaskirche. He was otherwise dependent upon the usual outside sources for additional income.

The *Accidentia*, also referred to as *Zufälligkeiten* ("outside sources

---

[33] Magdeburg, Landeshauptarchiv, Zeitzer Akten, Rep. A 29 d I No. 258.
[34] Magdeburg, Zeitzer Akten, A 29 d I, 73.
[35] Magdeburg, Zeitzer Akten, A 29 d I, 37.
[36] Leipzig, Stadtarchiv, Jahresrechnungen.

of income"), were, as has already been mentioned, a constant source of irritation for all concerned. An example from Schleusingen may be cited:[37] in 1672 Johann Balthazar Stenger was hired as organist at the modest basic salary of 60 Gulden, but had been given to understand that there were many prospects for supplemental income. Within two years, anticipating the sense of Bach's statement in his letter to Erdmann, Stenger complained that he could not manage with the money and felt himself taken advantage of because

> in my present single state it is most difficult to make ends meet, and also because the *Accidentia* which were promised me to amount to 40 Gulden don't come to more than 4. . . .

Similarly, Johann Methes Holzhey, J. B. Stenger's successor in the post, who was compensated with 70 Gulden from the municipal funds and 10 from the church treasury, complained that the money was not sufficient and that there was nothing left over for his professional advancement, as we would express it today:

> . . . Although I had at first thought that the 80 Gulden put at my disposal would be sufficient, I must now admit, particularly in view of current hard times, that it is impossible for me to buy even the basic necessities. This is further aggravated by the fact that I receive no extra allowances and have no additional means of income. Therefore it is impossible to buy bread and wood or to pay the rent, not to mention that there might be anything left over for my professional advancement, or to buy instruments or procure useful materials. . . ."

Just as badly off in the cities were the *Stadtpfeifer* ("town pipers"), *Ratsmusiker* ("municipal musicians"), *Kunstgeiger*, ("formally trained violinists")* and other musicians, regardless of their professional designations. In the previously mentioned account books in Leipzig of 1724/25, for example, the four town pipers are listed at 18

---

[37] *Acta die Bestellung und Besoldung derer Organisten bey der Stadt Schleusingen betreffend 1654-1756,* Stadtarchiv Schleusingen.

Kunst meaning art and *Geiger* meaning fiddler or violinist. Here perhaps used as the opposite of the so-called *Bierfiedler,* meaning those who played primarily in taverns and pubs. *Tr. Note.*

Groschen per week, adding up to an annual salary of 39 Taler. In this group the first name is no less than that of the trumpet player Gottfried Reiche. Bach's parts for the Clarin* testify to the fact that Reiche must have been a first-rate musician. Perhaps his accomplishments declined with age, for J. S. Bach makes a judgment in his petition to the council in Leipzig on August 23, 1730, on the *Stadtpfeifer, Kunstgeiger* and the players as a whole:

> Modesty prevents me from making candid judgments with respect to their abilities and musical knowledge. Yet one must also consider that they are partly retired and partly out of practice.

J. S. Bach also knows other causes:

> ... since many cannot concentrate on perfecting, not to mention distinguishing, themselves because of concern over their means of support ...

Strangely enough, he feels the conditions at the court in Dresden to be more attractive than those in Leipzig, for he believes—as we have seen, most incorrectly—that the "musicians there need not be concerned about their means of support."[38] These four town pipers appear once again in the account books of the Thomaskirche, with a remuneration of 10 Taler plus 2 Taler as a New Year's bonus. Also listed are the so-called *Kunstgeiger,* with a salary of 21 Taler and 21 Groschen. They were, however, not entered in the municipal records and thus had no steady income from the council. The income of these musicians was very erratic and based upon irregular employment. Thus, for example, the town pipers could demand 5 Taler for a wedding with procession (church service) and an additional 5 Taler if they also played at the dinner. The three *Kunstgeiger* could be had for 3+3 Taler for the same services. Something designated as a *halbe Brautmesse* (a shorter service), at

---

[38] Bach-Dokumente, Band I: *Schriftstücke von der Hand Johann Sebastian Bachs,* ed. by Werner Neumann and Hans-Joachim Schulze, Kassel-Leipzig 1963.

*The Clarin was a word for trumpet in the 17th and 18th centuries. Players were especially trained in the art of producing the highest harmonics (*Clarino blasen*), and it was this training which enabled the trumpeters of Bach's time to play rapid passages in high positions without valves. *Tr. Note.*

which less music was performed, was correspondingly less expensive. For an additional fee, the bridal party could also have trumpets and drums, instruments which a century earlier had been reserved only for the privileged classes.

We have some basis for comparing the wage scale in Leipzig with that in Hamburg. There Telemann had at his disposal eight town musicians and two *Expektanten*, that is, musicians who at first served without pay, in the expectation of one day being able to fill a vacant municipal post. In addition, he could fall back on 15 *Rollbrüder*, thus designated because their names were entered in a roster (*Rolle*) along with their duties and rights. Nevertheless, Cantor Telemann had great difficulty in staffing his church performances, for unlike the situation in Leipzig and in other places, Latin school students were not at his disposal. On the other hand, he was probably able to hire theater musicians. Yet in 1730, when he needed more than 100 church musicians and not less than 74 trumpet players for the tower music, as was the case for the commemoration of the *Augsburger Konfession,** he was in great difficulty. For their participation at any of the five main churches in Hamburg, nine singers and eight town musicians (instrumentalists) each received 1 Taler, while trumpeters and drummers received 1 1/2 Taler. In addition, as the instrumentation of G. Ph. Telemann's cantatas appears to show, the trumpeters customarily left the church before the sermon.

A dismal picture of the condition of the town piper is portrayed by Wolfgang Caspar Printz in a novel ascribed to J.S. Bach's predecessor in Leipzig, Johann Kuhnau, entitled *Musicus vexatus* (1690). Until the 19th century there existed a well developed system of exploitation of apprentices and journeymen called the *Stadtpfeife* (pipers' training system). The apprentices usually received more beatings than nourishment, and by the time a trainee was released after a total of eight years (five years as a journeyman), he had experienced much hardship. The complaints over the miserable conditions continued and as the guild system, inherited from the Middle Ages, slowly gave way to a more independent life for musicians, the economic struggle for survival became more and more intense. This was particularly true in Leipzig in the 18th

---

*The *Augsburger Konfession* (1530) was Martin Luther's summary of his basic beliefs. Articles 1-21 deal with the beliefs and teachings of the Lutheran Church, while Articles 22-28 speak of the former abuses as found in the Catholic Church. *Tr. Note.*

century. Cities had grown in population and the municipal *Stadtpfeifer* and *Kunstgeiger* often could not meet the demands for public and private performances. As a consequence, the non-organized musicians at first filled the vacuum and eventually tried to set up a guild-like structure. In Leipzig, Christoph Stephan Scheinhardt, first mentioned as a shawm player and later as a tower musician and instrument builder, organized such a group of *Bierfiedler* known as the *Scheinhardtsche Compagnie*. They were in direct competition with the municipal players (*Ratsmusikanten*), to the extent that the latter thought it prudent to come to an understanding with Scheinhardt with respect to dividing the work. Scheinhardt, for example, supported the *Neukirchenmusik*, organized by a student of G. Ph. Telemann, and received a modest compensation for it.[39] Additional competition for the town musicians came from the regimental oboists (later the military musical regiments) who, in the 19th century, were to play a significant role in providing popular musical entertainment for large segments of the population. (They were also called upon to perform more ambitious and challenging music.) It is possible that J. S. Bach already had associations with such musicians, for he became godfather no less than four times for one such regimental oboist.[40]

In the often quoted letter to his former school comrade from Ohrdruf and Lüneburg, Georg Erdmann, J. S. Bach calculates his income in Leipzig at 700 Taler. It is difficult to verify and itemize this figure, which far exceeds the base pay of 100 Taler. We know that Bach had many pupils, some of whom came to Leipzig from great distances. The records also show numerous interest payments from endowments, etc., which were, to be sure, very small. Thus one finds, for example, in the previously mentioned records of 1724/25 the entry, among others, "from Wolfgang Berger's Endowment, 1 Taler and 16 Groschen for the Cantor at St. Thomas School," and again the same sum from another endowment. The church records show also a payment of 21 Groschen. One example reads: "To the Cantor... for funeral obsequies, 3 Taler and 8 Groschen," while

---

[39] The origins of *Neukirchenmusik* and the struggle between the Town Musicians belonging to the guilds and the *Scheinhardtsche Compagnie* are clearly portrayed by A. Schering in: *Johann Sebastian Bach und das Musikleben Leipzigs im 18. Jahrhundert*, Leipzig 1941.

[40] I am indebted for this information to Prof. Werner Neumann, Director of the Bach Archives in Leipzig.

another legacy provides 10 Groschen and 6 Pfennige. The main source of income came from the singing of the St. Thomas boys' choir at memorial services, so that one can understand Bach's heartfelt sighs when he writes to Erdmann,

> ... but the air has been healthy and thus even such [*Accidentien*] as the ordinary funeral services from which there were over 100 Taler in income last year are lacking.

Even one hundred years before, the Cantor at St. Thomas, Johann Hermann Schein, who like Bach advanced from *Capellmeister* to *Cantor* (letter to G. Erdmann), had all sorts of problems with his school colleagues, related to the disbursement of monies derived from funeral services and the singing of the boys' choir. Soon after his appointment, a schoolmaster by the name of Rhenius wrote to the council in Leipzig:

> It is after all true that the Cantor (Schein) is no better than any other colleague, so that he should not receive three or four times the pay, especially because one can dispense with his services more than anyone's, as was evident this whole year and in other previous times also, in view of the fact that the teachers' aides (*Locaten*) covered his classes at school.[41]

It is enlightening to fix J. S. Bach's position in relation to salaries of his time in Leipzig, whether one bases it on his official (100 Taler) municipal salary or the 700 Taler he mentions himself. It can be assumed that municipal employees also had additional incomes, insofar as they were affiliated with church and school. The annual ledgers list, for example,

The Mayor	1570	Taler
Town Judge	650	Taler
Head Architect	570	Taler
Director of St. Nicolai	350	Taler
Pastor at St. Thomas	350	Taler
Director of St. Thomas School	175	Taler
The 3rd Teacher at St. Thom.	87	Taler and 12 gr.
The Cantor at Nicolai School	66	Taler and 21 gr.

---

[41] A. Prüfer, *Johann Hermann Schein,* Leipzig 1895.

184

If one attempts cautiously to convert these incomes according to the suggested methods of economic historians, by means of grain, flour and baked goods prices, using Bach's own estimate of an annual income of 700 Taler, one arrives at a figure which would compare to the monthly salary of 600-700 German Marks in the year 1968.[42*]

Yet such a comparison can lead to false conclusions with respect to present-day life. Lodging at the St. Thomas School was included in J. S. Bach's salary. He did not have regular expenses for transportation, and a servant was in those days easily obtained for a few Taler. In addition, the Cantor's wife probably found ways and means of obtaining butter, eggs, cheese, poultry, etc., from the surrounding countryside at more reasonable prices than we can today calculate from the prevalent prices in cities.

How did things stand with the much more business-minded G. Ph. Telemann in comparison to his friend and colleague J. S. Bach in Leipzig? In his autobiographies Telemann has written about the amounts brought in from his numerous posts. As was the case for the music director at the Thomaskirche in Leipzig, Telemann's salary from the city of Hamburg for the post as *Kantor* and church music director (*Kirchenmusikdirektor*) represented only a portion of his income; the main difference was that, thanks to Telemann's enterprise, the flourishing public musical life of Hamburg was able to offer far more lucrative sources of income than were available to Bach in Leipzig. This was probably an important reason for not trading his position in Hamburg for the post of Cantor at St. Thomas in Leipzig when it became vacant through the death of Georg Kuhnau. Telemann reports that he angered Kuhnau when, although still a student, he received a considerable sum for the cantatas he wrote for the Thomaskirche. For his admittedly short tenure as musical director of the Neukirche, the council of Leipzig only awarded him an annual 50 Taler. About his activities in Frankfurt, he proudly tells that he received 350 Gulden plus 10 *Achtel* of grain as municipal director of church music, and that he received an additional 50 Gulden salary as secretary for the *Frauenstein* Association, plus 40 more for wood, as well as free lodging. For being chairman of the *Tabakskollegium* he mentions another 100

---

[42] Compare especially the above cited study by U. Hain, *J. S. Bach als Leipziger Bürger* and also A. Otten, *Die soziale Stellung.*

*A salary in West Germany in 1968 of some DM 600-700 would have corresponded to the wages of an unskilled worker in a factory or in construction or road building. *Tr. Note.*

Gulden. How he comes to the total figure of "approximately 1600 fl.," which he mentions in connection with an appointment to the post of *Kapellmeister* in Gotha, is not clear. It is likely that even at that time he may have promoted a whole series of activities for the purpose of obtaining additional income. He speaks, for example, of wedding serenades that he composed for the wealthy citizens of Frankfurt. He judiciously dedicated a great festival cantata to the child's father on the occasion of the birth of a royal prince and had it performed "in the open air on a stage on top of the *Römerberg*." It is very likely that this *Gelegenheitsmusik* ("music for special occasions") brought him more money than J. S. Bach got from Count Keyserlingk for the *Goldberg Variations*, for which he received a golden goblet filled with 100 gold pieces.

Telemann was probably also well paid for his church composi- tions. The city of Frankfurt, for example, paid him 24 Reichstaler for his dedication of a year's church cantatas in 1714. At a later date, the composer placed a higher valuation on his compositions, for after his move to Hamburg he petitioned for the maintenance of his status as a citizen of Frankfurt, in turn for which he promised to deliver a cycle of cantatas every third year for 50 Reichstaler (= 75 Gulden). The citizens' tax was, upon his request, deducted from this sum.[43] He was not numbered, however, among the dignitaries of the city, for the letter of notification informing him of his call to Hamburg was filed in the municipal archives under the records pertaining to artisans (musicians). Nevertheless, his basic salary, not to mention the considerable additional income, would have to be thought very handsome, even exceeding by 25 Gulden the 325 Gulden per year which the Rektor of the *Gymnasium* received. In addition, Telemann was given 20 *Achtel* of grain, a certain quantity of wood, etc., further supplemented by the regular fees obtained from the singing of the choristers (for example, 15 Kreuzer per burial).[44] In comparison to Telemann's 350 Gulden, Dr. Burgk, a municipal attorney and trustee, received an annual salary of 550 Gulden in 1714, plus 20 *Achtel* of grain and wood as well as a per diem allowance, about which we unfortunately have no information. He was also exempted from

---

[43] Frankfurter Bürgermeisterbuch 1721 f. 42, Almosenkasten Ag II, 8 (Almosenkasten = municipal church administration charity funds).

[44] Stadtarchiv Frankfurt a.M. Dienstbriefe Kasten 16/15.

various tasks such as watch duty.[45] The actual total salary is always difficult to determine for it was usually drawn from a number of different sources within the municipal budget.

According to the records in Hamburg, the municipal treasury paid G. Ph. Telemann the sum of 1300 Marks per year at the start, and after 1723, when the composer was offered the Cantor post at the Thomaskirche in Leipzig, it was raised to 1600 Marks. This figure remained the same until his death. In the case of Hamburg it is instructive to examine a typical range of salaries paid to the leading citizens from municipal funds and compare these figures with what was paid Telemann. The sums listed below represent annual salaries:[46]

	1722-1755		After 1766
Mayor	approx. 4000 M.		5000 M.
Trustees	2800-3200 M.		3500-4000 M.
Senators	approx. 2000 M.		2500 M.
Kantor Telemann	1300 M.		1600 M.
Senate Secretaries		1200-1500 M.	
Senior Advisors	approx. 1000 M.		1250 M.
Commander of the Municipal Guard		1050-2200 M.	
Professors	900-1350 M.		1500 M.
Head Master at the Johanneum		600 M.	
Janitors of the Senate House		350 M.	
Streetsweepers		200-300 M.	

In contrast to J. S. Bach and many of his professional colleagues, Telemann was obviously not dependent on additional pennies of income. For example, he received a fixed sum of 350 Gulden for funeral services, and in addition, 160 Gulden from the treasuries of the five main churches in Hamburg for general supervision of their musical activities, plus an additional 18 Gulden for serving at the installation of church officials, as well as 36 Gulden for serving at Passions. Various legal actions reflect that he was able to average

---

[45] Ibid. Dienstbriefe Kasten 10/5. Information kindly supplied by the Municipal Archives of the city of Frankfurt a.M.

[46] Kindly supplied by the Staatsarchiv Hamburg.

another 90 Gulden from city printers as his share of the sales income from textbooks and Passion Music. For the direction of the opera at the *Gänsemarkt* he himself gives the figure of 300 Gulden. For a period of time he also received 100 Taler from each of the courts at Eisenach and Bayreuth for being non-resident *Kapellmeister*. If one adds up these various incomes and converts the sum to Taler, one arrives at a figure of at least 1400 Taler. This would already represent twice the income that J. S. Bach had in Leipzig, and does not even include the money (about which we have no exact information) which Telemann received for composing the *Kapitänsmusiken* for the the festivals of the Hamburg Municipal Guard. Monies were further derived from public concerts which he promoted, unlike any other German musician of his time.

Here too, one would do well to make some comparisons. During Telemann's last years, a North-German day laborer received 6 Schillings for a 12-hour day in the winter and 8 in the summer, and a man working the harvest, 16. For 16 Schillings one could buy 6 pounds of pork[47] (1 Mark = 16 Schillings). In contrast, the price of admission to Telemann's concerts in Hamburg was on the average 24 Schillings, three day's pay for a laborer. Evidently, the musical life of Hamburg was something designed for the well-to-do of the city-state.

It is obvious that the mosaic which has been presented here, gathered from separate records, cannot give a complete picture. But even if one were better informed about details, the world of difference between the *Bierfiedler*, dependent upon tips, and the internationally known castrati of the 18th century would still exist. In general, little has changed in this respect to the present day. One can still contrast the modest village organist with a star of the Metropolitan Opera. The problems involved with research in the economic area of the sociology of music have been suggested. Many detailed studies will be required before we have a more exact overall picture, one which will bring together the many isolated facts which we have at our disposal.

---

[47] Compare E. Waschinski, *Währung, Preisentwicklung.*

CHAPTER SEVEN

The Musician as Music Dealer in the Second Half of the 18th Century

.

KLAUS HORTSCHANSKY

A history of music dealing with the trade in manuscripts and printed music has yet to be written. Though there are many studies dealing with this important aspect of music history, they are limited in the main to a description of the dealer or publisher in music, and perhaps with the printing process. While these aspects were often closely related, it seems especially desirable to investigate the particular economic, personal and social characteristics of the professional dealer in music, particularly from a cultural-historical perspective.

The present study attempts to supply several views of a period in which trade in music was just coming into its own, paving the way for the large-scale operation which developed in the 19th century and became established as a separate specialty alongside the book trade. The musician will be the object of this study, and consideration will be given to his role as a part-time dealer in music as well as to his sociological position in relationship to the professional merchant in music. It is hoped that the conditions depicted here will justify this special study of a period characterized by change. The music business in England, France and Italy was, in part, determined by different circumstances, which accounts for this study being limited to Germany and the neighboring lands, Switzerland, Austria, Denmark, etc.

In discussing the music and music book trade one must distinguish between those who were active in it full-time and those who were part-time merchants. Both groups still existed in the 18th century on almost equal footing. It was not until the 19th century

191

that the part-time merchant in music was gradually displaced by the full-time dealer. Such activities as sales, distribution and lending were conducted as side-lines by the cantor, organist, or orchestral musician, whose positions already provided a fixed annual income. The full-time dealers were those who operated commercial sales firms sometimes attached to their own publishing houses. For these businessmen there were only occasional digressions into related fields, such as managing concert series, or even dabbling in composition.

I • PART-TIME MERCHANTS

Up to the end of the 18th century, a considerable part of the music business was in the hands of the musicians themselves. For a long time musicians had sold music manuscripts for profit. They had copies made of music they owned, rented their manuscripts so that they might be copied, or they offered for sale copies they had produced themselves of both their own compositions and those of others.[1] It has been verified that even Johann Sebastian Bach sold music manuscripts.[2] These practices were in part still current as late as the first decade of the 19th century, when the emphasis switched from cantatas and music for keyboard instruments to "music for singing," for opera. In the News Letter No. 5 of the *Allgemeine Musikalische Zeitung,* 7 (1804/05), col. 18, a musician by the name of Ludwig, employed "at the National Theater in Frankfurt a.M.," gave "public notice" that it had been "his primary occupation for many years to collect the music of the latest and best arias, duets, trios, etc.," and that he was now "able to serve all music lovers who might honor him with a request, to their complete satisfaction."[3] On January 4, 1800, *Musikdirektor* Karl Cannabich of Frankfurt a.M.

---

[1] Detailed vouchers relating to lending and copying practices are supplied by W. Braun, "Die alten Musikbibliotheken der Stadt Freyburg (Unstrut)," in: *Die Musikforschung,* 15 (1962), pp. 142-144.

[2] G. Kinsky, *Die Originalausgaben der Werke Johann Sebastian Bachs,* Wien etc. 1937, p. 27; W. Neumann, "Einige neue Quellen zu Bachs Herausgabe eigener und zum Mitvertrieb fremder Werke," in: *Musa-Mens-Musici.* In Memory of Walther Vetter, Leipzig (1969), pp. 165-168.

[3] In the Central Library in Zürich there is a manuscript for the score of a quartet from V. Righini's opera, *La Presa di Gerusalemme* which bears the comment: "to be

192

published an "index of operas" in the supplement of the *Staats-und Gelehrten Zeitung des Hamburgischen unpartheyischen Correspondenten*. The music could be bought from him, for the most part, as copies. In addition, composers were continuously offering for sale their own works in manuscript form. The development of the system for the lending of music paralleled the development of lending libraries for the public.* The latter were established not only by dealers in books and music, but also by individual musicians. For example, a catalog issued around 1815 by the Director of Music at the University in Kiel, Germany, Georg Christian Apel, who also served as *Stadtkantor* and organist, bears the title: *Musikalische Leihbibliothek oder Verzeichniss der Musikalien und musikalischen Schriften, die für den einer jeden Nummer beygefügten Communicationspreis zu haben sind bey...*, 4 Abteilungen, Kiel (ca. 1815) [Lending Library of Music or Catalogue of Music and Music Supplies, available at the indicated price].[4]

In the daily newspapers of the 18th century there were repeated advertisements in which newly printed editions were offered for sale by organists, cantors and conductors. This kind of operation, however, had two disadvantages. In the first place, there were too few musicians with sufficient capital to collect an inventory with enough variety to make such an undertaking lucrative. Secondly, problems with the law could arise whenever the book and music sellers who had received a privilege from the ruling powers took action against such unwanted competition. A similar situation existed in the altercations between book dealers and bookbinders

---

obtained in Frankfurt from the musician Ludwig," cf. G. Walter, *Katalog der gedruckten und handschriftlichen Musikalien des 17. bis 19. Jahrhunderts im Besitze der Allegemeinen Musikgesellschaft Zürich*, Zürich 1960, p. 108.

[4] Staatsbibliothek Berlin, Sign. Ab 1101. Attached: *Index of Music Supplies sold by G. Chr. Apel in Kiel... For the use of Owners of the Catalogue of the Music Lending Library*, 4th Section, Kiel (ca 1815). In the Preface to this Index it is stated on page 2 that: "In addition to the items listed here, the latest works of quality publishers in Germany, as well as those of the finest firms abroad can be had through me as soon as they appear... Also available are good pianos, guitars, genuine Italian strings, lined manuscript paper, portraits of famous composers, etc." I am indebted for the above reference to a doctoral candidate in Kiel, Mr. Uwe Haensel. Also see O. Jahn, *Gesammelte Aufsätze über Musik*, Leipzig 2/1867, pp. 6 f. On the topic of Music Libraries also compare E. Preussner, *Die bürgerliche Musikkultur*, Kassel 2/1950, pp. 195 f.

*What is meant here is a commercial library serving the public, as opposed to what is today called a public library, meaning a non-profit institution supported through taxation or philanthropic donations. *Tr. Note.*

who repeatedly attempted to enter the field of sales. In this case it was not merely a matter of competition, but a matter of prestige and honor for a free and independent businessman (the dealer) who considered himself a member of the middle class, as opposed to a craftsman (the bookbinder) who occupied a lower rank as a member of a guild.[5]

With the advent of subscriptions to music parts and scores in the 18th century, musicians were able to expand their commercial ambitions. In addition to offering the subscribers a special price, the sellers of subscriptions (middlemen) received a small commission in the form of free copies or even cash. There was no financial risk involved and the musician thus assumed the function of a middleman, whether it was between the publisher and the customer, or between the composer himself and the public. Like any good middleman, he praised the merchandise and invested money in advertising. So, for example, the *Hofmusikus* in Mecklenburg-Schwerin, a man by the name of Hardenack Otto Conrad (or possibly Benedikt Friedrich?) Zinck, had advertisements placed in the newspapers in which he offered to accept subscriptions for Carl Philipp Emanuel Bach's *Herrn Doctor Cramers übersetzte Psalmen mit Melodien zum Singen bey dem Claviere*, Leipzig 1774, as well as for the first collection of *Claviersonaten mit einer Violine und einem Violoncell zur Begleitung*, Leipzig 1776.[6] Similar offers were made by a cantor, Johann Samuel Petri, active in Bautzen, and the organist of Bautzen, Johann Ludwig Stallmann. Stallmann was soliciting subscriptions for a sonata collection of Johann Wilhelm Hässler, while Petri was advertising for Carl Friedrich Cramer's *Magazin der Musik*.[7]

One can partially assess the scope of the activity of musicians as middlemen by consulting the lists of subscribers' names printed in many editions. In the lists reproduced below, only orders of five or more copies of a given edition have been included. This sampling

---

[5] Compare also A. Kirchhoff, *Kleinbuchhandel und Colportage in Leipzig an der Wende des 17. Jahrhunderts*, in: *Archiv für Geschichte des Deutschen Buchhandels*, 8 (1883), pp. 91 ff.; F. H. Meyer, *Buchbinder und Buchhandel*, ibid. 10 (1886), pp. 159-173, and 15 (1892), pp. 63-72; J. Goldfriedrich, *Geschichte des Deutschen Buchhandels*, Vol. 2, Leipzig 1908, pp. 96-119.

[6] O. Kade, *Die Musikalien-Sammlung des Grossherzoglich Mecklenburg-Schweriner Fürstenhauses*, Vol. 1, Schwerin 1893, pp. 121, 125.

[7] H. Biehle, *Musikgeschichte von Bautzen bis zum Anfang des 19. Jahrhunderts*, Leipzig 1924, pp. 51, 49.

reflects the fact that there are musicians here from various areas of central Europe and from different professional backgrounds:

Bissmann, Johann Andreas, cantor in Frankfurt/M.
> 6 copies of J. Brandl, *6 Lieder von Schubart und andern Dichtern*, op. 6, Heilbronn [1793].[8]
> 12 copies of J. W. Hässler *6 leichte Sonaten fürs Clavier*, Tl. 2, Erfurt 1787. (D-Lr)[9]
> 6 copies of F. L. Ae. Kunzen, *Compositionen der . . . Oden und Lieder*, Leipzig 1784. (D-KIl)
> 6 copies of J. L. Willing, *3 Sonaten fürs Clavier. . . mit Begleitung einer Violine*, Tl. 2, Leipzig 1788. (D-Dl)

Dussek, Franz Xaver, piano teacher in Prague
> 9 copies of C. P. E. Bach, *Clavier-Sonaten. . . für Kenner und Liebhaber*, Slg. 2, Leipzig 1780 (D-KIl)
> 9 copies of the same, Slg. 3, Leipzig 1781. (D-KIl)
> 11 copies of the same, Slg. 4, Leipzig 1783. (D-KIl)
> 7 copies of the same, Slg. 5, Leipzig 1785. (D-KIl)
> 9 copies of the same, Slg. 6, Leipzig 1787. (D-KIl)
> 6 copies of J. W. Hassler, *6 leichte Sonaten fürs Clavier*, Tl. 3, Erfurt 1788. (B-Bc)
> 4 copies of J. F. Reichardt, *Musikalisches Kunstmagazin*, 2. Bd., Berlin 1791. (D-SW)

Hässler, Johann Wilhelm, organist and for a time manufacturer of plush hats in Erfurt; he founded a music lending library in 1784.[10]
> 7 copies of C. P. E. Bach, *Sturms geistliche Gesänge*, Slg. 1, Hamburg 1780. (D-KIl)
> 6 copies of J. F. Hobein, *Lieder*, Wolfenbüttel 1778. (D-KIl)
> 6 copies of the same., *Lieder*, Slg. 2, Wolfenbüttel 1779. (B-Bc)

---

[8] The Subscription-Index is reproduced by H. W. Schwab, *Sangbarkeit, Popularität und Kunstlied*, Regensburg 1965, p. 121.

[9] Since subscription lists are not found in all copies of a given printing because they were either lost or only bound in with a given number of copies, the sources for the editions listed here have been indicated in parentheses, using the symbol of the Répertoire Internationale des Sources Musicales (RISM). In order to avoid using the bold type employed in this index for the symbol of the country, a hyphen has been used to separate it from that of the city symbol.

[10] *MGG* V (1956), Sp. 1300.

12 copies of K. R. H. Ritter, *Versuch einer Sammlung vermischter kleiner Stücke fürs Clavier*, Bremen 1786. (B-Bc)

5 copies of J. H. Rolle, *Mehala*, Kl. A., Leipzig 1784. (D-Mbs)

12 copies of J. H. Rolle, *Melida*, Kl. A., Leipzig 1785. (D-LÜh)

6 copies of J. D. Scheidler, *Sammlung kleiner Klavierstücke*, Gotha 1779. (D-GOl)

6 copies of J. G. Schicht, *Die Feyer der Christen auf Golgatha*, Kl. A., Leipzig 1785. (D-Dl)

6 copies of Corona Schröter, *25 Lieder*, Weimar 1786. (D-LEu)

6 copies of D. G. Türk, *6 leichte Klaviersonaten*, Tl. 2, Leipzig 1783. (B-Bc)

12 copies of E. W. Wolf, *6 leichte Clavier-Sonaten*, Weimar 1786. (D-LÜh)

Kellner, Johann Christoph, cantor and court organist in Kassel

5 copies of F. B. Beneken, *Lieder und Gesänge für fühlende Seelen*, Hannover 1787. (D-G)

6 copies of J. W. Hässler, *6 leichte Sonaten für Clavier*, Tl. 3, Erfurt 1788. (B-Bc)

6 copies of J. D. Scheidler, *Sammlung kleiner Klavierstücke*, Gotha 1779. (D.GOl)

6 copies of J. A. P. Schulz, *Uzens lyrische Gedichte*, Hamburg 1784. (D-KIl)

6 copies of D. G. Türk, *6 leichte Klaviersonaten*, Tl. 1, Leipzig 1783. (D-LÜh)

6 copies of D. G. Türk, *6 leichte Klaviersonaten*, Tl. 2, Leipzig 1783. (D-Bc)

12 copies of D. G. Türk, *6 kleine Klaviersonaten*, Tl. 1, Leipzig 1785. (B-Bc)

6 copies of J. L. Willing, *3 Sonaten fürs Clavier... mit Begleitung einer Violine*, Tl. 1, Leipzig 1787. (D-Dl)

Kreusser, George Anton, concertmaster in Mainz

6 copies of F. H. Graf, *Deux Quatuor a Flute traversiere, Violon, Viola et Violoncell...*, (Augsburg before 1782). (CH-Zz)

34 copies of W. A. Mozart, *Il Dissoluto Punito*, Kl. A., Mainz [1791]. (D-Mbs)

Lang, Johann Georg, concertmaster in Koblenz
  10 copies of J. André, *Gesang zur Elmine,* Berlin 1782. (B-Bc)
  11 copies of G. Benda, *Sammlung Vermischter Clavierstücke,*
    Tl. 1, Gotha 1780. (D-Mbs)
  10 copies of J. N. Forkel, *Clavier-Sonate und eine Ariette mit*
    18 Veraenderungen, Göttingen 1782. (B-Bc)
  6 copies of F. H. Graf, *Deux Quatuor a Flute traversiere,*
    Violon, Viola, et Violoncell..., (Augsburg before 1782).
    (CH-Zz)
  10 copies of J. W. Hässler, *Clavier- und Singstücke,* Slg. 1,
    Erfurt 1782. (B-Bc)
  10 copies of J. W. Hässler, *Clavier- und Singstücke,* Slg. 2,
    Leipzig [1785/86]. (D-Mbs)
SchiØrring, Niels, Royal Chamber Musician in Copenhagen
  30 copies of C. P. E. Bach, *Sturms geistliche Gesänge,* Slg. 1,
    Hamburg 1780. (D-KIl)
  30 copies of C. P. E. Bach, *Sturms geistliche Gesänge,* Slg. 2,
    Hamburg 1781. (D-KIl)
  40 copies of C. P. E. Bach, *Clavier-Sonaten... für Kenner und*
    Liebhaber, Slg. 5, Leipzig 1785. (D-KIl)
  8 copies of J. N. Forkel, *24 Veränderungen fürs Clavichord,*
    Göttingen 1791. (B-Bc)
  15 copies of J. A. P. Schulz, *Uzens lyrische Gedichte,* Ham-
    burg 1784. (D-KIl)
  6 copies of J. A. P. Schulz, *Religiöse Oden und Lieder,*
    Hamburg 1786. (D-KIl)
  10 copies of J. A. P. Schulz, *Chöre und Gesänge zur Athalia,*
    Kiel/Hamburg 1786. (D-KIi)
Türk, Daniel Gottlob, University Music Director, cantor and
  organist in Halle
  8 copies of G. Benda, *Sammlung Vermischter Clavierstücke,*
    Tl. 1, Gotha 1780. (D-Mbs)
  10 copies of J. G. Gebhard, *Sammlung vermischter kleiner und*
    leichter Klavierstücke, Tl. 1, Barby 1786. (D-LEm)
  8 copies of N. G. Gruner, *6 Sonaten für das Klavier,* Tl. 2,
    Leipzig 1783. (B-Bc)
  8 copies of J. W. Hässler, *6 neue Sonaten fürs Clavier,*
    Leipzig 1779. (D-Dl)
  6 copies of J. W. Hässler, *6 leichte Sonaten fürs Clavier,* Tl. 2,
    Erfurt 1787. (D-Lr)

12 copies of K. R. H. Ritter, *Versuch einer Sammlung vermischter kleiner Stücke fürs Clavier,* Bremen 1786. (B-Bc)

6 copies of A. Salieri, *Armida,* Kl. A., Leipzig 1783 (D-KIl)

10 copies of J. K. G. Spazier, *Lieder und Gesänge,* Halle 1781. (D-Bhm)

11 copies of J. G. Vierling, *6 Sonaten für das Klavier,* Leipzig 1781. (B-Bc)

8 copies of H. O. K. Zinck, *6 Clavier-Sonaten,* Hamburg 1783. (D-KIl)

The number of copies ordered by these musicians might well have been higher. One should keep in mind that the people listed in printed subscription lists most often dealt with middlemen and only infrequently went directly to the publishers themselves. In the above list, the following musical professions are represented: cantor, organist, director of music, orchestral musician, concertmaster and piano teacher. Noticeably absent is the *Stadtmusikus* [municipal musician]. Feeling his career to be secure because of the closely defined regulations of his guild, he rarely participated in the free enterprise activity of middleman. There are only a few exceptions, such as the town musician Matthes in Berlin, who ordered 30 copies of Christian Heinrich Müller's *Drey Sonaten, fürs Clavier, als Doppelstücke für zwo Personen mit vier Händen,* Berlin 1782.[11] He expressly had the words: *"in Commission"* added.

A small incident, a dispute printed in the *Berlinischen Nachrichten Von Staats- und Gelehrten Sachen,* reflects the degree of interest musicians showed in acquiring a subscription business and the efforts they undertook to safeguard themselves against undesired competition. On December 17, 1774 (Nr. 151, p. 754), C. P. E. Bach published the following notice:

> Since Cantor Pochhammer of Berlin is not accepting a subscription to my oratorio, music lovers may address their inquiries to the *Musicus* Mr. Hering . . .

Pochhammer, provoked, replied on the 29th of December 1774 (Nr. 156, p. 782):

> Notice is hereby given to the honored public that the

---

11 Copy in Stiftung Preussischer Kulturbesitz, Deutsche Staatsbibliothek, Berlin.

report that I had refused to subscribe to Kapellmeister Bach's oratorio is groundless and false, because I had not been given the proper notice and instructions. I should like to take this opportunity to announce that I am accepting orders for an edition of fifty sacred songs with Klavier accompaniment by Director of Music Rolle.

These two public notices are, at first glance, confusing. An examination of the subscription market in Berlin, with respect to the compositions of Carl Philipp Emanuel Bach and the Magdeburg oratorio composer Johann Heinrich Rolle, reveals, however,[12] that there existed two competing groups, each trying through its liaison men to solicit subscribers. The works of Bach's son, who was at one time active in the orchestra of the prince in Rheinsberg and Berlin and who later also played in the royal orchestra, were repeatedly sought by the chamber music composer Johann Philipp Kirnberger, as well as by musicians Friedrich Wilhelm Riedt and Johann Friedrich Hering.[13] Through their official and private obligations, these musicians were associated with the very circle in which the songs, orchestral works, piano and chamber music of Bach could find acceptance. The oratorios of Rolle, on the other hand, were generally ordered by organists and the directors of the *Konzert der Musikliebhaber*, Karl Ludwig Bachmann and Ernst Benda.[14] Within this *Liebhabervereinigung* [amateur association] the compositions of

---

[12] Comparisons were made for the period 1773-1780 on the basis of the above cited newspaper.

[13] Compare the following advertisements appearing in the *Berlinischen Nachrichten* on January 19, 1773 (page 40): "An edition of *Sei Concerti per il Cembalo concertato*, Hamburg 1772, available through Riedt and Hering" — On November 11, 1773 (page 676): "Subscription available from, among others, Riedt and Hering of *Herrn Doctor Cramers übersetzte Psalmen*, Leipzig 1774" — On November 21, 1775 (page 687): "Subscription available through Riedt and Hering of *Claviersonaten mit einer Violine und einem Violoncell zur Begleitung*, 1 Slg., Leipzig 1776" — On October 6, 1778 (page 578): "Subscription through Kirnberger, Riedt and Hering for *6 Clavier-Sonaten für Kenner und Liebhaber*, 1 Slg., Leipzig 1779" — On December 22, 1778 (page 736): "Subscription through Kirnberger, Riedt and Hering of *Heilig*, Hamburg 1779" — On February 8, 1780 (page 96): "Subscription through Kirnberger, Riedt and Hering of *Clavier-Sonaten . . . für Kenner und Liebhaber*, 2. Slg., Leipzig 1780."

[14] Invitations for subscribers by Bachmann and E. Benda for the works of Rolle are to be found in the *Berlinischen Nachrichten* on May 8, 1777, page 294 (*Abraham auf Moria*) and October 27, 1778, page 621 (*Lazarus*). Evidence for Bachmann's activity as a middleman is found in the printing of F. W. Benda's, *Die Grazien, eine Cantate im*

Rolle were cultivated, and here one could count on the sale of excerpts arranged for piano. Obviously, the public buying the works of Bach or Rolle could not be quite so rigidly split into two separate groups. A man like Pochhammer must necessarily have been an obstacle and was consequently circumvented quite unceremoniously. Although the events cannot be corroborated in detail at this time, Bach's public letter would seem to offer evidence of this.

Numerous notices and commentaries also provide evidence that musicians solicited subscriptions not only to receive the promised discounts, but moreover, to sell additional music. The above mentioned Hering published notices in Berlin such as the following (*Berliner Nachrichten*, Sept. 23, 1777, Beil. p. 596), when the ordered subscriptions had arrived and were ready to be picked up:

> Capellmeister C. P. E. Bach's second collection of his Clavier-Sonaten with Violin and Cello has arrived and can now be collected at *Musico* Hering's. . . upon presentation of a subscription receipt. There are also a number of additional copies available for those who might desire them.

The intent to sell is also clear in such entries as the following, from a list of subscribers:

> (Mr.) Caspar Daniel Krohn, organist at St. Peter's and St. John's churches: 55 copies, 26 for himself and 29 for previously named subscribers solicited by him.

This entry was taken from the first collection of Carl Philipp Emanuel Bach's *Sturms geistlichen Gesängen*, Hamburg 1780, listed under the city heading of Hamburg. The organist of the Hanseatic city was so encouraged by the success of his subscription solicitations that he wished to stock up for the future. Many other musicians emulated Hering in Berlin, and the organist Krohn in Hamburg. All of them carried on trade in music on a small scale, which characterized this kind of business.

Composers who published their own works were dependent upon such commission agents, since there was no structured organization for selling music on a large scale. In this manner the

---

Clavierauszuge, Leipzig 1789, where it is stated: "printed by Iohann Gottlob Immanuel Breitkopf, on Commission from *Cammermusikus* Bachmann and *Commercienrath*

public could be reached more quickly and effectively, and with a greater chance for profit than through traditional professional methods such as music dealers, post offices, or newspapers and address lists, where selective interests were not taken into account. In this way each musician sought to build up his own mailing list. An excellent example of this approach was the roster of C. P. E. Bach, reflected in a subscription advertisement in the *Berlinischen Nachrichten* of November 2, 1773 (p. 676) for *Herrn Doctor Cramers übersetzte Psalmen*, Leipzig 1774.

> ...upon advance payment of 1 Thlr. the following gentlemen, in addition to myself, will accept subscription orders from this date until Easter:
>
> In Berlin, Royal Cammermusicus [chamber musician] Riedt and musician Hering;
> In Braunschweig, Professor Eschenburg;
> In Bresslau, Senior Organist Hofmann;
> In Bückeburg, Concertmaster Bach;
> In Celle, Organist J. F. G. Beckmann;
> In Copenhagen, Royal Cammermusicus Schiørring;
> In Dresden, Cammermusicus Horn;
> In Eisennach, Kapellmeister Bach;
> In Göttingen, senior-year student and musician Forkel;
> In Gotha, Cammermusicus Cramer;
> In Hamburg, Mr. Bode, Mr. Westphal and bookseller Herold;
> In Hannover, Municipal Secretary Schilling;
> In Leipzig, Mr. Breitkopf;
> In Ludwigslust, Cammermusicus Zinck;
> In Parchim, Associate Rector Monich;
> In Petersburg, senior-year student and musician Kramer, by permission of his excellency, Chief State Attorney von Soimonoff;
> In Riga, Mr. Hartknoch;
> In Schleswig, Organist Zinck;

Hummel, in Berlin." This simply means that he felt himself to be in the position to be able to sell a large number of copies in Berlin and its environs.

In Stettin, Director of Music Wolf;
In Weimar, Kapelmeister Wolf.

Among the 23 "collectors" listed above, from twenty cities of central and northeastern Europe, one finds, in addition to professional musicians, two music dealers (Breitkopf and Westphal), two book dealers (Herold and Hartknoch), and four non-musicians (Eschenburg, Bode, Schilling and Monich). In other subscription notices there are even larger lists, always including a number of non-musicians.[15]

The participation of non-musicians in the subscription operations points beyond the economic aspect to a social consciousness which was conspicuous among citizens everywhere in the second half of the 18th century. Not only were musicians prepared to help each other with the sale of compositions which they themselves published, but even non-musicians stepped in with the same good will to lend a hand. A quotation from a letter by Georg Benda to the publishing firm of Breitkopf, dated January 5, 1780, serves as a good example:[16]

> In view of the fact that artists and scholars have tacitly agreed to aid and support each other in the publication of their works, may I be so bold as to request your support in publicizing the enclosed notice among music lovers in your area and to accept subscriptions from them . . .

This "tacit" agreement, aimed at achieving very concrete results, could also generate public recognition. Heinrich Wilhelm Freytag, cantor in Zeulenroda, itemized the names of those to whom he was indebted for the success of his *Schubartschen*(n) *Lieder mit Melodien zum Singen beym Clavier*, 1. Slg., Leipzig 1790. A total of 268 subscriptions had been sold, and he expressed his gratitude as follows:[17]

> While the inner knowledge of having done good is for every Christian a sweeter reward for his earnest strivings

---

[15] Comparisons made by the author in "Pränumerations- und Subskriptions listen in Notendrucken deutscher Musiker des 18. Jahrhunderts," in: *Acta musicologica*, 40 (1968), p. 165.

[16] Published in: *Der Bär*, 1924, p. 50.

[17] Copy in Bayerischen Staatsbibliothek in Munich.

than the most public expression of gratitude, it is nevertheless a most pleasant duty for me to list the following names with the greatest respect and to hereby acknowledge my gratitude for their efforts, rewarded by happy success, in the collecting of subscriptions. They are: . . .

Carl Philipp Emanuel Bach was indifferent as to who sold his music or who collected subscriptions for him, whether it was musician, a music dealer, or a non-musician. In a letter to Johann Joachim Eschenburg in Braunschweig, dated December 1, 1784, he wrote bluntly:[18]

Enclosed you will find 7 *Morgengesänge*—six are to be sold, and with the seventh, I have the honor of making you a poor gift. Whichever songs cannot be sold can stay with you until a friend will bring them back to me after the fair.

A compilation like the one on pages 195-198, listing the names of musicians, could easily be matched by similar lists which would illustrate subscription collecting by non-musicians.

Up to this point, one could classify as amateurs the avocational music and music book dealers. Yet they filled a need which existed at a time when commerce in music was still in its infancy. Although there was only a modest profit, they could build up their own music collections with the free samples which were given out. The music business,[19] which did not become well organized until the first half of the 19th century, could not and had no desire to oppose such voluntary activity. The book trade, already organized in the 18th century in the form of book dealer representatives, had, however, initiated numerous complaints against the *"Pfuscher und Stöhrer"* [bunglers and troublemakers], who were accused of accepting and collecting subscriptions. However, it is to be noted from the proceedings of regulatory commissions that these very book dealers did not wish to become involved with subscriptions and orders for

---

18. L. Nohl, *Musiker-Briefe*, Leipzig 2/1873, p. XLVI; also see pp. XLV, XLVIII.

19 *MGG* IX (1961) Sp. 1181; F. H. Meyer, "Mittheilungen zur inneren Geschichte des Deutschen Buchhandels von 1811-1848. I. Vereinsbildung und Vereinsthätigkeit," in: *Archiv für Geschichte des Deutschen Buchhandels* 8 (1883), pp. 234-238.

books published by authors themselves.[20] The life-long, almost hobby-like activity which musicians carried on without giving up their posts as professional musicians stood in contrast to the professional activity which would have been associated with the organization of a shop. Johann Ludwig Willing in Nordhausen,[21] Melchior Bernhard Veltmann in Osnabrück,[22] or Karl Anton Reichel in Danzig,[23] for example, carried on their profession as organists and also maintained a music business, in connection with which they each wanted to be known as *Organist und Musikhändler* [organist and music dealer]. M. B. Veltmann also had himself listed in the "index for subscribers" for Friedrich Burchard Beneken's *Lieder und kleine Klavierstücke für gute Menschen*, Hannover 1794.[24] In this manner, the organist, music publisher and technician Wilhelm Nikolaus Haueisen in Frankfurt/M. used the title *Organiste & Editeur de Musique* on music published by his company.[25] In Frankfurt, the organist Johann David Otto regularly placed advertisements in the *Kayserl. Reichs-Ober-Post-Amts-Zeitung*, indicating he would accept orders for printed music from the firm of Johann Julius Hummel in Amsterdam.[26] In 1766 the Kapellmeister for the elector of Trier, Cron, made it known that he had available in Pfaffendorf "all kinds of beautiful music."[27] Additional examples could easily be given.

---

20 F. H. Meyer, "Reformsbestrebungen im 18. Jahrhundert II. Die Thätigkeit der Buchhandlungs-Deputirten," in: *Archiv für Geschichte des Deutschen Buchhandels,* 13 (1890), pp. 227 f.

21 *MGG* XIII (1968), Sp. 689.

22 F. Bösken, *Musikgeschichte der Stadt Osnabrück*, Regensburg 1937, p. 157; W. Salmen, *Geschichte der Musik in Westfalen bis 1800*, Kassel, etc. 1963, p. 75.

23 G. Döring, "Carl Anton Reichel. Ein Lebensbild aus dem Künstlerkreise Danzigs," in: *Neue Preussische Provinzialblätter*, 3. Folge, Jg. 3, 1859, p. 89; H. Rausching, *Geschichte der Musik und Musikpflege in Danzig*, Danzig 1931, p. 399.

24 Copy in Staatlichen Institut für Musikforschung Preussischer Kulturbesitz in Berlin.

25 W. Matthäus, "Der Musikverlag von Wolfgang Nicolaus Haueisen zu Frankfurt am Main 1771 bis 1789. Geschichte und Bibliographie," in: *Die Musikforschung*, 22 (1969), p. 421. On the question of the music dealer's self-appreciation see also the author's "Selbstverständnis und Verantwortung des Musikverlegers," in: *Neue Zeitschrift für Musik*, 131 (1970), pp. 295-300.

26 For example, on April 28, 1759 (Bl. 2v), and January 24, 1764 (Bl. 2v). The relationship between Johann Julius Hummel in Amsterdam, Burchard Hummel in The Hague and J. D. Otto in Frankfurt is the subject of an essay by the author in: *Festschrift für Wolfgang Schmieder* (1971).

27 A. Standt, "Oeffentliches Musikwesen in Coblenz," in: *Zeitschrift für Heimatkunde von Coblenz und Umgebung*, 1 (1920), p. 77. Contains additional examples.

One could deduce that the establishment of a business not only produced additional income, but was designed to provide some support for an insecure existence. The fate of Georg Christoph Grossheim in Kassel lends support to such a deduction.

Grossheim, who was an instrumentalist in the court orchestra of Kassel from 1782-1785, describes his move into the music business in his autobiography of 1819:[28]

> And when Friedrich II died [1785], the orchestra was dissolved, my father reduced from an annual 500 Rthl. to 60, and my salary completely gone. I was forced to stay and support my family...by giving music lessons. My lot was cast, once and for all.... I had to devise new means for our support and founded a music trade. Up to then I had only known the Italian and French composers; Gluck and Grétry had been my models. Now I became familiar with Händel, Mozart and Haydn; in short, the music trade supplied me with a library...

According to this report, it would appear that Grossheim started his music business in the mid-eighties. Yet the official founding followed much later, for a new blow was to come first which deprived him of his livelihood once again. In the year 1800, Count Wilhelm IX had built a theater and hired Gossheim as his director of music. At the beginning of 1802 there were disagreements and Grossheim resigned his post. With this, as he emphasizes in the autobiography, he gave up "an annual income of 300 Rthr." (loc. cit., p. 17). It was around this time that he sought refuge in the music business which he ran jointly with Wilhelm Wöhler[29] (traceable until ca. 1827). In subsequent years, Grossheim was never again able to hold a post as a practicing musician. The post of teacher of music at a teachers' college, which he filled from 1784 until 1835, was not a regular appointment but considered merely a non-tenured, part-

---

[28] G. Heinrichs, "Georg Christoph Grosheims Selbstbiographie, mit Erläuterungen und Ergänzungen hrsg.," Homberg (distr. of Kassel) 1925, pp. 11-13 (*Beiträge zur Geschichte der Musik in Kurhessen...*, H. 4).

[29] Compare also G. Heinrichs, "G. Chr. Grosheim," p. 13; *MGG* V (1956), Sp. 946; *MGG* VII (1958), Sp. 727.

time position.[30] While the regular teachers at the seminary were accepted into the electoral ranks,[31] Grossheim was denied this honor and remained a mere adjunct teacher for more than fifty years.

In a few cases, even non-musicians devoted part-time efforts to the operation of a music business. One could point to Heinrich Philipp Bossler, the *Hochfürstlich Brandenburgisch-Onolzbachischen Expeditions-Rath* [royal commercial advisor] who operated a music business in Speyer which he called *Musik-Institut*,[32] at first with Hofrat Caspar Beecke and then later by himself. This firm is quite well known through the publication of Beethoven's early works. In Biberach a treasurer by the name of Johann Maximilian Kick, an ardent music lover since childhood, founded a music and instrument business in 1783.[32a]

The various forms of the music business mentioned to this point fall within the range of two extreme possibilities. At one end, musicians conducted an amateur music trade or operated agencies without deriving their main source of income from this activity. Either they did not need to rely on such income, or their conscientiousness as professional musicians kept them from actually changing professions, or a separation between the professions of musician and that of music dealer had not yet become a reality for them. A respected man like the university music director in Halle, Daniel Gottlob Türk, famous in his time, could hardly imagine himself professionally as primarily a dealer in music. Yet there were others who, at the other end of the spectrum, founded a music business and held on to their music posts as an avocation because they did not possess the drive and organizational initiative to conduct large-scale trade, though growth in the printing of music towards the end of the 18th century would have provided ideal conditions for doing so. This subject will be dealt with in the second part of this study.

---

[30] Salary: 1784 — 40 Taler; from 1785 — 50 Taler (in other words, less than the father's pension); after 1805 — 150 Taler; after 1822 — 200 Taler; after 1831 — 300 Taler, and with that sum, still less than his father once received as a violist in the orchestra of Friedrich II. Compare also loc. cit., G. Heinrichs, pp. 13 f.

[31] In the ranking of 1834 they were placed at the same level as pastors and necondary school teachers, the seventh rank, cf. G. Heinrichs, among other places, on p. 19.

[32] C. F. Cramer, *Magazin der Musik*, 1 (Hamburg 1783), pp. 135-137.

[32a] A. Bopp, *Das Musikleben in der freien Reichsstadt Biberach*, Kassel 1930, pp. 29, 35, 41.

II • BACKGROUNDS OF PROFESSIONAL MUSIC DEALERS

Towards the end of the 18th century in Germany and in Europe in general, there was an increase in the number of new music publishing firms. After a few innovators such as Bernhard Schott in Mainz, Johann André in Offenbach, Johann Michael Götz in Mannheim, the Dutchman Johann Julius Hummel in Berlin, and others who sought to establish themselves in this field around 1770, smaller and larger music publishers and dealers sprang up everywhere. Because the quantity of printed music available increased by leaps and bounds from 1790 to 1800, there was now clearly a need for large-scale businesses in music which could, on a wide geographic basis, replace the previous agent-type amateur activities of musicians, scholars and others. Everywhere music firms were established, providing a secure income on the basis of great demand from a music loving public (with the exception of some temporary periods of economic depressions). In 1843 the *Allgemeines Adressbuch für den Deutschen Buchhandel* ["General Directory of the German Book Trade"] contained a listing by Otto August Schulz[33] of 333 music dealers or book sellers who carried a selection of music in the area of central Europe. Most likely this represented scarcely half of the actual music dealers.

From a sociological point of view, it is interesting to discover what kinds of people were involved in the music trade, which factors led to their involvement, and what their attitude was towards their profession. The seven categories which follow are illustrated by specific examples.

1. *The route from book-seller to music dealer.* The firm of Breitkopf (later Breitkopf and Härtel) in Leipzig[34] provides the best example of an organization which was founded as a publisher and distributor of books and then turned to the printing of music and books on music. It is useful to outline the history of the firm. Bernhard Christoph Breitkopf, who founded the company in 1719, quickly established its reputation as a respected book publisher. In the middle of the 18th century a

---

[33] 5. Jahrgang, Leipzig (1843), 3. Abt., pp. 25-27. R. Schaal in *MGG* IX (1961), Sp. 1180 f., claims 30 music dealers for the 18th century in Germany.
[34] O. von Hase, *Breitkopf & Härtel*, 2 Bde., Leipzig 4/1917-1919; *MGG* II (1952), Sp. 256-265.

music copying department was added and a stock of domestic and foreign music maintained in manuscript and later in printed form. The scope of this aspect of the business can be ascertained from the Breitkopf thematic catalogue, published in six parts and sixteen supplements between 1762 and 1787.[35] With the invention by his son Johann Gottlob Immanuel of movable type for setting and printing notes, a new and lucrative field was opened. In addition to printing music for their own editions, Breitkopf became the music printer for numerous independent dealers in north and central Germany. At this time, though, the non-music publications were still an important part of the business. It became clear, around 1800 at the latest, that the music business had become the dominant concern of Breitkopf and Härtel, and other publications assumed a decided second place.

2. *The route from engraver and art dealer to dealer and publisher in music.* This development is rather similar to the one just outlined. That is, a later profession developed from a closely related activity and subsequently became the sole or dominant one. It would seem significant that the business of Breitkopf, a printer, dealer and publisher who dealt with type-set materials, became a music concern using the process of type-set notes, regardless of the fact that in the first half of the 19th century, new developments (lithography) completely altered typesetting procedures in the Breitkopf firm. The average print dealer dealt primarily with engravings, and probably only to a small extent with paintings and drawings. Therefore his move into the field of music is just as understandable as that of the engraver. In the second half of the 18th century, south of the Main river, music was generally printed by means of engraved plates and Breitkopf's procedure was almost unknown there. Some specific examples for this group are given below:

(a) Balthasar Schmid, the descendant of a Nürnberger family of craftsmen, was described at the time of his marriage in 1732 as an "experienced . . . copper engraver" and in 1734, in connection with the baptism of one of his children, as a

---

[35] *The Breitkopf Thematic Catalogue,* facs., ed. by B. S. Brook, New York 1966. It contained the opening themes of over 1400 works in all genres, available for copying at a fixed rate per page.

"musician and copper engraver."[36] His printed products date back to 1729. Around 1733 he also accepted a post as organist at St. Margaret's Church, and from 1737 on was organist at St. Augustine. In 1738 he founded his own publishing firm which was carried on by his widow and son, Johann Michael Schmid. It gained in importance through its association with J. S. Bach, C. P. E. Bach, J. L. Krebs, Christian Nichelmann, and others. From a socio-historical viewpoint, it is significant that many musicians were also familiar with copper engraving techniques. C. P. E. Bach, for example, had, as a seventeen-year-old, "himself engraved in copper"[37] a minuet of his own composition. On the title page to Georg Simon Löhlein's *Six Sonates pour le Clavecin*, op. 6, Leipzig 1776, one finds the reference "Gravé par l'auteur,"[38] and for the *Sonate sei per Chiesa e da Camera*, published by Leopold Mozart in his own edition in 1740, there is an indication of the engraver at the bottom of the violin part, "L:M: Fecit."[39]

(b) Bernhard Schott also began his career as a copper engraver.[40] His father Nikolaus had already worked on copper and music engraving on a part-time basis, and had sent his son to Strasbourg as an apprentice where he learned engraving, printing and type-casting. In addition, Bernhard Schott worked to perfect his musical education. In 1768 he founded a music printing concern in Mainz, to which he added a music publishing business no later than 1770. In addition, he dealt in writing materials, violin strings, and after 1787, even Burgundy wine.[41] In the beginning, he was

---

[36] H. Heussner, "Der Musikdrucker Balthasar Schmid in Nürnberg," in: *Die Musikforschung*, 16 (1963), pp. 349 ff.; Ibid., "Nürnberger. Musikverlag und Musikalienhandel im 18. Jahrhundert," in: *Musik und Verlag. Karl Vötterle zum 65. Geburtstag*, ed. by R. Baum and W. Rehm, Kassel, etc. 1968, pp. 320, 324, 328.

[37] W. Kahl, *Selbstbiographien deutscher Musiker*, Köln 1948, p. 38; G. Kinsky, *Die Originalausgaben J. S. Bachs*, p. 96, note 46; also compare in the same book pp. 40 ff.

[38] *MGG* VIII (1960), Sp. 1095-96, Illustration 2.

[39] An illustration of the title page, a dedication to Johann Baptist Graf Thurn-Valsassina and Taxis, as well as the last page of the violin part with the engraver's signature in: *Antiquariatskatalog* No. 133 of the family Hans Schneider, Tutzing 1968.

[40] *MGG* XII (1965), Sp. 50. U. Thieme/F. Becker, *Allgemeines Lexikon der bildenden Künstler von der Antike bis zur Gegenwart*, Bd. 33, ed. by H. Vollmer, Leipzig 1936, p. 267. Here mention is also made of non-musical engraving by B. Schott.

[41] A. Gottron, *Mainzer Musikgeschichte von 1500 bis 1800*, Mainz 1959, p. 212.

occasionally active as a practising musician (military musician in Strasbourg), and his special services as a clarinetist with the elector's court orchestra were charged to the court each time at 1 fl.[42] While Balthasar Schmid also composed music, however, nothing is known of any compositions by B. Schott.

(c)   The route from art dealer to music dealer is exemplified by the firm Artaria, in Vienna.[43] Carlo, Francesco and Giovanni, coming from a northern Italian family of art dealers, founded a business in Mainz in 1765. In 1770, Carlo and Francesco founded their own art dealership in Vienna. In 1776 the Viennese firm also established the music business and began publishing music in 1778. Finally, in 1785, Artaria set up its own music engraving workshop. The firm experienced an expansion and growth which was intimately connected with the music of the Viennese classic and post-classic period. There were many similar firms which, by making the change from art to music dealing, filled a gap left by the book industry.[44]

3.   *The route from "officially employed" musician to publisher and dealer in music.* Here the reference is to musicians who eventually gave up performing, either willingly or through the pressure of circumstances, to make music publishing and sales their main profession.

(a)   Nikolaus Simrock, for example, who was French hornist with the electoral orchestra in Cologne from 1775, was assigned the task of "purchasing and developing the library of wind music for the elector" (payment authorization of 1787).[45] Since about 1780 he had already been operating a

42 K. Schweikert, *Die Musikpflege am Hofe der Kurfürsten von Mainz im 17. und 18. Jahrhundert,* Mainz 1937, p. 68.

43 A. Weinmann, *Vollständiges Verlagsverzeichnis Artaria & Comp.,* Vienna 1952, pp. 4 ff.; same author, *Wiener Musikverleger und Musikalienhändler von Mozarts Zeit bis gegen 1860. Ein firmengeschichtlicher und topographischer Behelf,* Vienna 1965, pp. 14 f.; *MGG* I (1949-51), Sp. 729-735.

44 A. Weinmann, *Beiträge zur Geschichte des Alt-Wiener Musikverlages,* Reihe 2, Folge 7: *Kataloge Anton Huberty (Wien) und Christoph Torricella,* Vienna 1962; Ibid., Folge 10: *Verlagsverzeichnis Pietro Mechetti quondam Carlo,* Vienna 1966, pp. VI-VII; Ibid., Folge 12: *Verzeichnis der Musikalien des Verlages Joseph Eder — Jeremias Bermann,* Vienna 1968, pp. V-VII.

45 E. H. Muller [von Asow], "Zur Geschichte des Hauses Simrock," in: *Simrock Jahrbuch,* 1 (1928), p. 3. compare also *MGG* XII (1965), Sp. 722 f.

business on the side, dealing in music as well as carpets, prayer books, stationery and musical instruments. When in 1792, at the age of forty, he was dismissed by the elector Maximilian upon the dissolution of the court orchestra, he turned his full attention to his business and at the same time expanded it into a publishing firm. A socio-psychological interpretation of this type of development would be summarized as follows: Simrock carried on extra-performing activities to augment a relatively secure income. When he lost his post, however, he preferred not to search for a new performing position, in view of the unstable times, but rather to establish himself as a businessman.

(b) Joseph Schmitt's career also led from a secure post to the establishment of a music business in Amsterdam.[46] It is known that until 1771 he served as *Regens Chori* in the Cistercian Monastery of Eberbach in the Rhineland, where he became an ordained priest in 1757. He appears also to have been involved in the procurement of music. Shortly after 1771 it seems that he left Eberbach; the reason is not known. He settled in Amsterdam and in 1772, or at the latest in 1773, founded a music dealership and publishing house, which included facilities for music engraving. This firm, along with the old established firm of Hummel, was among the leading publishers in Holland. In the last years before his death, from 1788 to 1791, Schmitt was also conductor of the *Felix Meritis* concert society in Amsterdam. As the composer of numerous works, he was the embodiment of the music dealer who, in addition to his commercial activities, continued actively to practice music and compose. On some of the title pages of his own compositions he identified himself as *Marchand de Musique*.[47]

4. *From "free-lance" musician to music dealer and publisher.* Another entry into commerce in music was made by the free-lance musician who founded a music business either to supplement his income or to make the transition from an insecure life to the middle-class existence of a businessman. Typical of this group are (a) J. André in Offenbach and (b) F. A. Hoffmeister in Vienna.

---

[46] A. Dunning, *Joseph Schmitt*, Amsterdam 1962, pp. 18-24, 30-32, 35-37.
[47] A. Dunning, *loc. cit.*, pp. 69, 75.

(a) Johann André was so attracted to music that he did not wish to take over the paternal silk factory and went instead to the theater, composed *Singspiele,* did translations, and later, in Berlin, served until 1784 as conductor at Theophil Doebbelin's theater.[48] Whether he wanted to provide some security against what might have seemed, after all, a rather precarious existence at the theater, or whether an inherited inclination for business was stronger than he had thought, the fact remains that as early as 1774 he organized a music engraving business in Offenbach. At the same time he opened a music publishing house which he allowed almost to run itself for the first ten years. At the end of his period in Berlin, he devoted his full enthusiasm to the concern and developed it into one of the leading firms of its kind in Germany.

(b) After completing his study of law, Franz Anton Hoffmeister[49] became an extraordinarily prolific composer and remained so for the rest of his life. It appears, however, that he never held an official music post. In order to provide some financial security for himself, he founded a music publishing house in 1784 together with the Viennese book dealer Rudolf Gräffer. Just one year later he became independent, and in 1788 he expanded his firm to include an art and retail music business. He opened a branch in Linz in 1792/93. In Leipzig in 1799, on one of his occasional concert tours, he met the organist Ambrosius Kühnel. Together in 1800 they organized the *Bureau de Musique,*[50] which later developed into one of the largest music publishing businesses—C. F. Peters, in Leipzig. The first partner, Ambrosius Kühnel, about whom there is otherwise little known,[51] can be classified under category (3), for he held the post of organist at the electoral court at Schloss

---

[48] *MGG* I (1949-51), Sp. 455-459; O. E. Deutsch, "Musikverlags-Nummern. Ein Nachtrag," in: *Die Musikforschung,* 15 (1962), p. 155.

[49] *MGG* VI (1957), Sp. 547-550; A. Weinmann, *Die Wiener Verlagswerke von Franz Anton Hoffmeister,* Vienna 1964; Ibid., *Wiener Musikverleger,* pp. 21 f.

[50] H. Lindlar, *C. F. Peters Musikverlag,* Frankfurt etc. 1967, pp. 9-10.

[51] *MGG* X (1962), Sp. 1118. H. Lindlar, *loc. cit.,* p. 9. Here Kühnel is classified as a book and art dealer as well as an organist.

Pleissenburg in Leipzig, only to give it up to devote himself exclusively to the lucrative music publishing business.
5. *From music-lover (non-professional) to music publisher and dealer.* This category is, from the socio-psychological point of view, the most interesting. Here a musically gifted person seemed to prefer the more secure profession of music dealer to the precarious future of a professional musician. Whether it was simply a question of an actual or an assumed lack of ability, or whether it was the fact that the status of a professional musician also underwent a change which now made such a decision more dependent upon socio-psychological factors, still needs to be established. In any case, the two examples below illustrate the route to music dealer.
(a)   In 1818, Hans Georg Nägeli wrote in a manuscript entitled *Short History of my Professional Life*,[52]

From my earliest years I had displayed most definite inclinations towards music; yet my father, though a fairly well-to-do businessman, was so greatly in debt, due to enterprises in agriculture, that I was not in a position to consider music as my hobby, or even to buy a good instrument or music. In the year 1791, at the age of eighteen and with the help of some local music lovers here, I was able to found a small music business and lending library. I was so successful that I was not only able to satisfy my musical aspirations, but in the course of ten years accumulated capital that was very conservative-ly valued at 20,000 Zürich Gulden. Consequently, several friends joined me in establishing a publishing business as well. This was also successful ... and, according to the newspapers, brought a first-rate reputation to my estab-lishment throughout half of Europe, whereas previously it had enjoyed a reputation as the only such business merely in Switzerland. There was no doubt that in a few

---

[52] Published by R. Hunziker, "Hans Georg Nägeli. Einige Beiträge zu seiner Biographie," in: *Schweizerische Musikzeitung,* 76 (1936), p. 611 f. Compare also by the same author, *Der junge Hans Georg Nägeli. Achtzehn Briefe aus den Jahren 1790-1808,* Zürich/Leipzig 1937, pp. 7, 34 (125. Neujahrsblatt der Allgemeinen Musikgesellschaft in Zürich); H. J. Schattner, "H. G. Nägeli. Pestalozzianer, Musikerzieher, Chorbildner, Verleger Kunstwissenschaftler," in: *Schweizerische Musikzeitung,* 105 (1965), pp. 285-286.

more years I would have been a rich man. Then the war came...

As late as 1794 he could say of himself, "Being the only music dealer here, so that all the music lovers in and around Switzerland send me their orders, I have very substantial sales."[53] The ultimate fate of Nägeli as a music dealer and publisher, as well as the fact that he did not become a rich man, are of no further interest here.

(b) The father of Johann Karl Friedrich Rellstab was a small bookseller in Berlin and also published books, primarily of a religious nature. Johann Karl Friedrich turned this into a music publishing business and also set music type. His was one of the few concerns other than Breitkopf's that achieved some importance. Seen from this point of view, Rellstab's route to the music publishing business would seem to be similar to that of the firm Breitkopf in Leipzig. Yet his son Ludwig Rellstab, later a well known music critic, writes in his memoirs *Aus meinem Leben* about the motives which caused his father to carry on his grandfather's business:[54]

He felt the need to expand the field of his activities, both as a creative artist and as a benefactor of the arts. He was about to accept a position as music director in Riga when misfortune befell his father [paralysis, stroke, d. 1788], and he was forced to exchange an independent career as an artist for that of the somber commercial sphere. Yet he was so possessed of the spirit of music that he could not have abandoned it altogether. Consequently, he solved the problem by making it a part of his business. His firm soon became one of the most famous in Germany.

Clearly, Ludwig Rellstab is speaking here of the choice between the "independent career as artist" and "the somber commercial sphere," which was also the alternative faced by

---

[53] Letter to M. Clementi, dated Jan. 28, 1794, published by R. Hunziker, *Der junge H. G. Nägeli*, p. 8, Letter No. 2.

[54] Vol. 1, Berlin 1861, p. 7. Compare also *MGG* XI (1963), Sp. 215. No evidence has been found to date to substantiate the planned post in Riga; yet it is clear that Rellstab, even according to his own words, had originally set himself the goal of becoming *Musiker von Metier*. Compare also O. Guttmann, *Johann Karl Friedrich Rellstab. Ein Beitrag zur Musikgesch. Berlins*, Phil. Diss. Leipzig, Berlin 1910, pp. 20, 16.

J. André, son of a manufacturer, who was able, to a degree, to combine the two. Rellstab relinquished all claims to the life of an artist and became a businessman, but found some satisfaction and an outlet for his artistic leanings by having regular musical performances in his home.

6. *Music dealer and publisher through inheritance.* In order to complete the picture, mention should be made of the route of traditional succession within a family business. When Johann Anton André the 3rd, upon the death of his father Johann André in 1799 (mentioned above), took over the business at age 24, he broke off what had begun as a successful musical education.[55] In this case, it was more from a sense of duty than from a decided preference for the business world. Yet this choice had been even more difficult for his father to make.

7. *From a non-related profession to music dealer and publisher.* All the previously mentioned routes originated in a somewhat related basis or field. In this last category one can bring together all those who came to the field from an unrelated or at least distantly related profession. Carl Gotthehl Siegmund Böhme, the successor to Carl Friedrich Peters, a firm still known by that name today, was a manufacturer before he bought the Leipzig firm, and was thus already familiar with commercial enterprises.[56] On the other hand, Jakob Christoph Hug who, together with his brother Caspar, took over the firm from Nägeli, had been an evangelical pastor in Zürich.[57] Whether it was the love of music or the prosperous firm which prompted him to change his profession is a question which would have to be investigated in detail.

The typology, presented here, of possible routes leading to the profession of music dealer and publisher should be considered only preliminary. The lack of biographical data, particularly with respect to facts unrelated to publishing or technical details, was felt to be a serious gap in the research of the stated task. Then, too, questions of a commercial-legal nature related to the founding of a music business have been little researched, and thus were hardly considered in this outline. One of the many accomplishments of the French Revolution was the introduction of the free right to exercise a

---

[55] *MGG* I (1949-51), Sp. 459 ff.

[56] H. Lindlar, *C. F. Peters Musikverlag,* p. 12.

[57] *MGG* VII (1957), Sp. 859.

trade in France, adopted soon thereafter in other countries. As a result of this development, mandatory guild membership, no longer enforceable, was finally abolished. In Prussia from 1810/1811 on, the right to conduct a business depended only upon paying a business tax and obtaining a certificate of good conduct from the police authorities. In fact, the old world of monopolistic commercial privileges had already begun to crumble in the last decades of the 18th century.[58] In the sphere of the book trade there was a noticeable increase in the development of new businesses, about which the old established firms could do little from a legal point of view. Everywhere, even in the smallest provincial towns, competition sprang up. As a rule, licenses were granted. Even as late as the second half of the 18th century there were no general or specific governmental regulations concerning the establishment of a book business. The book trade was an unskilled trade,[59] and not until after 1772 did Austria require proof of apprenticeship, sufficient knowledge of the best authors, and adequate working capital in order to establish a business. In 1801 Prussia followed suit with similar stipulations. If book dealers could set themselves up more or less at will, how much easier must it have been in the up-and-coming field of the music dealer.

As has been shown, the music trade developed between two extremes. At one end were the professional merchants and artisans (book and art dealers or printers and engravers) who saw an opportunity for growth and expansion as well as considerable profit in a field that lay very close to their original sphere of interest. At the other end, for similar economic reasons, were music enthusiasts, who chose the life of a businessman, fully integrated into middle-class society, over that of the artist. Between these two extremes were all those who chose one profession but could not stay away from the other. They remained musicians, either in a permanent post or as free-lance composers, conductors or soloists, and also carried on a music business activity. The emphasis might have been on one or the other. The music enterprise could be either full-time or avocational, quasi-amateur or carried on using the traditional sales and distribution procedures. According to the importance the music business assumed in the life of each individual, one can also speak of

---

58 Compare also J. Goldfriedrich, *Geschichte des Deutschen Buchhandels*, Vol. 3, Leipzig 1909, pp. 556 ff.

59 J. Goldfriedrich, *Geschichte des Deutschen Buchhandels*, Vol. 2, p. 96; Vol. 3, p. 561.

the various motives or purposes that were associated with their enterprise. The activities of agents and sellers described in the first section seem to have been equally affected by material and idealistic motives. A man such as Daniel Gottlob Türk in Halle was probably less concerned with the modest additional income he might receive than with an idealistic goal of doing something to fill an existing gap in the music trade, and thereby bringing music to the public. To the degree to which he could educate his fellow citizens to appreciate music, he could also expect to find a fertile field for his own musical work. In the liberated society of the late 18th century, eager to absorb culture, music was no longer isolated from the average citizen. If commerce in music was carried on as a business enterprise, it was either because there was a need for supplementing the salary received from a musical post, or because it permitted the musician to lead a less perilous existence as an independent composer or conductor, professions which, in general, were poorly paid. It is significant that many music dealers began publishing operations by bringing out their own editions. Such was the case, for example, with F. A. Hoffmeister and L. Koželuch[60] in Vienna and J. Schmitt in Amsterdam. Undoubtedly they hoped to obtain greater returns this way than by selling their works for a lump sum.

In all these efforts to reconcile, either voluntarily or out of necessity, the profession of a musician with that of a businessman, there is reflected a latent crisis in the musician's life at the end of the 18th century. J. W. Hässler, in a biographical preface to his *6 leichte Sonaten fürs Clavier*, 2. Tl., Erfurt 1787, says, concerning his father,[61]

> He (the father) loved music, insofar as it gave him pleasure, but called it a "breadless art" if one made it his primary profession. He could not be convinced that there were distinctions between *Bierfiedler*, *Musikanten* and *Tonkünstler*.*

---

[60] Compare A. Weinmann, *Verzeichnis der Verlagswerke des Musikalischen Magazins in Wien, 1784 bis 1802 "Leopold Koželuch,"* Vienna 1950, pp. 4 ff.

[61] P. III, also printed by W. Kahl, *Selbstbiographien*, p. 55.

*As always in these essays, such terms are difficult to translate and the authors themselves do not indicate what the concepts meant at a given time. One can assume, certainly, that a *Bierfiedler* was one who played at pubs, taverns and modest weddings, or other such festivities. The *Musikant* was probably the municipal musician, and the *Tonkünstler*, most likely, would come closest to our concert artist or virtuoso. *Tr. Note.*

The case of Nikolaus Simrock was typical. Because he held a post until 1792, he carried out his musical trade privately and as a sideline. When the electoral orchestra of Cologne was dissolved, he was forced to turn his full energies to his trade. The gradual transformation of the social structure from an aristocracy to a middle-class society, as exemplified most dramatically by the French Revolution, could not fail also to touch upon the various musical professions. Their function and status changed. Though there had been earlier disbandings of court orchestras,[62] they were the result of feudal whim and not of the breaking up of a social class, which experienced only brief efforts towards restoration in the 19th century. In the wake of these developments, the artist lost his position within the social order and was turned loose in his special field. Those who did not wish to take this step preferred, as the emphasis of this study has shown, to be incorporated into the social structure as merchants and businessmen. Rellstab may have had before his eyes the picture of an aging Wilhelm Friedemann Bach who, from 1774 on, vegetated in Berlin without a post. A significant factor promoting integration of the new music dealer profession into the social order at the end of the 18th century was the conferring of titles by the monarchies, who meant them to be status symbols for certain professions. In 1797, Bernhard Schott was awarded the title of Electoral Councillor in Mainz. Peter Wilhelm Olsen, the music and instrument dealer in Copenhagen, was given the title of Royal Danish Commercial Councillor.[63] Johann Julius Hummel became a Royal Prussian Commercial Councillor, a title which he did not neglect to include in his advertisements in the *Berlinischen Nachrichten Von Staats- und Gelehrten Sachen*.[64]

---

[62] It would be of sociological value to investigate the subject of what happened to such dismissed orchestral players. The problem has been hinted at by, for example, W. Lidke, *Das Musikleben in Weimar 1683-1735,* Weimar 1954, pp. 83-86. [63]

A. O. Schulz, *Allgemeines Addressbuch für den Deutschen Buchhandel,* Jg. 15, Leipzig 1853, Abt. 1, p. 136. [64]

To the best of the author's knowledge, the editions appearing in Berlin from the publishing house of Hummel do not bear the title *Kommerzienrat* (commercial councillor). Yet, in the J. W. Lustig translation of F. W. Marpurg's *Aanleiding tot het Clavier-speelen,* Amsterdam 1760, according to the plates, he wishes to be known as *Muziekverkooper* [music dealer]. On the title page for P. Ricci's *Sei Trio per due Violini e Violoncello obligato,* op. 3., he is called *Mercante e Stampatore di Musica* [music dealer and printer] (cf. illustr. in *MGG* XI, 1963, Sp. 429).

CHAPTER EIGHT

The Origin and Social Status of the Court Orchestral Musician in the 18th and early 19th Century in Germany

·

CHRISTOPH-HELLMUT MAHLING*

*The author is currently preparing a more exhaustive work on this subject entitled: *German Orchestras and Orchestral Musicians from 1700 to 1850. Tr. Note.*

While research in musicology has greatly emphasized investigation of biographical data on outstanding personalities, for example, the lives of the great virtuosi, it has paid little attention to and even ignored that middle group of practising musicians, represented most prominently by the orchestral musician. With the exception of references in works about particular court orchestras, it was not until the beginning of this century that one could find a number of works which dealt exclusively and in an organized manner with the social and economic problems of the orchestral musician.[1] Such studies were, however, generally written by economists and all but disregard the historical point of view. In addition, they take into consideration their own contemporary period or only the most recent past, and are therefore of limited value here. An exception to this is a work which was brought to my attention after completion of this study and which, based upon extensive investigation of the conditions in Weimar, is in general agreement with the conclusions

---

[1] R. Eitner, "Die soziale Stellung der Musiker im 18. Jahrhundert," in *MfM* XXII (1890); H. Ritter, *Ueber die materielle und soziale Lage des Orchestermusikers*, Munich 1901; P. Marsop, *Die soziale Lage der deutschen Orchestermusiker*, Berlin and Leipzig 1905; H. Waltz, Die Lage der Orchestermusiker in Deutschland mit besonderer Berücksichtigung der Musikgeschäfte, Diss. Heidelberg 1906 (*Volkswirtschaftliche Abhandlungen der Badischen Hochschulen* 8, Heft 4, Karlsruhe 1906); F. Stempel, *Die soziale Lage der Orchestermusiker—Ueber das Lehrlingswesen—Militärkonkurrenz*, Berlin 1910; St. Krehl, *Musikerelend. Betrachtungen über trostlose und unwürdige Zustände im Musikerberuf*, Leipzig s.d. (1912); L. Krieger, *Die soziale Lage der Theatermusiker*, Diss. Heidelberg 1913; W. Schatz, *Die Zünfte der Spielleute und die Organisation der Orchester-Musiker in Deutschland*, Diss. Greifswald 1921; G. Materne, *Die sozialen und wirtschaftlichen Probleme des Musikers*, Diss. Mannheim 1953.

presented here. It is entitled *Socio-economic position of the court orchestral musician at the Weimar court in the first half of the 19th century—exemplified by Johann Christian Lobe.*[1a] This study by Beate Grimm underscores the similarity of conditions at various courts.

In order to get the most comprehensive picture of orchestral musicians, whether they stood in a fixed service relationship to a court[2] or were employed by an individual nobleman, one must take the broadest possible view of the concepts of "origin" and "social status." Thus, one should consider the question of origin from the point of view of geography as well as social class. In this connection one should know, for example, whether the orchestral musicians came from close by, from areas distant to the residences, or from districts or areas which could be termed "talent pools." One should also consider from which social classes they were primarily recruited. Did they come from musicians' families and thus carry on a tradition, or from a musical environment, or possibly even from a non-musical background? The musical education as well as the general schooling of the orchestral musician are additional factors which must be considered.

Then, too, one must take into account such factors as income, the buying power of money, and the general standard of living, in order to be able to determine the social status of a particular group. In order to avoid too narrow a perspective, one should also consider the question of the orchestral musician's position within society, his individual status within the structure of the orchestra itself, and the gradual changes which took place with respect to these relationships in the course of time.

The mentality and intelligence of the orchestral musician are also important considerations if one wishes to understand the position of the individual with respect to his fellow musicians. One should also define the relationship between town musicians, pipers and *Kunstgeiger* on the one side and military musicians, primarily court and field trumpeters and drummers, as well as hautboists, on the other. Indeed, these very distinctions define their positions and roles. The relationship of the orchestral musician to that of the practising amateur can also provide revealing insights.

[1a] Beate Grimm, *Die sozial-ökonomische Lage des Weimarer Hofkapellisten in der ersten Hälfte des 19. Jahrhunderts—dargestellt am Beispiel Johann Christian Lobes,* unpublished Ph.D. dissertation, Leipzig, 1964.

[2] e.g., *Accessiste* (trainee) or *élève* (pupil).

The situation with respect to the availability of sources and the question of research methods offer difficulties in some of these areas. The musicians' education can often be only partially substantiated, since in the case of many musicians there are no extant written documents between the entry in the baptismal register and the inclusion of the name on a payroll list. It is equally difficult to determine today what the average cost of living was, and whether the average musician was able to afford anything beyond his daily needs. In his study of 16th century German court musical groups,[3] Martin Ruhnke was faced with the same problems. There are literally no basic studies of the economics of the situation. Moritz John Elsas' *Outline of the History of German Prices and Wages*[4] is to this day still the only work in this field. Thus, there are two possibilities: either one attempts to ascertain the actual cost of specific goods for a given time period on the basis of research in archives and thereby determine the actual standard of living, or one can compare the pay of the orchestral musician to that of other court servants or other groups. One would in either case have to work out the social hierarchy and, of course, one should attempt to combine the two investigational procedures as far as possible.

A further difficulty arises from the fact that a given wage, as well as payment in kind, sometimes so stipulated, did not necessarily always represent a musician's total income. There was a wide range of possibilities for augmenting a given wage. One could consider, for example, music lessons,[5] the production of concert series under the

---

[3] M. Ruhnke, *Beiträge zu einer Geschichte der Deutschen Hofmusikkollegien im 16. Jahrhundert*, Berlin 1963, especially pp. 95-134.

[4] M. J. Elsas, *Umriss einer Geschichte der Preise und Löhne in Deutschland vom ausgehenden Mittelalter bis zum Beginn des neunzehnten Jahrhunderts*, Vol. 1, Leiden 1963, Vol. 2, Part A, Leiden 1940; Vol. 2, Part B, Leiden 1949.

[5] Compare here, among others, G. Bereths, *Die Musikpflege am kurtrierischen Hofe zu Koblenz-Ehrenbreitstein* (*Beiträge zur Mittelrheinischen Musikgeschichte* Nr. 5), Mainz 1964, p. 79; Fr. Rochlitz, *Für Freunde der Tonkunst*, Vol. 3, Leipzig 3/1868, p. 75; Fr. W. Marburg, *Historisch-kritische Beyträge zur Musik*, Vol. I, Berlin 1754, p. 157 (education of the oboist, Johann Christian Jacobi); *loc. cit.*, p. 156 (education of the violinist, Leopold Raab); *loc. cit.*, p. 547 (The concertmaster Graun gives lessons to the violinist Iwan Böhm).; B. Grimm, *Die sozial-ökonomische Lage der Weimarer Hofkapellisten . . .* p. 60 (Lobe is given flute and violin lessons by the chamber musician and senior orchestral player, Ernst August Riemann) and p. 81 f. (Gottfried Röder gives music lessons on the side because of poor wages received as an orchestral player). O. E. Deutsch, *Schubert. Die Dokumente seines Lebens*, Kassel 1964, p. 12: "Wenzel Ruzicka, a violist with the *Burgtheater* and the Court Organist, was also a piano teacher at the

musician's own direction,[6] playing for churches or theaters which did not maintain their own orchestra[7] and also appearances with foreign virtuosi. Thus, for example, court musicians in Munich received "the customary 60 Gulden from the Royal Theater treasury . . ."[8] for accompanying the violinist Laub in "entr'acte music." This was in accordance with the directive of January 10, 1848. Frequently, there was additional pay for playing theater music. Other sources of additional income were the copying of music manuscripts[9] or the selling of strings, reeds and other instrument supplies.[10] What the actual income was from such activities can be determined only in a few individual cases.

What follows is an attempt to contribute to our understanding of the questions which have been posed.

I • GEOGRAPHIC ORIGINS OF THE ORCHESTRAL MUSICIAN

While it was a matter of course that there would be a number of foreign singers at least at the larger German courts, this was generally not the case for orchestral personnel. The primary exceptions were the positions of conductor and concertmaster, for which musicians from France and Italy were often chosen. The

---

Church Hostel, taught the boys to play the viola and cello, and even tutored them in figured bass. For this he received 100 fl. at the beginning. . ."

[6] Thus, for example, in the year 1760, the violinist Konrad Rovantini was able to produce public concerts together with the court musicians in Koblenz. G. Bereths, *Musikpflege am kurtrierischen Hofe*, p. 147.

[7] See also, among others, *ibid.*, pp. 241-242.

[8] Munich, Hauptstaatsarchiv (HStA) Staatstheater 13286, Hofmusik 1834-1861.

[9] Fr. W. Marpurg, *Beyträge*, Vol. V, Berlin 1760, p. 8: "Many a poorly paid musician is required to maintain himself by copying out music, that is, the musician must obtain the concertos, arias, trios, etc., and write them out for others. . ."

[10] If such supplies were not procured centrally, it was customary for a member of the orchestra to be charged with such responsibilities. This was the case, for example, in Stuttgart for many years. Also see G. Bereths, *Musikpflege am kurtrierischen Hofe*, pp. 26 and 144. In addition there were still other possibilities for earning additional income. The "French Horn virtuosi" and, in 1790, the Böck brothers, "court musicians in Munich, at the same time carried on a jewelry business with beautiful rings etc." W. Chr. Müller, *Aesthetisch-historische Einleitungen in die Wissenschaft der Tonkunst*, Part II, Leipzig 1830, p. 178.

majority of the personnel came *aus deutschen Landen*. This is verified by the available source material.[11] The geographical range of German lands from which musicians were recruited was primarily determined by the size of the court. The smaller courts generally relied upon musicians from the residence itself or from the local area.[12] Even here, if there was an exception, it was most probably the conductor. This limitation was due mainly to a lack of financial resources available to court orchestras. Consequently, one felt gratified if one could manage to satisfy musical needs with local musicians without too great an expense. Although similar conditions prevailed at medium and large courts, there was the advantage that they had a larger budget at their disposal and did, in fact, pay them accordingly. This, in turn, meant that such orchestras attracted musicians from all over Germany and even other parts of Europe.[13] Yet it should be noted that even in such orchestras the musicians came primarily from districts under the jurisdiction of a particular ruler.[14] In no case can one speak of an orchestra which was composed largely of foreign musicians. When foreign musicians were employed in orchestras, they usually came from Italy, France and Bohemia. Bohemia produced not only good string players, but also, and above all, brass players, and particularly horn players who were frequently mentioned by name.[15]

---

[11] In addition to material found, for example, in the archives of 1782 in Stuttgart which have been cited in Appendix I, one could find similar evidence in such works as: Fr. W. Marpurg, *Historisch-kritische Beyträge*, Berlin 1754 ff.; C. Fr. Cramer, *Magazin der Musik*, Hamburg 1783 ff.; W. Chr. Müller, *Aesthetisch-historische Einleitungen*, Leipzig 1830; in the *Musikalische Real-Zeitung*, Speier 1788 f.; in the *Allgemeine Musikalische Zeitung*, Leipzig 1798 ff.

[12] According to Fr. W. Marpurg, *Beyträge*, Vol. III, Berlin 1757, pp. 77-80, of the twenty-five musicians in Schwarzburg-Rudolstadt only five did not come from the immediate vicinity.

[13] Compare here also the references given by Fr. W. Marpurg, *Beyträge*, Vol. II, Berlin 1756, pp. 567-570, with respect to the court orchestra in Mannheim.

[14] Compare also the references given by C. Fr. Cramer, *Magazin der Musik*, Hamburg 1783, pp. 145-147 where he speaks about the Court Orchestra in Kassel: "... from the area of Hesse," and "from Cassel" there were some twenty musicians. The remainder of the total of thirty musicians divided with respect to geographic origin as follows: 3 from France, 1 from Silesia, 1 from the district of Meiningen, 1 from Saxony, 1 from Würzburg, 1 from Fritzlar, and 2 of unknown origin.

[15] In Fr. W. Marpurg, *Beyträge*, Vol. II, Berlin 1756, pp. 567-570, for the court orchestra in Mannheim, and in the same work, Vol. I, Berlin 1754, p. 271, for the court orchestra in Gotha. Also see D. A. v. Apell, *Gallerie der vorzüglichsten Tonkünstler und merkwürdigen Musik-Dilettanten in Cassel von Anfang des 16ten Jahrhunderts bis auf gegenwärtige Zeiten*, Cassel 1806, p. 47.

As a rule, pay scales were based upon ability and not nationality. As an example, in September 1753, "two violinists from Italy," Piero Pieri and Martiale Greiner, were "taken into service" in Stuttgart. Each was "awarded an annual wage of 700 Gulden."[16] In comparison, a wage survey,[17] undated but most likely from the year 1755, lists a "violinist Kurtz" at 750 fl., but the "violinist Luiggio Schiassi" at only 300 fl. Martiale Greiner's salary was in fact reduced by 50 fl. to 650 fl. This kind of wage reduction could be related to actual performance accomplishments, or at least they were a factor in arriving at a wage figure. But one cannot in any sense speak of decidedly preferential treatment for the foreign orchestral musician.

The German orchestral musicians came mostly from cities with a *Residenz*, from free imperial cities, or from smaller towns and their immediate environs. However modest, there was usually some musical activity in even such small places, and here then also existed the opportunity to acquire a musical education. Only when there was no opportunity for employment at one's own court did one make the decision, generally with the permission of the local ruler, to seek employment away from home. Such a move, however, ordinarily took place within three larger geographic regions whose borders were rarely crossed. These were north Germany, central and east Germany, and southwest Germany. Another explanation for the relatively limited mobility among orchestral musicians is perhaps their basic inclination towards middle-class sedentary life.

II • SOCIAL ORIGINS OF THE ORCHESTRAL MUSICIAN

The majority of orchestral musicians came from the middle class. Many were the sons or relatives of families already employed by the courts.[18] New generations also came from the ranks of the

---

16 Stuttgart, HSt A, A 21.

17 Stuttgart, HSt A, A 21. Compare also J. Sittard, *Zur Geschichte der Musik und des Theaters am Württembergischen Hofe*, Vol. 2, Stuttgart 1891, pp. 175-177 and Supplement (Beilage) II.

18 Compare here the biographical data mentioned by Fr. W. Marpurg, *Beyträge*, Vol. I-III, Berlin 1754 ff., and in particular Vol. I., pp. 554 ff. Here the professions of the fathers are given, such as court conductor (*Hofkapellmeister*), court musician (*Hofmusikus*), captain of dragoons (*Dragoner Hauptmann*), or regimental bandmaster

"honorable artisans."[19] This was primarily because such recruits could be trained within the ranks of the town pipers' associations, which anyone who could offer proof of an "honorable" status could join. Only rarely does one come across representatives of the lower and upper classes among orchestral musicians, though the "Court and State Roster" of 1752[20] in Munich does list under the "Electoral Instrumentalists" three members of the von Cröner family who advanced to positions as Concertmaster, Assistant Concertmaster and Leader of the Violins.[21]

In Stuttgart there also existed special conditions. Here, with the founding of the *Hohe Karlsschule*,[22] members of less advantaged classes were able to receive a free musical education. As evidence one could cite the origins of three or four court musicians listed in the payrolls of 1782 as orchestral players, former students of the *Karlsschule*.[23] The violinist Johann Georg Mayer[24] and the flutist

---

(*General-Regiments-Capellmeister*), chief clerk (*Ober-Secretär*), and clerk (*Secretarius*). The father of Joh. Rud. Zumsteeg was a "retired footman"; also see H. Mendel—A. Reissmann, *Musikal. Konversations-Lexikon*, Vol. 11, Berlin 1879, p. 507. In 1791, the widow Bürger, whose husband had been an "administrator in the church in Heidelberg," requests that her eldest son Josef Bürger be accepted "into the orchestra in Munich as a violinist." Munich, Staatsarchiv für Oberbayern, HR. Fasc. 463, Nr. 227.

[19] Fr. W. Marpurg, *Beyträge*, Vol. I, Berlin 1754, pp. 197 and 431. Here are biographical sketches of Johann Joachim Quantz and Christoph Nichelmann. The father of J. J. Quantz was a "smith" and that of Chr. Nichelmann, a "tailor." On April 21, 1762, "Aegidius Puppelle, son of a beer brewer from Trostburg," makes application to be accepted into the court orchestra of *Hörtzog Clement* in Munich; Munich, Staatsarchiv für Oberbayern, HR Fasc. 463, Nr. 228. On the occasion of the wedding of Joh. Chr. Lobe's father in the year 1796, the senior Lobe is designated as a citizen and "stocking weaver" (B. Grimm, *Die sozial-ökonomische Lage der Weimarer Hofkapellisten*, p. 49).

[20] *Hof- und Staatskalender* of Munich for the year 1752, p. 47.

[21] Compare, for example, *Hof- und Staatskalender* of Munich for the year 1776, p. 67. The conferring of the title of nobility followed in the year 1749. See F. G. Lipowsky, *Baierisches Musik-Lexikon*, Munich 1811, p. 59.

[22] From 1776 to 1794 it had the status of a university; see R. Uhland, *Geschichte der Hohen Karlsschule in Stuttgart*, Stuttgart 1953 (*Darstellung aus der Württembergischen Geschichte* 37).

[23] For example, see Stuttgart HStA, A 21 Bü 955.

[24] Johann Georg Mayer was born on January 17, 1757, in Urach. For this and what follows refer to Stadtarchiv und Kirchenbücher des Pfarramts II in Urach. In the *Hof- und Staatskalender* of Stuttgart for the year 1782, on p. 75, he is designated as a violinist under the name *Georg Mayer*. This is conceivably the same as a "violinist and

Johann Friedrich Mayer[25] came from Urach. They were probably brothers, though there is some question about this since the father is listed as having different professions. Other evidence seems to support the contention that they were brothers.[26] In any case, it is certain that they both came from modest backgrounds, for the father is listed as a "night watchman"[27] as a "cow herd"[28]—most likely at the ducal stud farm in Gütersheim,—and finally, as an "assistant toll collector."[29] The father of the bassoonist and court musician Johann Philipp Mohl was also employed at the ducal farm in Gütersheim, in this case as a "farm laborer."[30] As a last example, one could mention here Johann Benjamin Friedrich Maier of Stuttgart.[31] He was the son of Johann Leonhard Maier, a "musician with the Swabian District Regiment."[32] In evaluating these examples one should not overlook

court musician, Georg Maier" mentioned by W. Pfeilsticker, *Neues Württembergisches Dienerbuch*, Vol. I: *Hof—Regierung—Verwaltung*, Stuttgart 1957, under par. 903 for the years 1794/95. I should like to express my gratitude to Dr. Eberling, Director of the Stadtarchiv in Urach, for this information and his cooperation.

[25] Johann Friedrich Mayer was born on March 17, 1760, in Urach. The *Hof- und Staatskalender* of Stuttgart for the year 1782, on p. 75, lists him as a flutist. In the *Kalender* for the year 1815, on p. 96, he is for the first time designated as flutist as well as a *Stadtmusicus*, a town musician. In 1824 his name no longer appears. According to the records, he died on December 6, 1827, as a *Hof- und Stadtmusicus* (court and town musician). Also see W. Pfeilsticker, *Neues Württ. Dienerbuch*, Vol. I, par. 903.

[26] In the entries the father is once called "Simon" and once "Simson Mayer," but the mother, both times "Anna Maria," born "Ruoff."

[27] In the entry for the birth of Johann Georg.

[28] In the entry for the birth of Johann Friedrich.

[29] On the death notice entry for Johann Friedrich. See also W. Pfeilstricker, *Neues Württ. Dienerbuch*, Vol. II: *Ämter-Klöster*, Stuttgart 1963, par. 2977. Here the entry states: ". . . died as gatekeeper on May 8, 1810, at the age of 87 years and 4 months, ducal servant."

[30] Urach: Stadtarchiv und Pfarramt II (*Kirchenbücher*): Mohl (also Moll), Johann Philipp, born in Urach on June 15, 1757. Father: Ludwig Moll, haymaker; Mother: Maria Magdalena, born Harter. Also see *Hof- und Staatskalender* of Stuttgart for the year 1782, p. 76, under the heading *Fagott*. W. Pfeilsticker, *Neues Württ. Dienerbuch*, Vol. I, par. 904, indicates that he was a "bassoon player and court musician" from 1794/95 on. A certain Küfer Mohl (and Moll) who appears in a council record of Urach in 1810 was most probably a brother of Johann Philipp.

[31] "Court Musician in Stuttgart" born 1756. The *Hof- und Staatskalender* for the year 1782, p. 75, indicates a certain "Court musician, Benjamin Mayer" as a violist. Whether the previously mentioned violinist Leonhard Mayer was the father of Johann Benjamin Friedrich, which was certainly in the realm of possibility, or whether he was someone else cannot be said with certainty here.

[32] W. Pfeilsticker, *Neues Württ. Dienerbuch*, Vol. I, par. 903.

the fact that the fathers of all these musicians were employed by the Duke. This fact may have made the admission of their sons to the *Karlsschule* easier, though such a background does not appear to have been an absolute requirement.

By far the greatest number of orchestral musicians appear to have come from families of musicians[33] or from families where music making was an important activity. Friedrich Ernst Fesca, for example, later to become concertmaster of the court and theater orchestra in Karlsruhe, was exposed to music from an early age, though his father was not a musician but a chief clerk (*Ober-Secretair*) for the municipal magistrates in Magdeburg. The father was, however, an accomplished cellist and pianist, and because the mother had formerly been a singer in the service of the Duchess of Kurland, it is not surprising that there was music-making in the Fesca home.[34] All of this must certainly have had a decided influence on the later career of the son. It was also often the case that music was considered to hold a special place specifically within the framework of a general education, for example, in institutions such as the *Thomasschule* in Leipzig or in Jesuit Colleges.[35] Frequently musical careers developed from such an education.

It was a different story when there was a tradition that had to be carried on. Here then, principles and rules of the artisans played their part. It was considered necessary that at least one son carry on the father's profession, if talent permitted it. Naturally there were cases, even then, where parents sought to prevent a child from contemplating a career in music, although usually without suc-

----

[33] See, for example, W. Chr. Müller, *Aesth. —hist. Einleitungen*, Vol. II, pp. 205-206: "Domnich, a famous family of virtuosi on the French Horn. The father, Fr. D., was court hornist in Würzburg. Three sons were already accomplished players at the age of 12 . . . The third son was in the orchestra in Meiningen."

[34] Fr. Rochlitz, *Für Freunde der Tonkunst*, Vol. 3, Leipzig 3/1868, pp. 73 f.

[35] Charles Burney, *The Present State of Music in Germany, the Netherlands and the United Provinces.* . . London, 1773, cited according to the edition of P. Scholes, *Dr. Burney's Musical Tours in Europe*, Oxford, 1959, vol. ii, p. 306: ". . . and, further, I was informed that in all the towns throughout the empire, where the Jesuits have a church or college, young persons are taught to play upon musical instruments, and to sing. Many musicians have been brought up here, who afterwards have rendered themselves eminent. This will in some measure account for the great number of musicians with which Germany abounds, as well as for the national taste and passion for music."

cess.[36] Once a child's musical training had been completed, of which the basic rudiments were often taught by the father, it was usually possible for him to play along with his father in the "home" court orchestra, often without compensation. This frequently provided the opportunity later to succeed his father as an employee. On April 12, 1806, for example, "Joseph Friedel, Royal Court Music Apprentice and trained tympanist," submitted the following appeal in Munich:

> Since my father, the Royal Court Tympanist Friedel, is forced because of advanced age and physical infirmity most humbly to request his dismissal and retirement, I, as a tympanist, having officially completed my training and having served four years as court tympanist, and as supported by the enclosed testimonial, having served in your court orchestra as a violinist for almost 2 years in order to be better qualified in general as a musician and to be better able to carry out the duties of a court tympanist to the greatest possible satisfaction, most humbly entreat your royal majesty to officially appoint me to my father's position with salary according to that status.[37]

Such almost "guild-like" conditions often resulted in several members of the same family becoming orchestral musicians and playing in the same orchestra. The *Verzeichniss der Churfürstl. Maynzischen Hof- und Kammermusik, wie sie im Jahre 1742 gestanden* ("role of Mainz Court musicians for 1742") lists, for example, four *Herren Schwachhoffer,* all of them brothers, as members of this orchestra,[38] and Hector Berlioz reports in his memoirs, in connection with his journey though Germany in 1840/41 concerning the

---

36 Fr. W. Marpurg, *Beyträge,* Vol. III, Berlin 1757, pp. 46 ff. "Leben Johann Christian Hertels... Entworfen von... Hrn. Johann Wilhelm Hertel."

37 Munich, Staatsarchiv für Oberbayern, HR Fasc. 466, Nr. 457. One could also cite the example of the cellist Franz Danzi, who received his first lessons from his father, first cellist of the electoral orchestra in Mannheim, and who was accepted into the orchestra at an early age (see W. Chr. Müller, *Aesth.-hist. Einleitungen,* Vol. II, p. 214). Also compare Fr. Rochlitz, *Für Freunde der Tonkunst,* Vol. 3, pp. 106 ff. Other examples are found in G. Bereths, *Musikpflege am kurtrierischen Hofe,* pp. 71 and 111.

38 L. Chr. Mizler, *Neu eröffnete Musikalische Bibliothek,* Part Four, Leipzig 1743 (Neudruck Hilversum 1966), Vol. II, 122-124. Concertmaster Ignatius, the cellist Joseph, the violinists Andreas and Antonius Schwachhoffer (also Schwachhöffer). Fr.

orchestra in Braunschweig: "The musicians Müller are even more numerous than I had supposed; I counted seven of them, brothers, sons, and nephews, in the Brunswick orchestra."[39] This brief summary should amply demonstrate that orchestral musicians usually came from the ranks of the middle class.

III • THE EDUCATION AND TRAINING OF ORCHESTRAL MUSICIANS

In the 18th century there did not yet exist centralized, specialized training institutions for musicians, and the necessary schooling was obtained primarily in one of three ways. The first possibility, existing in relatively few places, was through an organized program within the framework of the school.[40] In such institutions the emphasis was, however, generally on vocal training rather than on instrumental instruction. For those who desired more than a general knowledge of music and who wanted to develop their abilities on one or more instruments, there existed as a rule only the second or third possibility, private instruction or training in a *Stadtpfeiferei* (town pipers' school).

As previously mentioned, private instruction often began within the family, from the father or other relatives, and was usually continued by professional colleagues.[41] When a pupil did not specialize in a specific instrument from the very beginning and at first was given instruction only in the fundamentals of music, the

W. Marpurg, *Beyträge*, Vol. II, Berlin 1756, pp. 475-477, "Die Königl. Capell- und Cammer-Music zu Dresden 1756." Here under the listing for violinists the "brothers Francesco Hunt, senior, and Johann Baptista Hunt, junior"; and similarly a violinist "Felice Pincinetti, senior," and cellist "Antonio Pincinetti, junior, brothers." Also a "father and son", the oboists "Anton and Carl Besozzi." See also G. Bereths, *Musikpflege am kurtrierischen Hofe*, pp. 48-49.

[39] *The Memoirs of Hector Berlioz*, trans. and ed. by David Cairns, New York, 1969, p. 309.

[40] Refer to fn. 109 on page 000.

[41] Fr. W. Marpurg, *Beyträge*, Vol. I, Berlin 1754, p. 548: "Mr. Johann Gottlob Freudenberg ... who started the study of music with his father continued his studies under the Royal Polish Chamber Musician Mr. Fickler, until in the year 1743 he was hired as a violinist with the Royal Prussian Orchestra." Joh. Cr. Lobe began his study of the flute with his father who played "Clarinet, Violin and Flute as a side-line" (B. Grimm, *Die sozial-ökonomische Lage der Weimarer Hofkapellisten*, p. 60).

teachers were usually the organist for theory and keyboard instruments and the cantor for vocal training.[42] This would serve as the foundation for further training, and it was customary to construct a musical education on as broad a base as possible so that one could have the greatest flexibility for later professional opportunities.[43] It appears also to have been the custom to place musical training in the hands of experienced working musicians.[44] In those cities and residences where there were orchestras, their members were available for private instruction.[45] If, for example, funds were not available for further training, such additional musical education could be continued within an orchestra.[46] At an institution such as the *Hohe Karlsschule* in Stuttgart, instrumental instruction was given by members of the court orchestra, where

---

[42] Fr. W. Marpurg, *Beyträge*, Vol. I, 1754, p. 432 and *Beyträge*, Vol. II, 1756, p. 93.

[43] Fr. W. Marpurg, *Beyträge*, Vol. I, 1754, pp. 549-550: "Mr. Johann Gabriel Seyfarth . . . His most distinguished music teachers were the organist Walther in Weimar for piano, the conductor Fasch and concertmaster Höck for composition and violin." He later became a "Chamber Musician and Violinist."

[44] In a letter dated April 29, 1782 to Breitkopf in Leipzig, Leopold Mozart writes: ". . . In the meantime I have an income from two pupils, the 12 year-old son and the 14 year-old daughter of H. Marchand, Theater Director in Munich. I have been entrusted with their education and I have hopes of making the boy into a great violinist and pianist, the girl into a good singer and pianist . . ." *Mozart. Briefe und Aufzeichnungen*, GA, Vol. III, Kassel 1963, p. 205. Also see the letter dated April 3, 1784, to Sebastian Winter in Donaueschingen, *op. cit.*, pp. 308-309. W. Chr. Müller, *Aesth.-hist. Einleitungen*, Vol. II, pp. 259-260: "J. N. Hummel, born in 1778 in Presburg, son of a musician, later Grand Ducal Kapellmeister and holder of the French Legion of Honor, began his musical education at the age of 4 with his father. Upon the dissolution of the seminary training college in Wartberg where the father was employed, the family moved to Vienna, where the father became the conductor for Schikaneder and placed his 7-year-old son, recommended by his mature playing, with Mozart, in whose house the diligent boy lived until 1787. . . " Hummel was later *Kapellmeister* in Stuttgart (1816), and from 1819, in Weimar.

[45] Also see, for example, *Musikalische Real-Zeitung*, Speier 1789, Sp. 406/407 and U. Götze, *Johann Friedrich Klöffler*, Diss. Münster 1965, p. 4.

[46] In a petition dated April 8, 1791, the previously-mentioned widow Bürger of Heidelberg writes to the Court Orchestra in Munich concerning the acceptance of her son: "Since he has progressed so far on the violin that he can learn nothing more in his home town, and since he has now reached his sixteenth year, time for additional training for which no funds are available. . ." she requests that her son be taken "into the Munich orchestra at a salary of only a few hundred gulden. . ." Munich, Staatsarchiv für Oberbayern, HR Fasc. 463, Nr. 227. Compare here also B. Grimm, *Die sozial-ökonomische Lage der Weimarer Hofkapellisten. . .* pp. 10 ff.

often the same teacher taught several different instruments. For example, Johann Friedrich Seubert of Marbach, from 1769 on listed as a violinist on the court civil service roster,[47] gave lessons from 1771 on in "violin, oboe, flute, French horn and bassoon."[48] J. F. Seubert's versatility is probably indicative of an education received in a *Stadtpfeiferei*. It also makes clear how comprehensive the training of an orchestral musician had to be until about the first half of the 19th century. Not until later did one specialize in a single instrument. This became a necessity in order to cope with greater technical demands.

By far the greatest number of orchestral musicians appear to have received training in the *Stadtpfeifereien*.[49] Money was probably an important factor. As dreary as apprenticeship time might have been, the money required for such training with piper associations, if there actually was a fee, was far less than that required for private lessons. In this way members of less advantaged groups could choose music as a profession and become "usable" instrumentalists. Whether an individual was actually able to obtain a position after his apprenticeship depended upon his ability, but also on prevailing circumstances. The fact that one was able to perform on a number of instruments must certainly have been an advantage.

---

[47] *Hof- und Staatskalender* for the year 1769, p. 67.

[48] R. Uhland, *Geschichte der Hohen Karlsschule in Stuttgart*, Stuttgart 1953, p. 172.

[49] See also, for example, W. Chr. Müller, *Aesth.-hist. Einleitungen*, Vol. II, p. 131: "Bode, born in 1730 in Braunschweig, son of a soldier, tended sheep until his 15th year. He learned music as a craft from a town musician. He learned to play all the instruments with ease and played the bassoon well. He conducted concerts in Hamburg..." Or *op. cit.*, p. 230: "J. G. Voigt the elder, born in 1769 in Osterwiek, learned all the standard instruments with the town musician, studied theory on his own, and became organist in Leipzig and lead violinist for the Royal Concerts; from 1802 on composed sonatas, trios, quartets, and one concerto for violin. He died in 1811." As late as 1878 one reads in the *Musikalische Conversations-Lexikon* by H. Mendel and A. Reissmann, Vol. 9, Berlin 1878, p. 398, in the article, *Stadtmusicus:* "Though the town piper associations may have been pedantic and even caused us to laugh at times, they were on the whole very useful institutions and above all, marvelous places to obtain rudimentary training for royal court and military musicians. Rising through the ranks, having to learn numerous instruments, students of the town pipers became capable orchestral musicians, often more useful for ensemble playing than the graduates of conservatories, who were often spoiled with solo playing and who displayed artistic moodiness. Many great artists, still gracing court orchestras with their presence, have learned something valuable there which cannot be learned anywhere else. Hopefully the Municipal Choirs will remain with us!"

Along with this guild-like training, the town pipers appear to have also given private instruction, as Friedrich Rochlitz reports about Adam Hiller: "During the last period of his stay at the Gymnasium (in Görlitz) he learned to play most of the current instruments tolerably from a kindly town musician. . . ."[50] Of the "current instruments" two could be learned only in a very specific way: the trumpet and the tympani. Only a privileged court and field trumpeter or drummer had the right to give instruction in these instruments,[51] and only to one who had signed a contract for such instruction. A good picture of these conditions is given in Quantz's autobiography,[52] excerpts of which are given in the Appendix.[53]

While string players could enter a court orchestra only in a "direct" way, wind players had other options available to them—at the smaller courts, mostly via the town piper training, and at the larger ones, via military music. This was possible above all if one had proven oneself in service with the court band (to which one might have been summoned because no one else was available or the ensemble needed to be expanded). In Munich in the year 1762 Adam Fridl, "onetime hautboist for the Royal-Electoral-Infantry-Regiment," and his two older sons Michael and Carl were hired as court musicians "in recognition of their outstanding ability as lutanists and violinists." Their combined salary was 1000 fl. (400 fl. for the father and 300 fl. each for the sons). They were also "awarded a complete uniform" to be used at "performances."[54] By a proclamation dated March 21, 1765, in Stuttgart, the former "hautboist with the personal guard," Johannes Nisle, was appointed "oboist and chamber musician" with the court orchestra.[55]

---

[50] Fr. Rochlitz, *Für Freunde der Tonkunst*, Vol. 1, p. 6.

[51] See also Joh. E. Altenburg, *Versuch einer Anleitung zur heroisch-musikalischen Trompeter- und Pauker- Kunst*, Halle 1795 (Reprint Dresden 1911). This privilege was maintained until the beginning of the 19th century (although not very strictly towards the end of this period), and gradually, corresponding to their function, trumpeters and tympanists were placed on equal footing with other instrumentalists.

[52] "Johann Joachim Quantzens Lebenslauf, von ihm selbst entworfen," in Fr. W. Marpurg, *Beyträge*, Vol. I, 1754, p. 197 ff. English translation in P. Nettl, *Forgotten Musicians*, New York, 1951, pp. 280-319.

[53] See Appendix II.

[54] Munich, Staatsarchiv für Oberbayern, HR Fasc. 466, Nr. 456.

[55] W. Pfeilsticker, *Neues Württ. Dienerbuch*, Vol. I, par. 905. Also see W. Salmen, *Geschichte der Musik in Westfalen*, Vol. I, Kassel 1963, p. 225.

Since instrumental training often began at an early age,[56] it was not unusual to find young court musicians, perhaps between the ages of 16 and 25.[57] Even very young "gentlemen" were to be found in such positions.[58] In this connection one should not be misled by such indications in the membership rosters as "the younger" or "the elder." "The older Herr Baumer," a French horn player in Anspach and later also in Berlin, was, for example, only 19 years old and was in this way differentiated from a younger brother who was also a horn player.[59] The age of the average apprentice in the orchestras should also be seen in relationship to the ages of the regular court musicians. The roster for Stuttgart, included in Appendix I, shows that the average age of the musicians accepted into the court orchestra in the year 1782 was 24. In connection with this matter of age, and compared to today, one must take into consideration the shorter life expectancy of that time. In this regard one must also remember that some of the relatively low salaries were often merely "starting wages."

[56] For example, Friedrich Ernst Fesca received piano lessons already at the age of four, and at age nine, violin lessons. Fr. Rochlitz, *Für Freunde der Tonkunst*, Vol. 3, pp. 74-75.

[57] Josef Bürger was 16 years old when his mother asked that he be accepted "into the Munich Orchestra" as a "violinist." (Munich, Staatsarchiv für Oberbayern, HR 463, Nr. 227.) Fr. E. Fesca, who was born in 1789, accepted his first position as a violinist with the orchestra of the Duke of Oldenburg in 1806, that is, at the age of 17. (Fr. Rochlitz, *Für Freunde der Tonkunst*, Vol. 3, p. 76.) "Christian Gottfried Weber, born in Stuttgart on the 24th of July 1758, studied violin with the former court musician Göz..." and "came to the court in April of 1782," at age 24. (*Musikalische Real-Zeitung*, Speier 1789, Sp. 406-407.—The son of the cellist Johann Jäger in Anspach "was already in his eleventh year employed as a cellist with this orchestra, under his father's eye." (Chr. Fr. D. Schubart, *Ideen zu einer Ästhetik der Tonkunst*, Vienna 1806, pp. 162-163.) "Peter von Winter, born in Mannheim in 1754, son of an officer of the guard, studied violin at Cramer's school, and was already accepted into the orchestra in his tenth year...;" "Ramm, born in Mannheim in 1744, was employed as an hautboist at age 14 by the court band..." (W. Chr. Müller, *Aesth.-hist. Einleitungen*, Vol. II, pp. 177 and 152.) Johann Christian Cannabich also came to the Mannheim Orchestra at age 13. (H. Riemann, *Musiklexikon*, Vol. I, Mainz 12/1959, p. 273.) J. Chr. Lobe was accepted as a trainee into the Court Orchestra in Weimar at age 14. (B. Grimm, *Die sozial-ökonomische Lage* ... , p. 73.)

[58] In Koblenz in 1763, the 13-year-old son of the court tympanist took over his father's post as tympanist of the guard. In the same place the 14-year-old Wilhelm Ries was accepted as the successor to his father as a horn player. G. Bereths, *Musikpflege am kurtrierischen Hofe*, pp. 71 and 59.

[59] *Musikalische Real-Zeitung*, Speier 1790, Sp. 75.

If one keeps in mind the youth of many of the orchestral musicians, it is understandable that a ruler now and then would make it possible for a particularly gifted instrumentalist to continue his training at the expense of his sovereign. Thus, for example, the "court violinist Carl Dupreuil," employed in Munich in 1762 at a salary of 400 fl., studied intermittently with Tartini in Italy.[60] In the year 1799 "Joseph Hanmüller, Royal-Electoral Hornist," wrote from Nürnberg for a supplement towards his tuition expenses with the virtuoso Punto, indicating that he could not cover the cost by himself.[61] A testimonial by Punto was enclosed. In view of the fact that Hanmüller was receiving a salary of 250 fl. at that time and that Punto was a traveling virtuoso, making it necessary for a student to accompany him, the request would seem justified. It was self-evident that in such cases a musician was expected to return to the service of his royal employer and not accept a position elsewhere.[62]

IV • THE EDUCATIONAL BACKGROUND OF THE ORCHESTRAL MUSICIAN

In keeping with his social class origins, the orchestral musician was not usually educated beyond elementary school.[63] Exceptions in this respect were mainly those who had originally chosen another

---

[60] Munich, Staatsarchiv für Oberbayern, HR Fasc. 466, Nr. 404.

[61] Munich, Staatsarchiv für Oberbayern, HR Fasc. 467, Nr. 526.

[62] This is explicitly stated in the employment contracts for those coming from the Hohe Karlsschule in Stuttgart in 1782. For example, from the contract of Antonius Weil: "Thirdly, always remembering the bountiful and exceptional grace and good will which I have enjoyed from my youngest years on in Ducal Military Academy, receiving at the Duke's expense my training, education and up-keep, I shall promise to keep in mind the natural obligation ensuing therefrom and to serve with the greatest zeal and enthusiasm his most noble and gracious majesty and never to leave his majesty's service or to bind myself in the least obligation elsewhere without his majesty's express permission." Stuttgart, HStA, A 21 Bü 955.

[63] In 1778 the Royal School Regulation for the Education of Citizens in the Districts of City and Rural Schools for Bavaria (*Chürfurstl. Schulverordnung für die bürgerliche Erziehung der Stadt- und Landschulen in Baiern*) stipulated the following curriculum for these schools: Christian religion and morals, learning of the mother tongue, spelling and reading, handwriting, mathematics in the four basic skills, letter writing, government, etiquette, hygiene, health, agriculture, and natural history and nature study. *Bayer. Schulordnungen vom Jahre 1774 und 1778*, newly edited by A. Bock (*Päd. Quellenschriften*, Heft 3), Munich 1916. In contrast to the simple musician, the

career.[64] It appears, though, that in the case of "soloists" or "virtuosi" a broader education was generally desired.[65] Institutions such as the Hohe Karlsschule in Stuttgart, where pupils were given a general education above and beyond their instrumental training, were rare exceptions.[66] In general, the "practical," that is, instrumental training was usually started while pupils were still attending school, or directly after graduation. Whether such instruction was limited to learning to play one or more instruments, or whether it might include a broader curriculum covering, for example, theory, composition, etc., depended upon the individual teacher.[67] The

orchestral musicians were thus placed on a higher social level, having finished school, which does not seem to have been the rule for the former. Also compare here Johann Beerens Weiland, *Hochfürstl. Sachsish-Weisenfelsischen Concert-Meisters und Cammer-Musici, Musicalische Discurse,* Nürnberg 1719, p. 16: "...and if one only would restrain the bunglers and beerfiddlers who, as a group, have the same inadequate education, when they run off from school in their mended coats." On the other hand, B. Grimm reports in *Die sozial-ökonomische Lage der Weimarer Hofkapellisten,* p. 56, that Joh. Chr. Lobe was able to get through the fourth year of the Gymnasium with the support of the court. "This demonstrates that the ducal house was interested in obtaining court musicians who possessed a relatively good school education."

[64] As an example to which many others could be added, mention could be made of the "Royal Prussian Chamber Musician and Orchestral Player, Christian Friedrich Schale," who at the age of 19 began a study of Law at the University of Halle, and 3 years later accepted a post as Chamber Musician. Fr. W. Marpurg, *Beyträge,* Vol. II, 1756, p. 93.

[65] L. Mozart writes in the previously mentioned letter to Sebastian Winter in Donaueschingen, dated April 3, 1784, "My best wishes to you. I must close now, as there are 4 people here from Munich who have come to fetch the 15-year-old Marchand, who stayed here with me under my tutelage for 3 years and is now returning, a first rate violinist and pianist who also did very well in composition. In addition, he didn't do badly in Latin either, although he also made considerable strides in his primary additional subjects of French and Italian." *Mozart. Briefe und Aufzeichnungen,* GA, Vol. III, Kassel 1963, pp. 308-309.

[66] In the report on the *Anspacher Musik* the following is said about the previously mentioned "elder Mr. Baumer:" "This young artist is a first-rate horn player but he is also a most worthy student of advanced humanities who will surely not have to take a back seat among scholars. Through the generosity of his uncle he attended not only the Gymnasium in Anspach for several years but also the *Karlsakademie* in Stuttgart, where he sought to perfect himself not only in musical art but also in humanities, modern languages, and other skills." *Musikalische Real-Zeitung,* Speier 1790, Sp. 75-76. From this it is quite evident that economic means were an important factor in determining whether one could have an advanced education.

[67] In his short story, *Musikalische Leiden und Freuden* (*Schriften,* Vol. 17, Berlin 1844, pp. 300-301) Ludwig Tieck writes: "It sounds unbelievable, but it is nevertheless the

primary emphasis was always—as it is today—on increasing technical proficiency. To be sure, one always wanted to hire the "educated" musician, but what was actually meant was that musician who had the greatest technical education, the one who was most proficient on his instrument(s). Regardless of whether he was a soloist or a member of the orchestra, the instrumentalist was expected to be able to grasp the spirit of the works he was called upon to perform and to offer a suitable interpretation. Every effort was made to obtain those musicians who were technically competent . . . and could interpret "with taste." Since there were relatively few musicians who could meet these standards, many discussions arose as to the causes of this problem and how to solve it. For example, a question was put as follows: "Why are there so few musicians who can interpret with taste?" The answer to the questioner is excerpted as follows:

> The reasons for this state of affairs are manifold. Most professional musicians are only machines. Nature destined them to work with their hands and not with their heads. Even their teachers did not recognize this because they themselves were perhaps of the same constitution and therefore their products necessarily had to turn out the same. . . . The second cause can be traced to the way in which this science [music] is studied. Only a very few study music as a science, with the aid of other disciplines such as mathematics, algebra, composition and the other arts which, one can easily see, are indispensable if one wishes to achieve any kind of expression. This omission occurs either through lack of

---

truth that I sawed away at the violin in this manner for some six or seven years, without the urge ever really to have a basic understanding of music, or without his (the teacher's) thinking it might be a good thing to append some theory to our practical art."—Yet even purely instrumental instruction appears to have been deficient. So it is stated by J. Fr. Reichardt, *Ueber die Pflichten des Ripien-Violinisten*, Berlin and Leipzig 1776, p. 8: "Nothing is rarer than a violinist or cellist with a good, full tone. The true cause stems from the first instruction; one doesn't allow the student to play scales long enough, or perhaps at all. In order to make things pleasant, one gives him melodies and difficult things to play right away. This is like telling someone to draw figures before he can make dots and a straight line."

opportunity, through indifference, or from an inability to see the necessity.... Public institutions such as the secondary schools and the *Gymnasien* could do much to refine the study of music.... The choice of a way of life, the poor methods of studying music, the lack of spiritual development—these are the factors which produce such a small number of really musical instrumentalists... a number which grows relatively smaller and smaller.[68]

In a similar manner, J. F. K. Arnold's comments show to what degree a high value was placed upon the orchestral musician's broad education. Yet Arnold saw as one of the primary functions of the *Musikdirektor* the further development of such education:

The development and growth of an orchestra can be accomplished in a dual manner. It is either purely mechanical or purely aesthetic, or it is a combination of the two. For the first, nothing more is needed than industry and constant practice. The purely aesthetic education can be most reliably gained from a library of books on music, which the *Musikdirektor* should distribute to the musicians. At the beginning, such books would primarily be mere musical anecdotes, biographies of famous composers (something practising musicians always like to read), but in time the musicians might concentrate more on readings on the critique of pure artistic tastes.[69]

The educational level of an orchestral musician would clearly be valued more highly if he was a composer as well as a good instrumentalist. Yet it is noteworthy that such composer-orchestra-members wrote works primarily for their own instruments, and most often for their own use. Johann David Schwegler, a member of the *Hofkapelle* in Stuttgart, for example, was designated as "oboe

---

[68] Anonymous, *Philosophische Fragmente über die praktische Musik,* Vienna 1787, pp. 10 ff.

[69] J. F. K. Arnold, *Der angehende Musikdirektor oder die Kunst, ein Orchester zu bilden,* Erfurt 1806, pp. 134-135.

player and composer for his instrument."[70] The primary motivation for such compositions may therefore well have been the exploitation of a given instrument's possibilities and the demonstration of virtuosity.

The expansion of the orchestral musician's educational horizon meant not only that music was performed with greater understanding, but that it in turn contributed to a raising of the orchestral musician's "social prestige" within the social structure.

V • THE SOCIAL STATUS OF THE ORCHESTRAL MUSICIAN

Two factors basically determined social status, including that of the orchestral musician: first, the level of income, and second, the "social prestige" which he enjoyed within the social structure. Each factor taken alone could, at least in theory, determine a social rank. Yet it was most likely both factors together, each dependent on the other, which characterized social status. In spite of the difficulties already indicated, an attempt will be made to convey an idea of the financial status of the orchestral musician.

At the outset one must differentiate between conditions at larger versus smaller courts. Whereas in the former musicians were hired solely as musicians, in the latter, they were most often obligated to perform other duties as well. Because each court had a fixed budget and a related roster of positions, which in most instances had to be strictly observed, salaries were dependent upon the exact nature of the position held by an individual.

As the pay rosters of the court orchestras in Stuttgart and Munich show, the general salary range of the orchestral musician was somewhere between 200 and 500 fl. per year. Exceptions were made for the concertmaster and for outstanding instrumentalists, particularly wind players, when they were needed for the orchestra. If the annual compensation was less than 200 fl., there might have been a number of reasons for it. For one thing, the players might be

---

70 M. Mendel—A. Reissmann, *Musikal. Conversations-Lexikon*, Vol. 9, Berlin 1878, p. 195. Also see W. Chr. Müller, *Aesth.-hist. Einleitungen*, Vol. II, p. 142: "Barth, born in 1735, virtuoso on the oboe in Cassel and Copenhagen, composed for his instrument. His son and grandson were likewise virtuosi on the oboe."

considered "candidates for positions," trainees, or students who were considered "apprentices" and who, in many cases, were still very young. Such musicians received a kind of "expense allowance." Others might be musicians whose regular pay came from another "department," for example, from the Lord Chamberlain's budget, and who only received a "supplemental" amount for their service with the court orchestra.[71] The wages paid to a "regular" court musician made an average middle-class existence possible, with some thrift, under normal circumstances. There was even some consideration given to the differences in the cost of living. For example, the pay at larger courts was correspondingly greater than in smaller ones.[72] If there was a general rise in the cost of living, there was usually an adjustment made, either through a monetary supplement or other forms of compensation.[73] As will be shown, such so-called "normal conditions" were quite clearly not the rule. It is also a fact that the common falling into debt of the orchestral musician was due less to an "eccentric change in life-style" than to the conditions themselves.[73a] Some examples from Munich make this quite clear.

---

[71] In Stuttgart (probably in 1755) the "Hautboist Christoph Hetsch, a member of the personal guard, [received] a supplement of 80 fl." for his participation as second oboist with the orchestra. Stuttgart, HStA,A 21 Bü 11.

[72] W. A. Mozart mentions in a letter to his father, dated September 29, 1777, written from Munich: "For if we had to live on 504 f. in Salzburg, an equivalent in Munich would be about 600 or 800 f." *Mozart. Briefe und Aufzeichnungen*, GA, Vol. II, Kassel 1962, p. 22. In his *Musicalischen Discursen*, Nürnberg 1719, pp. 14-15, Johann Beer (Bär) had already made mention of the varying cost of living: "True enough, it is said that this or that one is receiving 500 *Reichs-Thlr.* in wages, but no mention is made of what it costs to live in a given place . . . and the salary must be adjusted correspondingly so that all musicians can support themselves and their families without having to take on additional work; for such incomplete information [concerning salaries] is of no use to anyone . . . "

[73] Compare here also the gradual rise in salaries in Munich up to 100 fl. and more around the year 1800. (Munich, Staatsarchiv für Oberbayern, HR Fasc. 457 ff.) Similar conditions can, however, be observed even earlier. For example, the violinist Ferdinand Blum received 200 fl. in 1745, in 1748, 300 fl. and thereafter 400 fl. From the 7th of March 1762 he received 500 fl. (op. cit., HR Fasc. 463, Nr. 183.) For information with respect to the changing price situation in Germany, see also N. B. Féltoronyi, *Diffusion du progrès et convergence des prix Allemagne—Angleterre 1792-1913*, Louvain-Paris 1966. Particularly informative here are the graphic representations.

[73a] Compare here also B. Grimm, *Die sozial-ökonomische Lage der Weimarer Hofkapellisten.*

If a member of a court orchestra earned an annual wage of 400 fl., he probably received only 380 fl., since 5% was generally withheld as a *Conditionssteuer,* a tax levied in order to provide a pension for the "Musician's widow." The above net wage would most likely have been paid in *quartaliter,* that is, in quarterly installments of 95 fl., amounting to approximately 31.67 fl. per month. If one calculates the Gulden at about 2 Marks,[74] this would yield a monthly income of some 63.34 Marks, for an annual salary of 760.08 Marks. In order to get at least some idea of the cost of living, a chart is given in Appendix III, indicating the adjusted prices as given by Elsas.[75] In view of the fact that these prices were given in the smallest denominations, that is, in *Denare* (Pfennige), the monthly income has to be converted. Since 1 Gulden was equal to 240 Denare, the figure arrived at amounts to approximately 7,600 Denare. It becomes apparent that even when rent money is deducted, it was possible for even a large family to manage on such a salary.[76]

In many cases, however, the road to such a "regular" appointment with a corresponding salary was most difficult and meant much privation. If one had the desire to obtain a court position, it frequently meant having to serve for an extended period of time without pay (*auf "freier Basis"*), or perhaps for a very modest compensation.[77] No thought was given to how an individual was to

---

[74] Compare also A. Blind, *Mass-, Münz- und Gewichtswesen,* Berlin and Leipzig 1923, pp. 84 ff. For general discussions on this subject see also M. J. Elsas, *Umriss;* L. C. Bleibtreu, *Handbuch der Münz-, Mass- und Gewichtskunde und des Wechsel-, Staatspapier-, Bank- und Actienwesens europäischer und aussereuropäischer Länder und Städte,* Stuttgart 1863; G. Wagner and F. A. Strackerjan, *Compendium der Münz-, Mass-, Gewichts- und Wechselcours-Verhältnisse sämmtlicher Staaten und Handelsstädte der Erde,* Leipzig 1855; Chr. and Fr. Noback, *Vollständiges Taschenbuch der Münz-, Mass- und Gewichtsverhältnisse,* Leipzig 1851. There are also further references in A. Schindler, *Biographie von L. v. Beethoven,* Münster 3/1860, Note after p. XXV, and also in L. Strecker, *Richard Wagner als Verlagsgefährte,* Mainz 1951, Appendix, Table XII.

[75] For further information, see Elsas.

[76] Of course the situation was different, above all, "when times were expensive" and the salaries did not keep up with inflationary prices. Thus, the "Court violist Joseph Palm" filed a petition for a supplement for "spa-treatment expenses" indicating his salary of 400 fl. as "meager," in the year 1798. He received a supplement of 60 fl.

[77] For example, the violinist Franz Xaver Joseph Dreer, in a petition of 1785, recounts that he came to the court in 1768 without pay. For 4 years he played without pay, 3 years at 100 fl., 4 years at 200 fl. and after 1781, for a salary of 300 fl. per year. He makes a request for another supplement of 100 fl. From the amounts mentioned

exist during this period of time. As a rule, he was dependent upon his family or other sources.[78] If such help was not available, there remained no other course than to go into debt. Such debts were often a burden for the rest of the musician's life,[79] and it was not

above, there was always deducted a 5% *Conditionssteuer*. When Dreer died in 1803, half of his salary was retracted. The other half, in the amount of 250 fl.—he had in the meantime been raised to a salary of 500 fl.—was divided. The concertmaster Moralt received 100 fl. (total income of 800 fl.), the violinist Joh. Baptist Moralt received 50 fl. (total income of 386 fl.), and the "uncompensated Anton Bohrer" (in the *Hof- und Staatskalender* of Munich in 1802 he is referred to as a "trainee" in the violin section) received 100 fl. (Munich, Staatsarchiv für Oberbayern, HR Fasc. 466, Nr. 390). One should note that in the settlement of a violinist's salary it was only violinists who were benefited and received a raise in salary. This kind of advancement within a group or class of instrumentalists was common practice. "As a result of the death of the court violist Mayer" (after the 1st of May 1789), for example, the sum of 253 fl. 18 x was made available. Count Seeau consequently made the suggestion that this sum be divided among the other violists: "For a long time now the younger and very poorly compensated court musicians in the viola section had to assist and substitute for the senior members and were always consoled with the settlement of such a vacancy." "The violist Toste" received a raise of 50 fl. in order "to increase his salary herewith to 300 fl.;" Rambo received 150 fl. "because of many years of exceptional and enthusiastic service . . . for an annual total of 250 fl.;" the violists Palm and Labeck, each 25 fl., "the former for a total of 225 fl., the latter for an annual 150 fl." (Munich, Staatsarchiv für Oberbayern, HR Fasc. 457, Nr. 13). Corresponding to Dreer's petition, the trainee Ignatius Albert requested in the year 1766 that he be appointed to a "regular post" since "he had been active at the court for six years as a contrabass player without any compensation." It was not until the fall of 1767 that he was appointed as "a real contrabass player, with an annual salary of 300 fl." What remained after the deduction of the *Conditionssteuer* was 285 fl. (Munich, Staatsarchiv für Oberbayern, HR Fasc. 462, Nr. 69.) In a petition dated April 20, 1800, the court musician Kapeller asked for a raise, claiming that he had already served for 3 years as a court musician but had no salary "save a gratuity of 50 fl., and since the new year 83 fl. 20 x. No need to say that it was not possible to exist from this." (Munich, Staatsarchiv für Oberbayern, HR Fasc. 464, Nr. 257.)

[78] On the 12th of May 1791, Count Seeau writes concerning the employment of the son of the widow Bürger, whose petition has been referred to a number of times previously: "In view of the fact that the electoral court at the present time still has three surplus violinists, who in part do not receive any compensation," there is a question as to when Bürger might be employed. It is suggested that until such time when he can be hired by the orchestra he be "given some [financial] aid as a supplement from the state treasury or perhaps from the ecclesiastical treasury . . . [and] that he [continue] to receive support in room and board from one of his good friends in the area." (Munich, Staatsarchiv für Oberbayern, HR Fasc. 463, Nr. 227.)

[79] The "Court Musician Georg Pranger," a violinist, pleads in 1788 and in subsequent years for a bonus or for advances on his salary to cover debt expenses. It

uncommon that even after his death, a widow or other relatives were required to continue "repayment."[80] Under such circumstances it is hardly surprising that an orchestral musician now and then fled from such "demands" by escaping to another state. In any case, a significant part of a musician's income often went towards the repayment of such debts. Making things more difficult was the fact that in spite of these conditions, the salary was not adjusted at all, or only very insignificantly. The actual appointment to a "regular" post often required years of waiting because, for example, an oboist could only be appointed when such a position became vacant. He could not be paid with the sum allocated, let us say, for a violinist.[81]

is claimed that these are so high because he "had worked 16 years as a trainee without compensation," and subsequently at a mere 100 fl. as a member of the orchestra. In 1790 he receives a "one-time bonus" of 100 Gulden and in 1793 he is allowed 50 fl. to enable him to retrieve his pawned clothes. On February 7, 1798, upon the death of Cannabich, he petitions "as the 52-year-old aspirant to a paying position"—since this might be the last opportunity—"to be able to receive the often requested but never yet granted *full* pay...." A late petition (1801) requesting free lodging is denied. (Munich, Staatsarchiv für Oberbayern, HR Fasc. 463, Nr. 213.) In the year 1757, the "Chamber-Musician" Luigi Schiatti, employed in Stuttgart at an annual salary of 300 Gulden, petitions for a raise to enable him to pay debts. (Stuttgart, HStA, A 21 Bü 617.)

[80] On April 30, 1799, upon the death of the violinist and court musician Plebs, his "widow is graciously granted an annual pension of 100 Gulden..." In November of 1801 the widow petitions for a pension increase, which is subsequently denied. Her petition was based, in part, upon the following: "My deceased husband Anton Plebs was employed as royal-electoral court musician, as a violinist. Yet for [the first] 9 years he served without pay; for the next 3 years, he received an annual wage of 100 fl., of which 5 fl. were deducted for *Conditionssteuer* out of which widows receive their pensions. For the next three years he received 200 fl. of which 10 fl. were deducted. For 20 years after that he received 300 fl. of which 15 were deducted. Subsequently, he received a final raise of an additional 200 fl., that is, for a grand total of 500 fl., and this lasted for 5 more years after which my husband died, after 45 years of marriage and with such an income..." In those first 9 years they had not only "spent" their savings but had to "go into debt." These debts had, however, not yet been cleared up. She claimed that because of the "current hard and expensive times" she could scarcely live off the current pension (100 fl.), let alone cover the remaining debt payments. She was now 65 years old. (Munich, Staatsarchiv für Oberbayern, HR Fasc. 463, Nr. 177.)

[81] In February, 1791, Marianna Fladt petitions for the employment of her son Anton as "Hautboist." Count Seeau replies that, although according to the Court Statutes "there should not be more than 2 hautboists ... and there are at present four, so there is a surplus," it should be stated in Anton Fladt's behalf that he is very capable and that he is deserving of support. He makes the suggestion to take on Fladt

Such was the situation for all musicians. The title *Hofmusikus* appears to have been used by all members of an orchestra, no matter what their particular status might have been. Officially, the title was customarily used only after a musician had been appointed to a specific post.[81a]

Of course it was a most fortunate situation whenever several members of a family were active at the same court. In such cases the total income could be quite considerable. As an example, one could cite the "former hautboist" Adam Fridl and his two sons, who had a combined income of 1,000 fl.[82] Wives and daughters of orchestral musicians were also found as "co-earners," as singers, actresses or dancers. For example, Mr. and Mrs. Heuzé in Kassel had a combined income of 2,000 Ecus, she as a singer receiving 1,000 Ecus, and he as a violinist and concertmaster, the same.[83] Fiorillo, as the *Kapellmeister* (conductor), also had a salary of 1,000 Ecus. In a letter dated November 12, 1778, Mozart reported to his father that he was happy "that Weber had done well for himself" and that father and daughter Weber were earning 1600 fl. in Munich.[84]

An orchestral musician's compensation could also be augmented by a *Gratification*, a bonus either for one specific occasion or covering a given period of time. In 1781, for example, "Joseph and Johann Toesky, the cellist Danzy" and "the violinist Ritschel" were awarded, and obviously not for the first time, a subsistence allowance of 100 fl. each, out of the "Marschallamts Cassa [treasury] as a bonus."[85] When the concertmaster in Munich, Karl Cannabich, was given a leave of absence to go to Frankfurt, probably in 1797/1798, his salary was divided among 14 musicians as a bonus[86] paid out, however, in monthly installments, so that it could be revoked at any time.

---

as a trainee but with the express comment that "he not receive a wage until such time when he might be given an official appointment, but that like all others he [be] obligated to serve in the little court theater." (Munich, Staatsarchiv für Oberbayern, HR Fasc. 466, Nr. 440.)

[81a] Compare B. Grimm, *Die sozial-ökonomische Lage,* p. 11.

[82] See above, p. 234.

[83] Marburg, HStA, Bestand 5, Hofsachen, Nr. 2585. Compare here also *Musikalische Real-Zeitung,* Speier 1789, Sp. 383.

[84] *Mozart. Briefe und Aufzeichnungen,* GA, Vol. II, Kassel 1962, p. 507: "... the two will make 1600 fl., for the daughter by herself makes 1,000 and her father 400 plus another 200 as *Souffleur* [prompter at the theater]. ..."

[85] Munich, Staatsarchiv für Oberbayern, HR Fasc. 457, Nr. 13.

[86] Munich, Staatsarchiv für Oberbayern, HR Fasc. 464, Nr. 253. For the exact distribution see Appendix IV.

Thus, while the orchestral musician did not have too much "mobility," he was able to exist if he had a regular appointment and was not too deeply in debt. The amounts listed in the payroll roster must in general be considered as a gross income which possibly included payment in kind.[87] References to such gratuities should, in any case, not be reckoned as additional income. Towards the end of the 18th century such "dual compensation" was no longer the obvious norm and wages were paid almost exclusively in money. It is not always possible to establish to what extent free room and board were included.

A further "facilitation" for the orchestral musician was the customary provision by the court of the "tools of his trade." Instruments[88] as well as the "expendables," such as strings and reeds, were supplied by the court. Obviously, and especially at the larger courts, they were anxious to achieve a uniform orchestral sound through a uniform quality of orchestral instruments. When the court did not supply the instruments, musicians received a

---

[87] Compare here the *Regulatif über die Fürstl Cammer-Hoff-und Kirchen-Music* from Stuttgart, probably from the year 1755. (Stuttgart, HStA, A 21 Bü 11.) Here the salary is itemized in an exact distribution. The violinist Martinez, for example, is listed with 800 fl., of which 400 fl. are paid in cash and the other 400 in kind. In a later payroll list he is listed with 1200 fl., but from the composition of the format, one can ascertain that he was again paid half in cash, the other half in kind. (Stuttgart, HStA, op. cit., Aufstellung vom 29. Juli 1774.) These *Naturalien und Materialien* (payment in kind), incidentally, were to be "paid at current market prices." (*op. cit.,* writing dated November 25, 1775.) In Munich, in the year 1791, the widow of the French horn player Wenzeslaus Kokert petitions for a supplement, since she still has an eight-year-old daughter. Her husband had served in the orchestra for 8 years. "His pay consisted of only approximately 300 fl., including clothing and wine, since he was one of the players with the least seniority. Even the wine and clothing allowances were lost in the well-known budget cut of 1788, so that we did not enjoy a salary of more than 150 fl." (Munich, Staatsarchiv für Oberbayern, HR Fasc. 464, Nr. 297.)

[88] In the employment contracts in Stuttgart from the year 1782 one stipulation, among others, states: "fourthly ... I shall, in general, serve to the best of my ability, treating the Duke's instruments with care so that they will not be neglected...." (Stuttgart, HStA, A 21, Bü 955.) Compare here also the instrument listings of the individual court orchestras, for example, in Stuttgart (HStA, A 21 Bü 629, listing dated June 2, 1787), or the one in Munich (HStA, Staatstheater 13527, Verzeichnis der Instrumente der Hofkapelle 1824-1881). Also in G. Bereths, *Musikpflege am kurtrierischen Hofe,* pp. 154-155, Inventory of music instruments at the end of the year 1782.

supplemental instrument allowance.[89] Printed music was always supplied. This state of affairs was, however, a source of concern for Marpurg in his *Beyträgen*, when he wrote:

"It is worth noting that although the very rich are too refined to carry money with them, it is generally only because of their money that they have any claim to eminence. Similarly, it is strange that many musicians don't own any music at all and often possess only very poor instruments; yet without them they can hardly be considered musicians."[90]

Since the orchestral musicians generally had to wear a uniform, the court administration would pay the costs of such "service dress" or would at least provide an allowance for this purpose.[91] If this had not been the practice, it would have been impossible for many musicians to afford a uniform, which cost a great deal in relation to their pay.[92]

---

[89] So it was, for example, in Koblenz in the year 1782, where wind players were given additional funds for the cost of reeds. The solo (*concertino*) winds were given 8 fl., since they required better quality reeds, while the *ripieno* players received only 4 fl. It was indicated that in the future all players would receive corresponding increases in their gross salaries to cover such expenses. Bereths, *Musikpflege am kurtrierischen Hofe*, pp. 159-160. Similar conditions prevailed in Stuttgart and Munich.

[90] Fr. W. Marpurg, *Beyträge*, Vol. II, 1760, p. 9.

[91] In Koblenz, at performances at the Akademie, the musicians were required to appear *in Livree*. For this purpose, each uniformed servant received a yearly allowance of 30 fl. in order to be able to buy himself a "citizen's suit." (Bereths, *Musikpflege am kurtrierischen Hofe*, p. 164.) In the year 1789 Joseph Haydn requests "along with all the court orchestral personnel ... in all humility, that Your Most Serene Highness permit the personnel to receive, as in years past, the monetary equivalent for the summer uniforms, rather than payment in kind, since many members are equipped with very new summer uniforms obtained through their own frugality...." The petition is approved and "the *Kappellmeister* is awarded a cash supplement of 150 Gulden; the other gentlemen, each 75 Gulden...." (J. Haydn, *Gesammelte Briefe und Aufzeichnungen*, Kassel 1965, p. 213.) As late as the year 1821, the "violinist Schemenauer" in Munich is awarded "60 fl. for the procurement of a uniform...." (Munich, HStA, Staatstheater 13488.)

[92] In the year 1821 a uniform cost as much as 85 fl., 12 kr., as is shown by the following breakdown for "the uniform of the court clarinetist Sebast. Werrle.

For the Merchant Rekenschuss (?)	27 f 28 kr.
For the Embroiderer Wagel (?)	16 f 24 kr.
For the Hatmaker	12 f 6 kr.
For the Tailor Lechner	29 f 14 kr.
Total	85 f 12 kr."

(Munich, HStA, Staatstheater 13488.)

The situation was considerably more difficult when an orchestral musician was married, was the "sole breadwinner," and possibly had to support a large number of children. Without "special supplements," which were generally granted in such cases,[93] it was impossible to support a large family.

It was particularly hard for a family when normal earnings were replaced at a relatively early time by pension payments, for reasons of illness or death. Such payments were most meager and hardly covered the bare necessities.[94] Even a "normal" pension was most modest. Depending upon income, they generally ranged from 30% to 50% of the regular income, though a minimum of 100 to 150 fl. per year seems to have been accepted as standard.[95] For example, the *Hofkapellmeister* Ignatio Fiorillo in Kassel received a normal salary of 1,000 Ecus per year, but his pension was only 300 Ecus annually.[96] Sometimes the amount of the pension was stipulated in the hiring contract.[97] In view of these conditions, it is understandable that the

---

[93] The French horn player Georg Eck requested an increased travel allowance for his move from Mannheim to Munich, because he had 8 children. He subsequently received, in addition to his previously awarded 125 fl., an additional "supplement of 75 fl." Munich, Staatsarchiv für Oberbayern, HR Fasc. 457, Nr. 13.

[94] For example, the 14- and 16-year-old children of the deceased "Court Cellist Alliprandi" in Munich received as "orphans," from 1801 until their 18th year, support of 100 fl. per year. Munich, Staatsarchiv für Oberbayern, HR Fasc. 462, Nr. 73.

[95] The court musician "Adam Friderich Comerrell" in Stuttgart, who had been employed at a salary of 325 fl., in 1757 petitioned for a pension supplement in view of the fact that he had a wife and three minor children to support and was receiving only an annual sum of 150 fl. He claimed that he was "too old to do any other additional work" and that he could not support his family from the pension. (Stuttgart, HStA, A 21) A similar petition was submitted by the "retired cellist" Ignaz Polz in Munich, in May of 1785. He also had a wife "and three minor children," but received a sum of 280 fl. per year from Duke Clement von Zweibrücken. With a raise he wished to pay off his debts gradually. The petition was at first denied, but in November of 1785, "since the condition of the treasury is not capable of supplying such charity payments," he was granted, annually instead of cash, two tubs of grain (*Schäffel Korn*). (Munich, Staatsarchiv für Oberbayern, HR Fasc. 463, Nr. 194.)

[96] *Musikalische Real-Zeitung*, Speier 1789, Sp. 383. Also see, Marburg, HStA, Bestand 5, Hofsachen.

[97] In the year 1765, the hautboist Joseph Sechi is hired at an annual salary of 1,000 fl. as "Court and Chamber Musician." Should he no longer be able to play he would then receive a pension of 300 fl. per year. When in 1776 he "stepped down," the oboist Xav. Jägerhuber received 500 fl., the oboist Michael Kristoph, 400 fl. and the surplus balance of 100 fl. reverted to the court treasury. Munich, Staatsarchiv für Oberbayern, HR Fasc. 472, Nr. 852.

archives dealing with the orchestral musician are filled with petitions asking for a raise in salary, in pensions, or for a supplement during a period of illness or upon a death in the family. In order to improve the situation for dependents and survivors of orchestral musicians, as well as pension benefits, so-called pension-funds or widows' and orphans' funds were established towards the end of the 18th century.[98] In addition to contributions by the musicians, as indicated previously (Conditionssteuer in Munich), these funds were supported by benefit performances[99] or other such "special performances."[100]

As late as the 19th century, the court orchestral employee was at the same time musician *and* servant. This dual function was a primary factor in determining his social status. While the larger courts could waive the obligations for musicians to perform additional duties, the smaller ones were dependent upon this dual role.[101] Only in exceptional cases did a smaller court have sufficient funds to maintain an orchestra whose musicians only fulfilled musical duties. Within the range of manifold approaches to the problem, two solutions appear to have been thought the most practical ones: either one looked for servants according to the instruments they could also play, or, as was more often the case, one simply directed musicians to specific court duties.[102] In the work

[98] Thus, for example, the Widows' and Orphans' Fund in Kurtrier. Bereths, *Musikpflege am kurtrierischen Hofe*, p. 163.

[99] J. Fr. Reichardt, *Vertraute Briefe geschrieben auf einer Reise nach Wien ... 1808/09*, Vol. 2, Munich 1915, pp. 94/95. Here it is reported in his "Twenty-third letter, Vienna, March 27, 1809," among other matters: "Yesterday (March 26th) the *Creation* of Haydn was performed at the Burgtheater as the annual Benefit Concert for Musicians' Widows...." Also compare from Munich, Staatsarchiv für Oberbayern, HR Fasc. 457, Nr. 13, Regulations on Pension Allotments for Widows and Orphans of October 1803.

[100] When in 1840/41, on his trip through Germany, Hector Berlioz discussed the possibilities of a concert in Stuttgart with the court *Kapellmeister* Lindpaintner, the latter said, with respect to the orchestra: "... as far as the players are concerned, you need only donate the modest sum of eighty francs to their pension fund, and to a man they will consider it an honor as well as a duty to perform your works under your direction and to devote several rehearsals to them." *The Memoirs of Hector Berlioz*, trans. and ed. David Cairns, New York, 1969, p. 275.

[101] Also compare here, among others, W. Salmen, *Geschichte der Musik in Westfalen*, Vol. I, Kassel 1963, pp. 216 ff.

[102] In the *Jahrbuch der Tonkunst von Wien und Prag*, [Vienna] 1796, it is said concerning the "Musical Constitution of Prague," among other things, "... thus it

previously cited, Gustav Bereths reports, in connection with the budget of 1783, on those *Musikintendanz* posts which the Kapellmeister felt could be reconciled with the duties of a court musician:[103]

> 1 court chaplain, also, as circumstances may require, instructor for the royal boys; 4 persons for the chancellery and registry, 1 as court quartermaster or court steward, 2 as porters, 1 as cupbearer and waiter, 1 as chamber lackey, 10 personal lackeys, 1 of the three hunt lackeys, 1 servant for the royal boys, in order to teach them music. In addition, also needed would be 2 court trumpeters, 1 court tympanist, 2 trumpeters [and] 1 tympanist of the guard, and 6 bandsmen,

a total of 34 persons out of an available total of 34 musicians. In this way the cost of court music could be reduced from 21,000 fl. to 7,500 fl. From this point of view we can see the orchestral musician as an average court servant of medium rank. The salary corresponded to the nature of the post and averaged between 150 and 200 fl. There would then be payment of a so-called "music wage," which on the average may have amounted to some 25 fl.[104]

---

was soon possible to place talented young musicians in an orchestra or band. It was not unusual for the nobility to do this on their own. The various houses, Morzin, Hartigg, Tschernin, Mannsfeld, Netoliz, Pacht, the Archbishop of Prague, and others, became the providers for many a young person; they recruited from their subjects, as well as from village school masters, trained children and brought them to the city. Here they maintained their own house music ensemble, dressed in uniforms, making up part of the servant staff. Their gun bearers were not allowed to put on a uniform before they were completely proficient on the French horn. Scarcely ten years ago, a servant was not considered trained, in Prague, unless he had musical training, and to this day, this is still a prerequisite for service in many a house." (pp. 105-106). —See also, Charles Burney, *op. cit.* supra n. 35, Vol. II, p. 134 with reference to Bohemia and Prague.

[103] G. Bereths, *Musikpflege am kurtrierischen Hofe*, p. 158.

[104] Thus, for example, in Koblenz, Joseph Anton Ries was "hired ... on March 13, 1755, as lackey and violinist ... his wage as a lackey was 120 rthlr. to which were added 13 rthlr. and 18 alb, as 'music-wage' " [this would equal some 160 fl. plus 18 fl. for a total of 178 fl.]. (G. Bereths, *Musikpflege am kurtrierischen Hofe*, p. 59.) Compare here also U. Götze, *Johann Friedrich Klöffler*, Diss. Münster 1965, p. 5. and pp. 9-10. J. F. Klöffler, as "District Treasurer" in Burgsteinfurt, drew a salary of 100 Rthlr. "in addition to free room at the court" as well as payment in kind. He was at the same time "Director of Music" at his court of Burgsteinfurt and conducted the Court Band.

Similar conditions prevailed at Prince Wallerstein's court, whose court orchestra is discussed in the *Musikalische Real-Zeitung* of 1788. In part, one can read: "Only a small number of orchestra members are paid as musicians; most are merely servants, and yet they get on very well with each other."[105] The musical consequence of such an orchestral make-up was that the works performed at small residences were often restricted to the music of a particular composer, works which did not require too much technical skill and which, with little practice, could be given a generally satisfactory performance.[106]

Comparing the incomes of court orchestral musicians with those of other court employees, or even with those of other professions, one finds that they were not as low as has generally been assumed to date. In Munich, for example, the town clerk Joh. Georg Joseph Albrecht Zech received an annual salary of 200 fl. cash in 1740, to which were added "annually 12 cords of beech wood, 1 ream of paper, and 8 measures of grain, as well as living quarters, which the previous town clerks had also been given...."[107] Also in Munich, a journeyman carpenter had an annual income of 80 Gulden in the year 1749.[108] A listing from the year 1759 gives an "indication of the amount a physician earned" in Munich, somewhere between 156 and 275 fl.[109] In contrast, as was already mentioned, the violinist Ferdinand Blum in the year 1745 earned, as a member of the court orchestra in Munich, the sum of 200 fl. In 1748 he earned 300 fl., later 400 fl., and finally, in 1762, 500 fl. (475 fl. after deductions).[110] In the year 1751, "Johannes Grönner [was appointed as] Court and Chamber violinist" with an annual salary of 500 fl.[111] But also in

---

[105] *Musikalische Real-Zeitung,* Speier 1788, col 53. Here is found a complete listing of the Court Band, Sp. 52/53.

[106] *Musikalische Real-Zeitung,* Speier 1788, Sp. 52: "News of the Royal Court Band in Wallerstein.... This ensemble, which plays mainly 4 composers: Haydn, Rosetti, who is similar to Haydn, Beeke and the current Court Concertmaster in Bonn, Reicha ... has as its *Komandeur* and *Musikdirektor* Capt. Beeke." Compare also L. Schiedermair, "Die Blütezeit der Ottingen-Wallersteinischen Hofkapelle," in *SIMG* IX (1907/08), pp. 83 ff.

[107] M. J. Elsas, *Umriss,* Vol. I, p. 773.

[108] *Ibid.* p. 712.

[109] *Ibid.* p. 762.

[110] Munich, Staatsarchiv für Oberbayern, HR Fasc. 463, Nr. 183.

[111] Munich, Staatsarchiv für Oberbayern, HR Fasc. 467, Nr. 500.

Stuttgart, none of the appointed court musicians received less than 300 fl., as shown by a roster from the year 1777, while, for example, the "Stagehand and organ-bellows pumper Rempp" received 150 fl., "Stagehand Huttner," 120 fl., "Theater Wig-Maker Pierre Bacle" 125 fl.; and finally "Theater Tailor-Apprentice Schmid" had to be satisfied with 150 fl.[112] As late as 1855 in Munich "the instrument Carrier Johann Maul" received a monthly compensation of only 6 fl. 15 kr. = 75 fl. annually.[113]

As far as salary is concerned, it is clear that the orchestral musician was at about the middle of the range of a court wage scale. One should keep in mind that by far the largest number of court servants had an annual income of no more than 200 fl. and mostly under 100 fl.[114] In rank order the court musician was, at least at the larger residences, placed in the center of the listing. This is apparent from the ranking listed in the *Hof- und Staatskalender* of Württemberg.[115]

The orchestral player always thought of himself as an obedient and loyal servant. He was thankful for the income and glad when his orchestra reached a respectable level of achievement. On the other hand, he was little inclined to set goals for improving conditions in the orchestra. For this there was too little motivation,[116] though this should not be interpreted to mean that he was

---

112 Stuttgart, HStA, A 21.

113 Munich, HStA, Staatstheater 13291. Compare B. Grimm, *Die sozial-ökonomische Lage...*, p. 11. In the year 1820 in Weimar, a "Court and Municipal Surgeon" received 100 Rthlr., a "Government Courier," 52 Rthlr. The latter corresponded to the wages of a trainee at the Court Orchestra.

114 Compare H. Eberhardt, *Goethes Umwelt*, Weimar 1951. In this volume: "Die Struktur der Weimarer Gesellschaft im Jahre 1820 auf der Grundlage ihres Einkommens." Also quoted by W. H. Bruford, *Culture and Society in classical Weimar*, Cambridge 1962, pp. 428-431. B. Grimm, in *Die sozial-ökonomische Lage der Weimarer Hofkapellisten*, p. 3, gives an "Income Pyramid" according to which, at the beginning of the 19th century, annual citizens' taxes indicate that 58% earned less than 100 Rthlr., 20% between 100 and 200, 13% between 200 and 400, 7% between 400 and 1000, and only 2% earned over 1,000 Rthlr.

115 Here the "Chamber, Court and Church Musicians" ranked beneath the "Ducal Gardeners, the Ducal Gentlemen at Arms" and the "Court Trumpeters and Drummers," but above the "other court officials" as well as the personnel of the "Stables, Hunt, and Stud Farms." This ranking, with only very minor changes, was kept at least from 1750 until 1810.

116 J. Fr. Reichardt, *Vertraute Briefe Wien*, Vol. 2, p. 132, Letter Number Thirty-six, Vienna, April 5, 1809: "Currently music suffers most from the lack of spirit among

not ready and willing to follow a good conductor or give his utmost when he was approached in the right way. It appears that the orchestral musician "not of the courts" perhaps played with greater enthusiasm and was maybe technically more proficient than his colleagues at the courts. One need only think of the Prague orchestra in this connection. This may have been because the "independent" orchestras put greater demands on the individual and forced him continuously to prove himself. In the court orchestras, in contrast, a musician was hardly ever dismissed because of poor performance, but rather because of improper behavior.[117]

If the musician as an individual was accommodating and pliable, he and his colleagues as a group were a body with whom it was not always easy to deal. It could happen that an orchestra might refuse to perform some extra duty, such as playing at court theater performances (at smaller residences), because of insufficient compensation.[118] Orchestral musicians appear to have also offered passive resistance whenever duties were imposed upon them which they felt went beyond what was customary, or when they were given works to perform which were new to them or which they felt exceeded their technical abilities. In a letter dated December 25, 1780, Leopold Mozart writes to his son in Munich about the rehearsing for *Idomeneo* and most accurately describes the mentality of the orchestral musician:

> Make every effort to keep the whole orchestra in a good mood, to compliment them and keep the players well disposed towards you by means of a little flattery, for I know your way of composing; it requires of all instrumentalists the most intense and constant attention, and it really is no fun when an orchestra has been working for over three hours under such pressure. Every musician,

---

the large number of servant-musicians. They almost never seem to display that enthusiasm without which a clean, strong ensemble is not possible. The majority complain about the poor salaries. . . ."

[117] For example, at the Electoral Court in Trier in 1769, the cellist Ignaz Wotschitka (Woschitzka) was dismissed after his salary had already been reduced from 600 fl. to 500 fl. in 1785 "because of his bad behavior." A part of his pay was used "to liquidate his debts." G. Bereths, *Musikpflege am kurtrierischen Hofe*, p. 87.

[118] Among others, see the previously mentioned incident at the Electoral Court in Koblenz in 1790. G. Bereths, *Musikpflege am kurtrierischen Hofe*, pp. 241-42.

even the worst violist, is most touched if one gives him a little praise privately, and will be all the more eager and attentive. After all, such little courtesies don't cost you anything except a word or two—I'm sure you know this already—I'm only saying it because one often forgets such things since one can't always do it right on the spot. When the opera is in production and staged—that is when you will really need to rely upon the enthusiasm and good will of the entire orchestra. The situation is then altogether different and every member will have to give even more of himself. . . .[119]

If one asks about the social position of an orchestral musician and whether he was still subject to discrimination during the period under discussion, it should be pointed out that a clear distinction was made between the performer who had a permanent appointment, that is, one who was on the payroll of a court or municipality, and the "independent" musician. While the latter received society's recognition only relatively late, the former was able sooner to command more and more esteem.[120] A clear sign of such recognition is the fact that after about 1840, even members of a court orchestra could be honored with decorations or other signs of respect.[121]

The court musician's standing with the average citizen was another matter. On the one hand, one was inclined to feel a common bond with someone who in many cases came from the ranks of the common people. Yet, as an employee of the court, he was also felt to be of a higher class and seen as a representative of a system which was basically hated.[122] Beyond this, the musician was still, as he had

---

[119] *Mozart. Briefe und Aufzeichnungen*, GA, Vol. III, Kassel 1963, p. 70.

[120] Also see G. Materne, *Die sozialen und wirtschaftlichen Probleme des Musikers*, pp. 41 f., and R. Eitner, "Die soziale Stellung," *MfMG* XXII (1890), p. 1. Also compare B. Grimm, *Die sozial-ökonomische Lage . . .* p. 100.

[121] Thus, for example, in Munich the violinist Jos. Leop. Holzbauer held the Medal of Honor of the Order of King Ludwig (probably from about 1839); the "Piccolist" Hr. Xav. Schwabl held the same medal (after 1843); the flutist Theobald Böhm held the title "Knight of the Order of St. Michael" (after 1839); and the cellist Karl Schönchen held the Ludwig Medal. This list could be expanded. The honors were bestowed without regard for the instrument which the individual played. (*Hof- und Staatskalender*, Munich, 1840 ff.) In Stuttgart in 1854 the flutist Krüger I is designated as "holder of the Great Gold Medal for Art and Science"(!) in *Hof- und Staatskalender* (p. 25). Later, among others, the title of "Professor" was also bestowed.

[122] Cf. Fr. Schiller, *Kabale und Liebe*, especially Act I, Sc. 1 and Act II, Sc. 4.

always been, considered as belonging to a group of unreliable, non-serious, lazy "characters." In fact, in the eyes of the average citizen the town musician, or the musician employed by the church, who also assumed the role of a citizen, appeared considerably more serious and honest than the orchestral musician [at the court]. The fact that the guild regulations were applicable to the town musician was also an important factor in this respect.[123] On the other hand, the average citizens more and more came to regard the orchestral musician as one of their own, and it was only in a predominantly middle-class society that the orchestral musician could achieve maximum social recognition.[124]

If one wishes to set up a ranking within the instrumentalists, the court orchestral musician would be in second place. The first place would be held by the traveling virtuoso. Following these two groups would be the town piper or town musician, along with the military musician later on, and lastly, the itinerant *Spielmann*.

At first the relationship between the court orchestral musician and the town piper was one of more or less equal status, for in general they performed much the same duties, although in separate spheres. A kind of "emancipation" of members of court orchestras took place as soon as they were relieved of the obligation to play *Gebrauchsmusiken*, here meaning music for social functions. This development began in Stuttgart, for example, in the year 1744, when court musicians were no longer required to play dance music (*Tantzgeigen*).[125] The fact that even afterwards town pipers and their journeymen were called upon occasionally to assist in court orchestras did not stop this development.[126] The only groups which from the very beginning maintained their distance from both court orchestral musicians and town pipers were the court and field trumpeters and drummers.

---

[123] Cf. K. Storck, *Musik und Musiker in Karikatur und Satire*, Oldenburg 1910, p. 320.

[124] K. Storck, *Karikatur*, p. 320.

[125] Stuttgart, HStA, A 21 Bü 611.

[126] For example, "on the 10th of January 1782" the "municipal winds" are called out from Böblingen, Ludwigsburg, Leonberg, Nürtingen and *"Canstatt" to go to Stuttgart, evidently to assist in the performance of the opera La nascità di Felicita.* (Stuttgart, HStA, A 21 Bü 958.) Also see J. Sittard, *Zur Geschichte der Musik und des Theaters am Württembergischen Hofe,* Vol. 2, Stuttgart 1891, p. 158 and Supplement (Beilage) IX.

A kind of predominance of particular groups of instruments or performers of such instruments does not appear to have existed within the orchestras, though a division into "soloists" and "ripieno" was the custom. It was accepted that the musician who was entrusted with the position of concertmaster and the more complex tasks, such as occasionally conducting the orchestra, received the highest pay and had the highest musical authority among the members. His "elevated position" was considered legitimate, particularly if he was generally known as a soloist and renowned master of his instrument, or even as a composer.

Parallel positions, quite separate, were maintained by the court and field trumpeters and drummers. In the first place, they did not fall under the jurisdiction of the court music administration. In the second place, they were organized in the manner of guilds, which explains many special privileges of which they were fully aware, and which they defended stubbornly.[127] Added to this was the fact that as officers they received better pay than members of the orchestras. Yet as early as the beginning of the 19th century, there appears to have been a "movement towards integrating" these musicians into a cohesive "orchestral" ensemble, which in most places was apparently completed by the middle of the century.[128] If it was previously stated that there appears to have been no "elevated" status for players of particular instruments, this was in part due to the fact that musicians were generally not identified with only one instrument.[129] It was, for example, customary, and

---

[127] Compare J. E. Altenburg, "Versuch einer Anleitung zur heroisch-musikalischen Trompeter- und Pauker-Kunst," Halle 1795 (Reprint Dresden 1911). Compare also Chr. H. Mahling, *Münchener Hoftrompeter und Stadtmusikanten im späten 18. Jahrhundert. Ein Streit um das Recht die Trompete zu blasen*, in: *Zeitschrift für bayerische Landesgeschichte* 1968, Vol. 31, No. 2, pp. 649 ff.

[128] Thus, for example, there is a differentiation made for the first time in the *Hof- und Staatskalender* for Stuttgart for the years 1807/08 among the trumpeters, between the *Hof-Musici* (court musicians) and the actual *Hoftrompeter* (court trumpeter) (pp. 69 f.). In Munich after 1849, or perhaps after 1856, the trumpeters seem to have been finally fully integrated into the orchestra. From 1892 on only the designations *Trompete* or *Trompeter* are used. (*Hof- und Staatskalender*, Munich, for the years 1849, 1856 and 1892.)

[129] Thus, in the year 1774 Johann Andreas Grünbein in Bentheim-Steinfurt was hired with the stipulation that "he play the clarinet with zeal and accuracy," and in concerts, "play violin, bassoon and cello, as may be required." W. Salmen, *Geschichte der Musik in Westfalen*, Vol. I, p. 227.

especially so at the smaller courts, for flutes and later also clarinets to be played by oboists. French horn players, and particularly trombonists, were expected to be able to play a string instrument. Many a musician whose "favorite instrument" was actually a string instrument was now and then used as a brass player. Later on even trumpet players were expected at least to be able to play the violin. So it was at the court in Salzburg in 1757, where "no trumpeter or drummer [was] hired by the royal court who could not [play] the violin well."[130]

Above all, it was the growing technical demands made upon the orchestral musician which necessitated a gradual specialization in one instrument, which now had to be played more skillfully than heretofore. This development, which at the same time gave the orchestral musician the rank of a "specialist," quite obviously had a positive influence on his social prestige. Yet this also had the effect, in the course of time, of placing him beneath the composer, the virtuoso, and finally, also the conductor, who were no longer, from an artistic and social point of view, "his kind." The orchestral musician was now only a reproducer of music and not, even in a limited way, creatively involved. With this development, "their [orchestral musicians'] individual ranking in society" as well as "their integration as a group took on added significance."[131] Now the group structure known as the "orchestra"—the union of instrumental musicians for a common professional goal—was their primary source of activity to a greater degree than before.

If one attempts to look in contemporary writings for comments which could throw light upon the orchestral musician and his position within the social structure, one will hardly find much related specifically to him.[132] General comments about the *Musikant*,

130 Fr. W. Marpurg, *Beyträge*, Vol. III, 1757, p. 197.

131 G. Materne, *Die sozialen und wirtschaftlichen Probleme. . .*, p. 42.

132 Also see, among others, P. Bülow, "Musik und Musiker in der neueren Deutschen Literatur," in *Zeitschrift für Deutschkunde* 46 (1932), pp. 736 ff.; K. Szöllösy, "Der Musiker.—Charakterologische Studie zur neueren Deutschen Literatur," in: *Jahrbuch des Deutschen Institutes d. Königl. Ung. Péter Pázmány Universität* Budapest 1936; H. Fr. Menck, "Der Musiker im Roman. Ein Beitrag zur Geschichte der vorromantischen Erzählungsliteratur" in *Beiträge zur neueren Literaturgeschichte* XVIII, ed. by Frh. v. Waldberg, Heidelberg 1931; H. Sorgatz, *Musiker und Musikanten als dichterisches Motiv*, Diss. Marburg 1939 (*Literarhist.-musikwiss. Abhdl.* 6, ed. by Fr. Gennrich, Würzburg 1939); G. C. Schoolfield, *The Figure of The Musician in German Literature*, Chapel Hill 1956.

who was ranked beneath the orchestral musician, are, in contrast, more frequently found.[133] For example, Jakob Michael Reinhold Lenz has the student Fritz comment, in his play *Hofmeister*, "It is a bad fellow who takes a chance with women and *Musikanten*, who are worth even less than women."[134] In Schiller's *Kabale und Liebe* there is also a picture of the simple town musician and a reference to his lowly social position. In all of these cases, it was obviously less the intent to depict conditions as such than to characterize particular traits, not only of the simple musician, but of certain lowly servant types.[135] In the short story by Ludwig Tieck, entitled *Musikalische Leiden und Freuden*, one first finds a short character sketch of the practising musician which, besides referring to the singer, makes specific references to the orchestral musician, but here, too, on the periphery, in a kind of "opposition role" in relation to the *Kapellmeister*:

> "So it went again as it has almost always gone," the Kapellmeister began, as they sat at the round table. "One works and works, one suffers and studies and finally looks with joy at the work, apparently successfully completed, and then it has to be turned over to these miserable, spoiled mechanics, who have learned nothing and who want to hold back, as if it were a phenomenal achievement, the precious little that they do know. Can there be a sadder profession than that of composer?"[136]

This picture of the orchestral musician who, though he knew his instrument, had little education and was, above all, uninterested,

---

[133] For example, E. T. A. Hoffmann, in his short story *Die Fermate*, sheds light upon the conditions for musicians in small towns when he has Theodor, thinking back to his youth, say, "All of Eden opened up before me, as it was likely to happen during the winter, when the town piper and his apprentices, aided by a few poor amateurs, would give a concert and I was able to play the tympani in the symphonies, owing to my good sense of rhythm. How foolish and laughable these concerts often were only came to me in later years." *E. T. A. Hoffmanns Werke*, ed. by V. Schweizer, Vol. 1, Leipzig and Vienna 1896, p. 220. Also see J. Fr. Reichardt, *Leben des berühmten Tonkünstlers Heinrich Wilhelm Gulden nachher genannt Guglielmo Enrico Fiorino*, Berlin 1779 (Reprint Leipzig 1967).

[134] J. M. R. Lenz, *Der Hofmeister oder Vorteile der Privaterziehung*, 1774, IV, 6. in: H. Kindermann, *Deutsche Literatur, Reihe Irrationalismus*, Vol. 8: *Kampf um das soziale Ordnungsgefüge*, 1. Teil, Leipzig 1939. p. 185.

[135] Also see K. Storck, *Musik und Musiker. . .* , pp. 72-73.

[136] *Ludwig Tieck's Schriften*, Vol. 17, *Novellen*, Berlin 1844, p. 291.

must have been quite accurate as a rule, for similar conclusions have been drawn previously during the course of this study.

In other literary works, the musician is generally depicted as a unique personality and artist who feels drawn to music and is either a success or a failure in his chosen musical profession. This world of "genuine art" did not exist as a reality for the orchestral musician who, in most cases, did not pick his profession because of some "inner need," and often had no secure place there. For this he was much too bound to the artisan tradition. Thus, for him it was necessary to make a "break with society." On the basis of his limited education he was not inclined to concern himself with questions of contradictions between the ideal and the real world. He was generally not even called upon to know something of aesthetic principles. So, from a spiritual perspective, there arose the sad image of an orchestral musician, a marked contrast to the unique, individualistic, searching, sensitive personality that, particularly since the period of Romanticism,* was the image one was led to believe in.

With respect to the orchestral musician's position in society, as indeed for most musicians within the time period under discussion, Friedrich Wilhelm Marpurg's statement in his *Historisch-kritischen Beyträge zur Musik* might well be considered an accurate assessment of the situation:

> It has already been said in other places that the performance of music brings the high-born and lowly onto equal levels. Yet this does not appear as a detriment to the former, for such persons must be most discerning as to whom they wish and can permit to be honored in this way, so that they themselves are not as a result dishonored. In general, they can permit very few to dine at the same table with them. If someone plays a solo for them or a concerto, that person can be permitted to come as close as professional musicians are to each other on such occasions.[137]

---

[137] Fr. W. Marpurg, *Beyträge*, Vol. V, 1760, p. 8

*Die Romantik—Romanticism, in Germany, was a short literary period of about 30 years at the beginning of the 19th century. *Tr. Note.*

APPENDIX I

(List of Ducal Court Musicians "who were taken into service on the 21st of November 1782.")*

1. Andreas Peter Malter	age 23	born in Stuttgart	Catholic
2. Ludw. Frid. Schweizer	age 22½	born in Nellingen	Protestant
3. Chr.an Leonh. Ludw. Majer	age 25¼	born in Stuttgart	Protestant
4. Joh. Benjam. Frid. Majer	age 26	born in Stuttgart	Protestant
5. Joh. Chr. Lud. Abeille	age 21	born In Bayreuth	Protestant
6. Joh. Georg Keller	age 23	born in Böblingen	Protestant
7. Christoph Weber	age 27¾	born in Bonnfeld in Pfalz	Protestant
8. Joh. Baptista Schaul	age 23	born in Stuttgart	Catholic
9. Joh. Jacob Haberle	age 25	born in Bittenfeld	Protestant
10. Ernst Hausler	age 22	born in Böblingen	Protestant
11. Joh. David Schwegler	age 24	born in Enderspach	Protestant
12. Joh. Rudolph Zumsteeg	age 22	born in Gausingen (Austria)	Catholic
13. Joh. Kauffmann	age 23	born in Kornwestheim	Protestant
14. Joh. Frid. Weberling	age 24	born in Stuttgart	Protestant
15. Joh. Georg Majer	age 26	born in Urach	Protestant
16. Joh. Hein. Schaul	age 24	born in Alldingen	Protestant
17. Ch.an Lud. Dieter	age 25	born in Ludwigsburg	Protestant
18. Jacob Adam Beurer	age 25½	born in Stuttgart	Protestant
19. Joh. Frid. Majer	age 22½	born in Urach	Protestant
20. Antonius Weil	age 24	born in Giver (Valence)	Catholic
21. Wilh. Frid. Hirschmann	age 26	born in Sindelfingen	Protestant
22. Philipp Mohl	age 25	born in Urach	Protestant
23. Lucas Breitling	age 25	born in Böblingen	Protestant

*Stuttgart HStA, A 21 Bü 954.

APPENDIX II

Curriculum vitae of Johann Joachim Quantz, written by himself.
(Excerpts from Fr. W. Marburg, *Historisch-kritische Beyträge zur Aufnahme der Musik*, Vol. I, Berlin 1754, pp. 197 ff.

"I was born on the 30th of January 1697, in the village of Oberscheden, located in the district of Hannover, between Göttingen and Münden. My father was Andreas Quantz, a blacksmith in the village. He had begun training me to be a smith from the time I was nine years old.... After his death two of his brothers, one a tailor, the other, a court and town musician in Merseburg, offered to take me in and teach me their professions, leaving the choice up to me.... Because of the fact that from the time I was eight years old I had to accompany my oldest brother, who took the part of a *Musikant* at the peasants' festivals, by playing the German bass fiddle without knowing how to read a single note ... music had taken such a hold of me that I had no other wish than to become a musician."

He "gave" himself "into apprenticeship under the town musician" and stayed with his successor after the former's death. "With him I stayed 5 and ¼ years as an apprentice and 2 and ¼ as a journeyman.... The first instrument which I had to learn was the violin ... followed by the oboe and the trumpet(!). I was most occupied with these three instruments during my years of apprenticeship. I was also not spared learning other instruments such as cornet, trombone, French horn, recorder, bassoon, bass viol, cello, viola da gamba, and God knows how many others, which a piper has to be able to play. It is a fact that because one has to learn so many different instruments, one always remains a bungler on each." Quantz also took "some lessons ... on the Clavier.... The ducal orchestra in Merseburg was at that time not very large. We therefore had to reinforce the group at court, as well as in church and at dinners.... The violin still remained my principal instrument.... In the course of time I hope to be able to make Dresden or Berlin my home."

For the time being however, he was a town piper in such places as Bischofswerder, Radeberg and Pirna. He declined an offer to come "as first violinist to Berenburg," as well as one to be oboist at another royal court, until "finally Count Moritz of Merseburg was willing to let me study the trumpet." But Quantz went to the town musician

Heine in Dresden. . . . "On the occasion of the Reformation jubilee, it came to pass that I had to play some solos on the trumpet." As a result of this, the "Capellmeister Schmidt" wanted to recommend that "the king permit me to complete my studies as a trumpeter and that I then be hired by the court as a royal trumpeter." But Quantz again rejected this. ". . . In March of 1718 the so-called Polish band, consisting of 12 persons, was being organized. Since 11 members had already been accepted and only one oboe player was still needed, I was recommended for the post. After an audition for the 'Director' Baron von Seyfertiz, I was hired. The annual salary was 150 Taler and free quarters in Poland, which was what the other members also got. In the summer of 1718 I traveled with this band to Poland and returned to Dresden the following spring.

"Now began a new phase of my career and a change from my former way of life. I was now to exchange the violin, which had been my primary instrument up to this time, for the oboe. But I was hindered from promotions on both instruments by colleagues who had seniority, something that disturbed me greatly. The annoyance over this situation caused me to take up serious study of the transverse flute, which I had up to then only practiced on my own. With this instrument I did not have to fear the resistance of those who were my colleagues at the time. . . .

"For some four months I studied under the famous flute player Buffardin in order to learn the instrument correctly." In the year 1728 he was made instructor to the then Crown Prince Friedrich of Prussia and "therefore had to come twice a year to Berlin, Ruppin or Reinsberg. . . . In November 1741 I was called to Berlin for the last time by his Majesty of Prussia and offered such favorable terms for service by none other than his majesty himself that I could not refuse any longer—an annual salary of 2,000 Taler for life, plus additional pay for any compositions, 100 Ducats for every flute I could deliver, exemption from playing in the orchestra, having to play only the royal chamber music [concerts] and finally, to be subject only to the King himself—for all of this I gave up my previous service, for I had never dreamed of being so advantaged. . . . Thus I left Dresden in December of 1741 to take up service to the king of Prussia."

APPENDIX III

cost per bushel = appr. 222.5 Liter	1706	1782	1792	1793	1799	1800
		HOLY GHOST HOSPITAL, MUNICH				
		1890 d		2520 d		
wheat		1 lt = 8,4 d		1 lt = 11,2 d		
		1260 d			3290 d	2577 d
rye		1 lt = 5,6 d			1 lt = 14,8 d	1 lt = 11,6 d
	1134 d	1754 d		3675 d	3885 d	3745 d
peas	1 lt = 5,1 d	1 lt = 7,9 d		1 lt = 16,5 d	1 lt = 17,4 d	1 lt = 16,8 d
	2275 d					
rice	1 lt = 10,2 d					
	560 d					
millet	1 lt = 2,5 d					
geese (each)			178 d			
butter (per lb.)	39,5 d					
lard (per lb.)	33,5 d	55,1 d	59,5 d	58,9 d		115,5 d
	133 d			262 d		1087 d
cabbage per 100	1 St = 1,33 d			1 St = 2,6 d		1 St = 10,9 d
beer (1.07 Liter)	1 lt = 10,5 d					
wool (per lb.)	52,5 d				105 d	
flax (per lb.)		56 d	31,5 d	63,0 d	87,5 d	
		945 d	980 d		1146 d	1165 d
salt (92.75 Liter)		1 lt = 10,2 d	1 lt = 10,5 d		1 lt = 12,4 d	1 lt = 12,6 d
		MARKET RECEIPTS, MUNICH				
	1302 d		2766 d	2490 d	4433 d	3771 d
wheat	1 lt = 5,9 d		1 lt = 12,4 d	1 lt = 11,2 d	1 lt = 19,9 d	1 lt = 17 d
	714 d		1918 d	1911 d	3558 d	2223 d
rye	1 lt = 3,2 d		1 lt = 8,6 d	1 lt = 8,5 d	1 lt = 15,9 d	1 lt = 9,9 d
		VARIOUS SOURCES				
meat (beef) per lb.	14 d				38,1 d	45,5 d
veal (per lb.)	14,2 d				34,4 d	42,0 d
pork						

Chart based on M. J. Elsas, *Umriss einer Geschichte der Preise und Löhne in Deutschland*.... The chart has been modified and converted to the smallest unit denominations.

1 Mass = approx. 1.07 Liter; 1 Scheffel = approx. 222.5 Liter;
1 Scheibe = approx. 92.75 Liter; 1 Liter = 1 Kilogramm.
1 Gulden = 60 Kreuzer (x); 1 Kreuzer = 4 Denare (d) [Denare=Pfennige]
1 Gulden (fl.) = 240 Denare

The chart clearly reflects the rising prices in the last third of the 18th century (up to as much as 200%). Even in those cases where no listing is given in later years, the relationship to the other prices can be estimated as, for example, with butter and lard.

Supplemental to the above chart are two further indicators of prices: in the year 1770 "a pair of silk stockings cost 5 fl. 30 x" and "1 pair of lace cuffs, 16 fl. 30 x." Both items were clearly mandatory for the "service uniform." (München, Staatsarchiv für Oberbayern, HR Fasc. 94b, Nr. 163).

APPENDIX IV*

The individuals listed below, members of the Electoral Court Music Establishment, divide the monthly salary of 81 fl. and 25½ Kreuzer of the concertmaster Karl Cannabich, who was still on leave, according to the formula indicated below:

	Annual Salary		Monthly Supplement	
Name	fl.	x	fl.	x
Assistant Conductor Danzy	500	—	8	20
1 violinist Freno	200	—	8	20
1 violinist Bürger	200	—	8	20
1 violinist J. Moralt	200	—	8	20
1 violinist Ruppert	50	—	3	20
1 violinist Schoenge	without salary		8	20
1 cellist Moralt	144	48	3	20
1 violist Geuthner	250	—	2	30
1 violist Moralt	without salary		6	40
1 flutist Cramer	without salary		6	40
1 flutist Kapeller	without salary		4	35
1 clarinettist Ruppert	50	—	6	33
1 horn player Vihat	200	—	4	10
1 double bass player Kugler	200	—	4	57½
			81	25½

*München, Staatsarchiv für Oberbayern, HR Fasc. 464, Nr. 253.

CHAPTER NINE

Social Obligations of the Emancipated Musician in the 19th Century

.

WALTER SALMEN

In the 19th century most poets, critics and the general public were prepared to give music a place of honor which elevated it far above all the other arts into the sphere of the "ethereal."[1] Franz Grillparzer, for example, wrote in his poem *In Moscheles' Stammbuch,*

> Music, you I praise above all,
> To you the highest prizes fall,
> Of the sister arts — three
> You the freest, truly free!
> ... To you, the prize most beautiful,
> — And to those to you devoted.

Whoever "devoted" himself to this art, whether as supporter, creator, or transmitter, received this elevation in rank, which in the case of particularly exceptional artists could take the role of a prophesying priest, even a god-like one.[2] There was a general consensus in certain circles of society that this art, so removed from the material world, should be released from the obligations of

---

[1] Also see W. Salmen, "Fragmente zur romantischen Musikanschauung von J. W. Ritter," in: *Fs. for J. Müller-Blattau,* Kassel 1966, pp. 235 ff. [*Fs. (Festschrift)* is a publication in honor of a famous person.]

[2] W. Wiora, *Komponist und Mitwelt,* Kassel 1964, p. 17; P. Kluckhohn, "Berufungsbewusstsein und Gemeinschaftsdienst des deutschen Dichters im Wandel der Zeiten," in: *Dt. Vj. f. Literaturwiss. u. Geistesgesch.* 14 (1936), p. 14. As early as 1782 Johann Friedrich Reichardt, in the *Musikalische Kunstmagazin,* vol. 1., p. 1, demanded that the artist should be a "prophet" of the arts; C. M. v. Weber and others repeated the same demand in the 19th century.

society and permitted an unbridled autonomy in a special world of its own. Consequently, works, at least in some forms (e.g., the string quartet), could abandon convention and social heritage and move into the sphere of pure subjectivity, an area in which the emancipated artist, as a genius among his contemporaries, presumed to reign far above his age. He was the new "ruler" of the middle class, the *uomo singolare*,[3] who was honored in a way previously reserved for the aristocracy or representatives of the church. The artist who, according to Novalis,* was the spokesman for a *Weltseele*, became aware of his "mission," the freedom to practice his art as an end in itself. The commonplace and the dull were loathsome to him, so that whenever possible, he withdrew from the demands of society in order to "live his own life" independently (J. F. Reichardt) or to dedicate himself "to his art" (R. Wagner). Instead of living life as a "bound servant," as Joseph Haydn had done, he strove for an existence as an "independent artist," one who had chosen the profession of composer as a spiritual career without strings attached. In keeping with this outlook, Richard Wagner, in 1858, bluntly rejected all offers of a "post" or "position" as being incompatible with his dignity.

Beethoven was the original model whose complete absorption in himself as a composer appeared to be a guiding example for others. As early as 1801, reflecting upon the meaning of his work, he had developed a self-awareness which led to the statement, "I live only within my notes." In 1808 he concluded:

> It must be the striving and goal of every true artist to achieve a position in which he can completely devote himself to the working out of larger works, and where he will not be distracted by other obligations or by economic considerations.[4]

Because Beethoven was able, for the most part, to achieve this independence for himself and shut out everything which did not fit

---

[3] H. Heckel, "Die Gestalt des Künstlers in der Romantik," in: *Literaturwiss. Jb. d. Görresges.* 2 (1927), p. 50.

[4] F. Prelinger, *Ludwig van Beethovens sämtliche Briefe und Aufzeichnungen*, vol. IV, Leipzig 1909, p. 40.

*Novalis, actually named Friedrich Leopold Freiherr von Hardenberg, 1772-1801, was one of the important poets of German literary romanticism. The term *Weltseele* means something akin to universal spirit. *Tr. Note.*

into his basic concepts, he was honored, even during his lifetime, as a god-like, all-powerful artist. Though at times he provoked his contemporaries because of unseemly "social rudeness" and his demonstrative "emancipation from all salon conventions" (A. Schindler), one was ready to permit this unique "independent genius" (Beethoven, 1826) such resistance to social pressures. In a letter to Goethe dated May 28, 1810, Bettina Brentano raved:

> The entire energy and force of humanity seem to revolve around him. He alone creates freely from within himself that which has not yet been thought of: the uncreated. Of what importance is intercourse with the world for him, who before sunrise is already at his sacred task and after sunset hardly looks up? ... No emperor or king is as conscious as Beethoven of his power, and of the fact that all power emanates from him. . . .[5]

In France, in 1828, Beethoven was even thought of as a *génie métaphysique et mystérieux*.[6] In a kind of transfiguration, Ernst Ortlepp wrote about the existence of this unique figure in 1831:

> There stands a lonely figure,
> At midnight,
> Upon the rock.
> Below him thunders
> The waterfall. . . .[7]

Georges Bizet went so far as to say: "Beethoven is not a human, he is a god."[8] How much the general public shared such views is clearly shown by the glorifying, "larger than life" monuments which began to appear after 1835.[9]

Inspired by the 18th-century model of genius which "knows only its own powers" (Moses Mendelssohn), other leading composers besides Beethoven took up their claims to unhindered independence after the fall of Absolutism. According to Franz Schubert's words of

---

[5] B. Brentano, *Goethes Briefwechsel mit einem Kinde*, v. 2, Berlin 1835, pp. 191 ff.

[6] *Le Globe* of May 14, 1828.

[7] E. Ortlepp, *Gedichte*, Leipzig 1831, p. 31.

[8] In the poem *Hommage*, Stéphane Mallarmé used a similar expression: "Le dieu Richard Wagner. . . ."

[9] J. A. Schmoll, called Eisenwerth, "Zur Geschichte des Beethoven-Denkmals," in: *Fs. for J. Müller-Blattau*, Kassel 1966, pp. 245 ff.

1818, the "artist prefers to be left to himself" and desires to be freed from the bonds of reality, something he attempts to attain through the magical "power of music" on "wings of song." In the same vein Carl Maria von Weber wrote in his diary on January 18, 1812, with notable insight:

> What life is filled with more unpleasant little incidents and wretchedness than that of an artist! He should stand there, free as a god, filled with a feeling of strength from within and steeled through his art! The world would seem to be his as long as he does not actually set foot in it. When all these dreams and strengths are gone, he finds himself in the shallow domain of the commonplace man.

In 1864, Peter Cornelius was convinced about his calling: "I have been summoned to be a musical creator and it is my most sacred duty—not to waste a minute." (letter to his brother dated Nov. 26, 1864) According to his *Memoirs*, Hector Berlioz considered it the greatest bliss for the exalted composer-conductor when, in the act of making music, the world could be forgotten:

> ... he listens to himself, is his own judge, and when he is moved and his emotion is shared by those artists near him, he no longer concerns himself with the reactions of the distant public.

Franz Liszt, who was considered a chosen priest "without a Temple" (Hugo v. Hofmannsthal), in 1857 expressed himself to J. W. v. Wasielewski:

> The pressure of custom and the bonds on the artist who is dependent upon the applause of the multitudes for his existence, advancement and reputation, are so strong that even the most courageous and well-intentioned, among whom I am proud to include myself, have a most difficult time preserving the individual self before the confused, unpredictable, prurient masses.

In a letter dated August 15, 1868, Modest Mussorgski wrote to Rimsky-Korsakov: "The artist is a law unto himself." Richard Wagner, who in boundless self-over-estimation at times thought of himself as the "model" artist, made an apparently irrevocable division of the world of the arts into two extremes—the masses and

270

the individual genius (i.e., "pleasure" from art and lonely "suffering" in art). In 1860 he wrote to Mathilde Wesendonk that these two categories could not be reconciled:

> You must know, my child, that those like myself look neither to the right nor the left, neither forwards nor backwards. Time and the world are nothing to us. Only one thing matters to us and determines our actions, namely, the necessity to release what is within us.

Many more quotations could be given to substantiate the concept of the superiority of the artist. Yet this would cast light upon only this one side, the proud, elitist attitude, a feeling that the composer is above social ties and conventions. It would overlook the profound crisis experienced by musicians and music. The egocentric artist who brought upon himself the burden of being responsible only to himself had to pay for this with a considerable loss of "security." This "withdrawal into himself"[10] led many an artist into a form of isolation which, though never complete, offered little hope of a way out, and produced a state in which conflicts were bound to develop.

While there had been awareness of the lonely, suffering artist ever since the time of Wilhelm Heinrich Wackenroder or Ludwig Tieck's short story *Musikalische Leiden und Freuden,* and even though there was also a kind of literary play with the concept of *Lebenskränklichkeit* (Thomas Mann),[11]* it should be remembered that such suffering was actually experienced. The crisis between society and the artist was movingly reflected in Beethoven's *Heiligenstädter Testament* (1802), Franz Schubert's *Klage an das Volk,* and Hector Berlioz's *Symphonie fantastique* (1830). They reflect suffering and loneliness within a reality which was felt to be intolerable. The disdain expressed by Berlioz in the phrase *épater le bourgeois* (to dumbfound rather than to serve the middle-class), and the degrading of the public to "philistines," "mob" or "rabble" resulted in a "suffering" which not infrequently ended in fear, emptiness and melancholy.

---

[10] *AMZ* 17 (1815), Sp. 582.

[11] W. Wiora, *Komponist und Mitwelt,* Kassel 1964, p. 57.

*While it is difficult to define this term succinctly, it can be said that it is related in Mann's works to the concept that the ascent to greater awareness in terms of the spirit is accompanied by a decline from the point of view of normality. Life and spirit are irreconcilable foes. *Tr. Note.*

When Frédéric Chopin reported from Vienna in 1830 to Jan Matuszyński ". . . everything around me is so sad, dull and gloomy," and when Robert Schumann in 1838 complained that his path was "quite lonely," they were not alone in their depression. In 1859 Giuseppe Verdi summarized it: "Our lot is resignation, that is all." In 1861 Richard Wagner confessed: ". . . not a soul asks about me . . . there is no demand for my art. . . ." When this lack of any connection to society demanded a "divine disdain of the world,"[12] the slim prospects for an understanding public were projected into the future. Not expecting the longed-for response during his lifetime, the composer placed his hope in an imagined public and in the "immortality" of the work of art itself.

This is surely what the aging Liszt meant when in 1874 he cited as his only ambition the desire "to fling a spear into the limitless distances of the future." In a similar manner Anton Bruckner wrote to Felix Weingartner in 1891, concerning the finale of the 8th Symphony, that this movement in its uncut version was meant "for a later age, and then only for a circle of friends and connoisseurs." Music as an end in itself, however, declines from the lack of an understanding public as easily as art, at the opposite extreme, perishes when it is meant merely for public consumption.

In spite of these examples of isolation from society, a complete separation from the world of the 19th century was relatively rare. The composer had become self-contradictory. Independent on the one hand, he wrote for a future age, while on the other, to provide himself with some degree of security, he wrote works that were sold as wares and was thus dependent upon society. At least in his "day to day existence" (Peter Tschaikowsky), even the most eccentric musician was "in need of help" (Richard Wagner). In 1825 Franz Schubert also complained that he was "slave to every miserable dealer" insofar as in some places composers did not yet enjoy the full fruits of their works through copyright protection.

Even though the Age of Romanticism disdainfully looked down upon ordinary utilitarian music, no musician could completely ignore the consumer and the demand for music for specific occasions. Many were forced to lead a kind of "dual life" (Peter

---

[12] In 1861 Liszt wrote, concerning Berlioz, that he had "neither friends nor supporters, enjoyed neither the radiant sun of the public, nor the gentle shadow of trusted friendship."

Tschaikowsky). Economic necessity forced the composer to make concessions to popular tastes or even to court the favor of the public. Consequently, works were produced which strove for "folk-like" familiarity and were merely mediocre, along with those which inclined towards the esoteric and spiritual.

Not only such personalities as Gioacchino Rossini were bent on pleasing the public and thus "doing a thriving business," but even Anton Bruckner fell into this category on occasion. At his inaugural lecture at the University in Vienna in 1875, he recommended the study of harmony and counterpoint to his students, for, among other things, one can "thus sometimes promote public interest by also writing occasional music, which will in turn again bring in the desired profits."

All too many composers were most eager to bow to the general commercialization of musical life, to play up to the daydreams of the masses and thus appear as brilliant and agreeable personalities. They thereby forfeited their chance for true independence. For example, in 1831, Gottfried Wilhelm Fink wrote in the *Allgemeine Musikalische Zeitung* concerning Henri Herz and his primary concern with effect:

> He desires nothing more than to be an obliging, well-practiced, highly urbane member of society who smiles in the proper fashion and has a pleasant manner of speech, which is, after all, what counts.

Heinrich Heine characterized Giacomo Meyerbeer as the "musical *maître de plaisir* of the aristocracy."[13]

Other composers, for whom life had become uncertain, found such a tribute all the more difficult to accept because, for them, this catering to the entertainment needs of the so-called "better classes" was like forced labor. Carl Maria von Weber reflected in 1814, for example, on the role of the artist as a "martyr to social life." In 1818 he complained, "Occasional pieces which are the May flies of the world of music are part of the shadowy side of this service obligation. . . ." Many were truly hard hit by the schism between the realities of unavoidable social dependence and a growing awareness of emancipation.

---

13 H. Heine, *GA* Vol. 8, p. 291.

A noteworthy readiness to resolve this conflict between opposing motivations—serving primarily the "better" society versus dedicating oneself to esoteric idealism—is observable from the late 18th century on. Those artists now freed from bondage to society sought, as free individuals, to obtain the support of those very connoisseurs and music lovers from whose control they had freed themselves. Instead of abiding by the existing service codes, which up to then had been traditionally assigned to this practical profession in the form of legal obligations, they now sought freely to choose their own obligations towards society and to consider each case on its own merits. In this way they thought it possible to integrate themselves into middle-class society.

A musician who had been dismissed from service, and who for a time might have lived isolated and alienated, did not usually remain in such an uncomfortable borderline state. He was inclined to depend upon the encouragement of his fellow man, upon his understanding and patience. Therefore, long before totalitarian states and ideologies forced him to do so, he strove on his own to find a humanitarian justification of his activities and to develop a positive relationship with his fellow man. He accomplished this through verbal affirmation of his "utility" as well as through musical works of art which were clearly related to the realities of the time. Philanthropic motivations, realized in the form of benefit concerts, gave testimony of an awareness of social responsibility. As early as 1777, Johann Friedrich Reichardt and, in 1786, Christian Daniel Friedrich Schubart wanted to prove their "usefulness to the fatherland" through "science and the arts."[14]

Popular composers like Johann Abraham Peter Schulz considered it a great honor at one time to have been called "a musician of the people."[15] In the same manner Carl Maria von Weber made a notation in his diary on December 31, 1817, stating it his duty ". . . to be useful and bring honor to the fatherland and art as an industrious artist!" This self-chosen service to one's people and homeland

---

14 J. F. Reichardt, *Briefe eines aufmerksamen Reisenden die Musik betreffend*, Vol. I, Frankfurt and Leipzig 1774, Preface identical to that in "An die Jugend," in: *Ephemeriden der Menschheit* 11, Basel 1777, p. 40; Ch. F. D. Schubart, *Musicalische Rhapsodien*, Stuttgart 1786, "Vortrab."

15 H. Gottwaldt and G. Hahne, *Briefwechsel zwischen J. A. P. Schulz und J. H. Voss*, Kassel 1960, p. 14.

suspended prior obligations to the aristocracy and church and, under the banner of an unbridled striving for all of humanity during the period of classicism,* was expanded to include all men on earth.

In the *Allgemeine Musikalische Zeitung* of 1801 (col. 442), in this connection, the question was posed: "What is the highest goal of all the arts?—Humanity, and not merely for the individual man but for our whole race." In the following year Ludwig van Beethoven affirmed in the *Heiligenstädter Testament* his "love of man and his propensity to do good." In 1816 he proclaimed himself to be a "friend of all humanity."

Such humanitarian motivations in music were put into practice in a number of ways. There was the *engagement* to work for the general well-being, characterized by the slogan of the French singer Adolphe Nourrit (1837), *l'art pour le peuple*.[16] There was also the support of social or patriotic movements and the creation of multi-level works of art, which the general public found appealing because of the mixture of the familiar, such as folk-song material, with the new.

Support of social or patriotic movements was largely activated by the French Revolution when former employees of the court, like Etienne Nicolas Méhul, were ordered to write *Hymnes patriotiques* which were played in 1796 in the Paris theaters before performances or during intermissions. Also commissioned was *l'Hymne chanté par le peuple à la fête de Barra et de Viala*.[17] In 1794 François-Joseph Gossec, E. Méhul, and other composers under the Robespierre regime received their orders for the public good:

> On the 15th of Prairial, Sarette received from the Committee of Public Safety an order signed by Carnot, Barrère and Robert Lindet, announcing the hymn (*Chant du Départ*) that was to be set to music for the 20th. As soon as Gossec had composed this music, Robespierre gave Sarrette the order to teach this patriotic song to the 48

---

[16] In *Le Nouveau Siècle*, Gustave Charpentier formulated the following motto to promote greater social awareness: "The artistic life of a country exists not only through the activities and creations of its artists.... To popularize art is one of the first duties of a democracy."

[17] A. Pougin, *Méhul, sa vie, son génie, son caractère*, Paris 1889, p. 117.

*The period of German literary classicism in its narrowest sense can be said to be between 1786 and 1805, from the time of Goethe's Italian journey until after Schiller's death. *Tr. Note.*

sections, making him responsible for its proper performance. Accordingly, teachers who were members of the *Institut Musical* divided up the different neighborhoods in order to teach the singing of this new hymn.[18]

Rather than being required to satisfy the desires of an aristocracy of leisure, the composer now living in the society of the Republic was asked to arouse collective support for the ideals of the Revolution through popular songs. Such an art, which had the goal of being functional, became constrained and inhibited in its development. Some 19th-century composers, for example Hector Berlioz, became active supporters of popular causes without coercion. Berlioz, who suffered particularly from a feeling of isolation and who enjoyed the intoxication of "massed musical power," was able to achieve his sonority ideal in an 1830 arrangement of the *Marseillaise* for soloists, choir, and orchestra. He dedicated this arrangement to "All who have a voice, a heart and blood in their veins!" The fact that this "All" referred not only (as it had generally) to the upper and middle classes, but also to the so-called fourth estate, is documented by his tendentious *Chant des chemins de fer* (Song of the Railways), op. 19, for tenor, choir and orchestra, written in 1846. It was dedicated to the "soldiers of peace" (*Soldats de la paix*), referring to the railway construction workers near Paris.[19]

Albert Lortzing, like Robert Schumann, wrote demonstrative hymns to freedom in 1848 and revolutionary sounding marches for piano. In 1834 Franz Liszt placed an explanatory preface to his *Harmonies poétiques et religieuses*, using the words of Alphonse de Lamartine, *"Ces vers ne s'adressent qu'à un petit nombre"* (These lines are addressed only to a select few). Giuseppe Verdi composed a monumental hymn for male chorus and orchestra called *Suona la tromba* (Sound the Trumpet), and Karel Křižkovský, a work entitled *Utonulá* (The Drowned Maiden). Johann Strauss chose to realize similar intentions in a more popular form and wrote the *Freiheitslieder-Waltzer* (Songs of Freedom Waltzes).

It is not particularly surprising, with the prevailing aesthetic views of the 19th century concerning the "purity of musical arts,"

---

[18] A. Poughin, *Méhul*, p. 108.

[19] Also compare G. Knepler, *Musikgeschichte des 19. Jahrhunderts*, Vol. I, Berlin 1961, p. 302.

that these compositions, conceived of as proclamations, were not accepted without opposition. One of the loudest spokesmen against what was considered a kind of democratic "derailment" was Johann Christian Lobe who, in 1860 wrote,

> As soon as the artist turns his thoughts to other ideas—the moment he becomes involved in a political uproar—he can no longer create anything artistic. All creativity, all fecundity, requires complete and exclusive dedication.[20]

The creation of a national as well as a utilitarian art was the common denominator of the era, from Finland to Spain. Those musicians who thought of themselves as servants to a state-organized people's movement strove to represent the voice of the nation.

Composers like Bedrich Smetana were concerned with raising the national idiom above that of the traditional classic one. Accordingly, each nation should be uniquely represented, even on the highest artistic plane. A realism became apparent, with local color and a depiction of the particular setting. There were national operas,[21] rhapsodies,[22] and medleys or symphonic poems in connection with middle-class aspirations for progress, as well as stylized dances and songs.[23]

In the 18th century, Johann Georg Sulzer had already demanded that musicians cultivate national elements, but now such innocent cultivation was weighted down with all sorts of non-musical effects. Composers were motivated by notions of bringing about unification or a *risorgimento* (resurgence of national pride), as well as by a conservatively oriented concern for preserving what was considered to be truly basic and genuine in the historic heritage.

Composers such as the Serbian, Stevan Mokranjac, the Russian, Michail Glinka, or the Czech, Leoš Janáček, hoped that by means of such conciliatory gestures of accommodation, a "folk inspired,

---

[20] J. Chr. Lobe, *Musikalische Briefe*, Leipzig 2/1860, p. 91.
[21] B. Szabolcsi, "Die Anfänge der nationalen Oper im 19. Jahr.," in: *Kongr. Ber. Salzburg*, Vol. I, Kassel 1964, p. 59.
[22] W. Salmen, *Geschichte der Rhapsodie*, Freiburg 1966, pp. 42 ff.
[23] Also compare I. Bengtsson, "Romantisch-nationale Strömungen in deutscher und skandinavischer Musik," in: *Kieler Schriften zur Musikwiss.* Vol. 16, Kassel 1965, p. 45.

socially realistic art form"[24] could be developed which would serve the common aspirations and needs. Leoš Janáček studied the folk music of Moravia and concentrated on collecting folk dances of his homeland, calling it his "sacred duty" (1891). Even prior to the Hungarians Béla Bartók and Zoltan Kodály, he sought to establish himself on behalf of his people, as early as 1888, as a scholar-composer. In 1889-90 he wrote the *Lachischen Tänze*, and in 1899 the *Ukvalské písně* for mixed chorus. As late as 1926, in a speech in London, he asserted with confidence,

> As soon as we are commonly brought together, away from our so-called art, to see the common source, the folk element, then we shall all become brothers. Music will then create a common bond and unite all men. The folk song is the bond between all peoples and nations and unites all humanity in a spirit of happiness and prosperity.

By thus justifying music derived from the people, Janáček, with many others, thought a faulty relationship with the world could be set straight again, that art and the people could be reconciled and the barrier between the high and low done away with.

Yet many composers were in time sorely disappointed, for instead of writing for all the people, they composed for the concert-hall public, the liberal middle class, and the music composed was a sentimentalized version of the original folk elements. In addition, there was the attempt to recreate a purposeful existence by striving for a group identity which had long ceased to exist and could therefore only be experienced second-hand.

Of course, this did not have to be the case. A productive synthesis of folk elements, of simple songs familiar to everyone, could be successful, but only when motivated by an inner musical need. A brief account of Ludwig van Beethoven's relationship to folk music is given below, since it is representative of such a synthesis.

As already noted, Beethoven was deeply moved by the idea of public responsibility and was inspired by both religious and humanitarian motives. This concept of bringing into harmony the creations of the artist and the summons to brotherly love was instilled in Beethoven from his earliest years, both by his teacher Chr.

---

[24] H. Hollander, *Leoš Janáček*, Zurich 1964, p. 50.

G. Neefe and by the electoral government of Cologne. Not only in the streets of the Rhineland but also in the music salons of Bonn in 1785 (as reported, for instance, by privy councillor von Pelzer) could one hear folk songs of the region.[25]

There was an attitude of tolerance and a concern with simple, natural things. Such youthful impressions were transformed by Beethoven in his earliest compositions in the form of joyous social songs, such as the drinking song *Erhebt das Glas mit froher Hand* (Raise the Glass with Joyous Hand, around 1787). In this kind of composition Beethoven, even later, abstained from injecting his own unique style and was more concerned with making the popular stanza style of *Lieder im Volkston* his own.[26]

Melodies of this kind could be learned and sung by everyone and were truly meant to be easily accessible to all. In the *Kriegslied der Österreicher* (Austrian Battle Hymn) (1797, GA No. 231), in the *Grenadiermarsch für eine Flötenuhr* (Grenadier March for a Musical Clock) from the middle period, or in the late musical offerings which he wrote into albums of friends (for example, the *Bundeslied,* op. 122, of 1823), he leaned toward popular forms without great pretensions.

Thus, Beethoven never completely abandoned the concept of satisfying the musical needs of his countrymen with such simple, socially functional music. Beethoven, who more than anyone at the beginning of the 19th century transformed musical forms into the sphere of the subjective, also provided settings for folk songs of various nations. Without ideological prejudice, Johann Friedrich Reichardt, Joseph Haydn, Leopold Koželuch, Ignaz Pleyel, Johann Nepomuk Hummel and Beethoven allowed this treasure to be shared again. Folk songs were, for Beethoven, not something to be rejected, but rather testimony to natural simplicity, the naive and beautiful, and to a lost fundamental force which deserved to be preserved and united with art forms.

As a citizen of the world, as Schiller put it, he approached this idea not as so many after him, in a narrow nationalistic sense, but rather, in spite of the then-limited sources available, from a European point of view. He collected *con amore*, aurally or from printed sources, Portuguese, Danish or Russian melodies. His search was directed towards a broad humanity and he was undoubtedly

---

[25] L. Schiedermair, *Der junge Beethoven,* Bonn 1951, p. 48.
[26] Also see H. Boettcher, *Beethoven als Liederkomponist,* Augsburg 1928, p. 63.

better-informed folkloristically than Mozart or Schubert. Beethoven was not bent on a chauvinistic self-portrayal in a national idiom,[27] but rather he was more interested in Herder's unity of mankind. Inspired by what was natural, Beethoven wanted to find that basic simplicity and praise it in his work. For one whose naiveté was lost, this could be accomplished only through a deliberate transformation, either by arranging no less than 185 songs, intended to be very easy to perform (*bien faciles à exécuter*) (op. 105) as well as a "useful business" (letter to George Thomson, dated November 23, 1809),[28] or by composing works based freely upon folk themes.

Some examples of the latter are the arietta *Ich liebe dich, so wie du mich*,[29] the string quartet opus 18, number 4 (secondary theme of the first movement),[30] the *Musik zu einem Ritterballett* of 1791, the string quartets of opus 59,[31] the andante of the Septett, opus 20, portions of the 6th Symphony, and in piano trios opus 70 or opus 97. Such use of traditional *Naturgesängen* may, aside from the musical aspects,[32] be understood as a gesture to accommodate the listener accustomed to hearing the conventional, for Beethoven was ever searching for approval and understanding. Beethoven was not as isolated from society as, for example, Schönberg in more recent times. Nevertheless, one cannot claim that he "created for the people," as the late Sergei Prokofiev said of himself. Also completely missing was an *engagement* with regard to doctrines or slogans, nationalism or socialism. Nor was there any attempt to convert through what might be called music education.

Beethoven was not inclined to support the concept of *l'art pour l'art* to the point of complete uselessness, or inclined to lend his support to the one-sided exploitation of art for utilitarian purposes

---

[27] Also compare W. Salmen, "Zur Gestaltung der 'Thèmes russes' in Beethovens op. 59," in: *Fs. f. W. Wiora*, Kassel 1967, pp. 397 ff.

[28] F. Lederer, *Beethovens Bearbeitungen schottischer und anderer Volkslieder*, Diss. Bonn 1934; M. Unger, "Zu Beethovens Volksliederbearbeitungen," in: *Musik 34*, 1942, pp. 210-12.

[29] W. Wiora, *Europäische Volksmusik und abendländische Tonkunst*, Kassel 1957, p. 224.

[30] E. H. Meyer, "Beethoven und die Volksmusik," in: *Aufsätze über Musik*, Berlin 1957, p. 90.

[31] W. Salmen, *Zur Gestaltung*, 1967.

[32] Particularly in late Beethoven there is a demonstrative sign of a return to simplicity and objectivity, a kind of revocation of subjectivity.

by a non-musical organization. He maintained the distance he needed to live for his art, but he also offered "the world" much that was acceptable. He did not completely leave the mainstream and was not forced to live without acceptance.

Since Beethoven's time, the composer has been free to choose whether he will live completely for his art and thereby assume the right of self-determination without limitations, or whether he will also place himself at the disposal of a socially determined art in the sense of Paul Hindemith's motto, formulated in 1959: "Think not of yourself; ask only, 'What can I do for my fellow man?'"